RIGHTS AS WEAPONS

Rights as Weapons

Instruments of Conflict, Tools of Power

Clifford Bob

PRINCETON UNIVERSITY PRESS

PRINCETON AND OXFORD

Published by Princeton University Press
41 William Street, Princeton, New Jersey 08540
6 Oxford Street, Woodstock, Oxfordshire OX20 1TR

press.princeton.edu

LCCN 2018964656
ISBN 978-0-691-16604-9

British Library Cataloging-in-Publication Data is available

Editorial: Eric Crahan and Pamela Weidman
Production Editorial: Kathleen Cioffi
Jacket Design: Layla MacRory
Production: Erin Suydam
Publicity: Tayler Lord
Copyeditor: Cynthia Buck

This book has been composed in Adobe Text Pro and Gotham

Printed on acid-free paper. ∞

Printed in the United States of America

10 9 8 7 6 5 4 3 2 1

To my wife Joan for her love and support

CONTENTS

RIGHTS AS WEAPONS

1

Introduction

THE USES OF RIGHTS IN POLITICAL CONFLICT

In Egypt's nationwide protests against the Muslim Brotherhood government in 2013, one of the loudest and most resonant cries was "Rights!"—for women, religious minorities, and secular Egyptians. Yet, on July 3, 2013, the liberal groups headlining the demonstrations welcomed a military takeover in which hundreds were soon killed, thousands imprisoned, and basic human rights greatly diminished. No doubt most protesters did not expect this bloodbath and rejected the Muslim Brotherhood's apparent plans for Egypt. Elected only one year before in a tumultuous vote, it had made constitutional and legal changes that scared many of those who supported a secular, rather than religiously inflected, government of Egypt. But in battling for another regime change so soon after the election and only two years after the fall of the Mubarak dictatorship, the protesters' eagerness to accept destruction of the country's first democratic government suggested that they had also used human rights strategically. By portraying the Brotherhood as Islamist radicals and inveterate rights abusers, demonstrators could frame themselves as victims, rallying support at home and abroad. Even as they allied with the military and refused at first to call its actions a "coup," liberals seemed to believe that they were protecting their rights. Yet by subverting the Muslim Brotherhood government that had so recently won power through a flawed but real electoral process, they also subverted rights. The dictatorship of General Abdel Fattah el-Sisi quickly committed far greater abuses than the Muslim Brotherhood had done. Most of the victims were suspected Brotherhood members. But liberals who had lived in Egypt during the Brotherhood government also fell victim, and many were forced to flee abroad.

The Egyptian liberals' use of human rights as a rhetorical weapon to undermine a flawed but struggling democracy might seem surprising. Rights are sometimes thought to transcend politics, furnishing a moral bedrock for societies and activists. For many, rights are progressive goals whose achievement brings peaceful reform. In some visions, rights embody humanity's best hope for achieving its highest aspirations. The United Nations promotes a universal rights culture as an antidote to conflict and domination. Many observers focus on rights' defensive uses: to protect the vulnerable and uplift the needy. For the influential legal scholar Ronald Dworkin, rights are "trumps" that safeguard individuals against invasive policies, repressive states, and oppressive cultures.[1]

Certainly they protect against these things, but rights, including liberal rights, can also be used as weapons of politics and for illiberal ends. How and why are rights used for aggressive purposes? In answering these central questions, this book focuses on the ways in which powerful forces use rights to batter weaker groups, smash minority ideas, or, as in Egypt, Thailand, and other states in recent years, unseat democratically elected governments. Groups such as Thailand's Yellow Shirts have argued that their movements are simply striving to protect the rule of law from governments that they decry as populist. Yet the rights language of such groups often masks a last-ditch effort to hold on to power when previously marginalized or repressed groups assert different views on social, economic, and political relations.

Nationalist battles involve the thrust and parry of rival rights—both individual and group. In places as diverse as Quebec, Scotland, and Catalonia, cultural, language, and minority rights are at the center of conflict. In Malaysia, India, and Nigeria, "sons of the soil" movements have won special rights to political, economic, and social status for indigenous majorities, even as "migrant" groups, both from overseas and from other regions of the same countries, seek their own rights. Nativist and populist movements in Europe demand cultural protections for majority groups in the face of mass migration from Africa and Asia.

Women's rights have been used in France, Belgium, Austria, and elsewhere to justify *burqa* bans. Although couched as a way of liberating Muslim women, the claim acts as a powerful attack on "unassimilated" Muslims. Meanwhile, Muslim women in these countries have begged to differ from their self-proclaimed defenders. They protest that wearing the burqa is itself a basic right. Internationally, women's rights served as post hoc justification for America's war against the Taliban and NATO's support for a corrupt new Afghan government. In another recent case, American and European governments have elevated LGBT rights to a central plank of foreign policy. The World Bank has followed suit, withholding development loans to poor countries, such as Uganda, for draconian laws attacking LGBT populations.[2] Yet traditional Catholics, Protestants, and Muslims in Africa and elsewhere view these policies as misguided international attacks on their right to live by the time-tested or majority-approved values of their own cultures. Many in the West condemn the resulting violations of LGBT rights in the name of majority cultural rights, but the societies targeted with internationally based rights claims see themselves as under threat by powerful outsiders.

Nor is there anything novel in offensive usages of rights. Natural rights, civil rights, and human rights have been used in such ways for centuries, not only to protect the powerless but also to boost dominant communities at others' expense. John Locke, philosopher and partisan of his day, stressed the right to "property" in "lives, liberties and estates."[3] He did so not only to weaken the British monarchy of James II in its conflict with Parliament, but also to increase the political power of the landed gentry and middle classes against propertyless Britons who also demanded rights.[4] In revolutionary France, the "Declaration of the Rights of Man" undermined the old regime but limited political rights to men of means. When radical women such as Olympe de Gouges issued a "Declaration of the Rights of Woman and the Citizen," they were rebuffed, then guillotined; women would not gain the vote in France until 1945. In nineteenth- and twentieth-century America, states' rights repeatedly stifled African Americans' claims to equality. These and many other cases reveal that rights are and have always been Janus-faced. They are used not only for defensive ends but just as much for aggressive purposes. They may protect the powerless, but just as commonly the powerful employ them to expand their influence.

This book focuses on this understudied aspect of rights, providing an answer to the puzzle of how rights may not only help achieve liberation but also end up justifying or facilitating oppression. The book provides the first systematic account of the multiple ways in which activists use rights in conflicts. In particular, I show how they invoke rights to *mobilize* their political forces, then *deploy* them against their foes—and how foes in turn *counter* these advances with their own rights tactics. The result is a new approach to understanding how political actors use rights as offensive weapons of conflict, not just as noble objectives to be achieved through selfless struggle.

I analyze the variety of ways in which all sides to conflict invoke rights, particularly highlighting aggressive usages by the powerful against the weak. Ultimately, this perspective helps explain why some who appeal to rights end up undermining them in practice.

Prior Perspectives

Until now, the scholarly literature has primarily contemplated the appealing first face of rights, largely ignoring the less attractive second face. The most optimistic accounts focus on individual human rights, chronicling their historical triumph and foreseeing their future victories. For some, such liberal rights represent a global "script" that magnetically attracts new adherents around the world.[5] In this view, rights inevitably expand over time and across space, and any delays or diversions are ascribed to governmental repression, cultural backwardness, or individual false consciousness. In this vision, rights' achievement will ultimately realize humanity's greatest dreams, raising it to its highest stage of development. In such an "indivisible" rights culture, as the United Nations asserts, "the improvement of one right facilitates advancement of the others," and "likewise the deprivation of one right adversely affects the others."[6] Missing, however, is the recognition that contending political forces often dress up their causes as human rights, whether individual or group. Vindicating the rights of one comes at the expense of another. In the name of rights, powerful forces have engaged in invasions, coups, and even torture.

Academics who take a more political approach to rights nonetheless continue to conceptualize them narrowly, portraying them as unequivocal goods attained through principled methods and high-minded persuasion. Movements for civil rights, women's rights, indigenous rights, and countless others are analyzed this way. It is seldom recognized, however, that in rhetorical, political, and legal conflicts over rights, they are means—potent tools to defeat opposing forces—not just ends. This is most obvious in the "cause litigation" common to highly institutionalized settings, such as American or Indian courtrooms. There rights are fought with and fought over—with direct consequences not only for the individual litigants but also for the societal groups whose interests they embody. It is equally true in other, less structured political contexts, such as newspapers, parliaments, public squares, and even battlefields. An invocation of rights, whether group or individual, can cover up less estimable goals, mobilize armed forces, shatter opposing coalitions, and destroy entire societies. This is why rights are so commonly used by the most powerful forces in modern societies, as well as by the weakest. Indeed, as this book shows, rights are multiform weapons and are popular not merely for their ostensibly progressive goals but also for their usefulness to all sides in all types of political disputes.

If scholars have recognized rights' instrumental uses, they have mostly seen them as defensive—as shields to protect the vulnerable or as hoists to raise the downtrodden. Michael Ignatieff has claimed that human rights are "universal because they define the universal interests of the powerless, namely, that power be exercised over them in ways that respect their autonomy as agents."[7] International relations specialists have highlighted the naming and shaming of violators as the primary means of vindicating rights. It is noteworthy, however, if often overlooked, that many basic rights are beloved of the powerful. A good example is property rights, which are staunchly upheld by a wealthy minority against insurgents claiming rights to food, education, work, and more. Oligarchs, who centuries ago had to protect their riches by employing private armies, have added rights as another arrow in the bulging quiver of protections they now use to maintain their status and the status quo.[8] Internationally, a gamut of rights are now invoked by Western states to justify armed interventions into weaker societies. Rationalized by concern for the most vulnerable, such interventions often advance only the interests of the most powerful.

Those scholars who do take note of material and political matters nevertheless have not sufficiently analyzed how rights operate in practice. Critical scholars, following Marx's footsteps, have noted that rights can be tools of the powerful but have seldom explored how they are actually used in politics. Others confine deep analysis of rights to specific historical or organizational settings. Lawyers and law professors, who use rights on a daily basis, demonstrate their instrumental aspects. But much of this scholarship examines rights and law within well-ordered national legal systems, particularly the United States or Canada. In such contexts, it is easy to see how litigation can be utilized as a tool. Judicial decisions can provide definitive judgments in favor of needy claimants. Less analyzed, however, are the ways in which broad political movements use rights outside institutionalized settings—to mobilize domestic support during moments of societal change or to draw international awareness to their cause.[9]

What explains this neglect, even though rights' weaponlike utility has been, as I suggest here, central to their rise? One reason may be that proponents of rights are so imbued with the righteousness of their causes and the assumed universalism of their goals that they are blind to rights' aggressive aspects—or even actively conceal them. The necessary strategic element in political conflict is seldom celebrated, at least not by the winners. Instead, theirs are triumphant tales of right over wrong. It is only those facing a rights campaign who cry that they are being attacked. Sometimes, of course, their protestations cover up their own controversial goals and repressive policies, which they themselves have draped in rights language (albeit a very different set of rights). Either way, there is much to be learned by analyzing rights as tools rather than being transfixed by their moral content.

It is true that pragmatically oriented analysts such as Ignatieff have noted that rights are "a fighting creed," one that demands "taking sides, mobilizing constituencies powerful enough to force abusers to stop[, being] partial and political."[10] The legal historian Samuel Moyn argues that human rights have risen to prominence as the contingent outcome of long-term if indirect competition with other visions of "utopia."[11] James Peck, Stephen Hopgood, and others have documented the ways in which human rights NGOs have sometimes tethered themselves to the violent foreign policies of powerful states.[12] This political realism is exactly right but limited in scope: it neither conceptualizes nor analyzes the ways in which proponents, both weak and strong, use rights in the pursuit of political goals.

Some, such as Ignatieff, claim that human rights are different from other forms of politics because they are "constrained by moral universals" that "discipline [activists'] partiality—their conviction that one side is right— with an equal commitment to the rights of the other side."[13] In fact, this is seldom the case. Rivals often portray rights conflicts as zero-sum, with full achievement of their foes' rights necessarily coming at the expense of their own. In most cases, opponents are so sure of their rectitude that they brook no concession on core values. Those who promote their causes with rights reject their foes' claims. Rights advocates denounce their opponents, even if they too come outfitted in a suit of rights. Governmental institutions may enforce particular rights, usually based on the influence of one side over those institutions. But such outcomes, variously portrayed as glorious wins, ignominious losses, or necessary but regrettable compromises, are seldom stable because the competing sides keep on fighting to achieve their rights more fully.

Some scholars recognize rights' political aspects but lament this fact or urge restraint. Richard Thompson Ford's *Universal Rights Down to Earth* typifies this view. He argues that activists overuse the concept of human rights. Instead, "only the most stark and discrete abuses" should be considered human rights issues, whereas "problems with more diffuse and complex causes are better understood as political questions."[14] Ford is hardly the first to decry rights' "proliferation" or "rightsification." For decades, academics of all political persuasions have pointed to the explosion of "rights talk" as a problematic development in national and international politics. In this view, the overuse of rights fragments societies, leading to an individualistic dissensus that ignores the common good. Others more sympathetic to the rights project criticize the expansion of new rights beyond a civil and political core. For international human rights lawyers and scholars, the ceaseless propagation of rights waters down their essence. This makes it difficult to build agreement around "fundamental" rights and rally action against the worst violators.[15]

Notwithstanding these critiques, political leaders, alert to rights' utility, ignore the dons' warnings. Rights continue their historic march, used by all sides in all manner of conflicts. They are not so much goals as means in these struggles. As Nicola Perugini and Neve Gordon show, for instance, Israel's Jewish settlers now employ indigenous and property rights to deprive Palestinians of land and ultimately to undermine Palestinian activism, if not Palestinian society itself.[16] In the United States, where the Supreme Court in 2015 affirmed the right to same-sex marriage, Democrats are already using the *Obergefell v. Hodges* decision to drive wedges into a Republican Party torn between conservative religious voters who oppose the decision and party leaders who, with an eye on electoral victories, are more divided. In this move, liberals follow a well-worn path: before the Court's decision, conservatives had used the ostensible threat that same-sex marriage posed to religious freedom as a means of wedging traditionalist Democrats away from the Democratic Party leadership as it became increasingly supportive of such marriages in the late 2000s.

All these examples of how aggressively rights can be used, how open they are to political manipulation, and how the powerful as well as the weak take advantage of them show that it is high time that scholars broaden their conceptual thinking about rights. I hope to contribute to this task by analyzing the varying ways in which rights are made to operate by political antagonists. This analysis will also illuminate the overwhelming strategic temptation to "rightsify"—to turn social problems into rights claims in contemporary conflicts.

Definitions and Preliminaries

PROPONENTS AND FOES

In this book, I focus much of my attention on rights "proponents" or "activists"—individuals, organizations, and states that formulate, raise, or advance rights claims on behalf of themselves or other groups. Activists are usually linked to "movements," defined broadly by Sidney Tarrow as "collective challenges, based on common purposes and solidarities, in sustained inter-action with . . . opponents."[17] "Opponents," "rivals," or "foes" are individu-als, groups, and institutions that fight against the proposed right. They too are part of movements—rival ones with their own set of activists promoting a contrary set of rights. Finally, beyond the main parties to conflict, conten-tion over rights involves third parties, those outside the opposing groups who hold resources that could help shift its outcome. Third parties some-times become so closely enmeshed with one side to conflict that they can be difficult to separate from it in practice. Nonetheless, I use this tripartite division to examine the various tactics that movements use in rights conflicts.

It should be underlined that these definitions of activists and move-ments encompass more than just the left-wing groups highlighted in the scholarly literature. My definitions span the political spectrum to include an ideologically diverse set of actors. The same goes for opponents of a rights movement, who are not necessarily conservative groups, as the foes of the right-to-life movement attest. More controversially perhaps, the definitions I use include individuals and groups regardless of their relation to governmental institutions and political power. Political party leaders, government officials, or even states themselves may be considered rights proponents in certain circumstances, even if in others they resist or repress rights claims from opposition activists. Notwithstanding these and other complexities, in the conceptual sections of this book, I distinguish the various conflicting parties and their tactics. In the empirical chapters, I seek to do so as well, although the task of categorizing key actors as pro-ponents or opponents is harder because of the dynamism and contention involved.

RIGHTS

What do I mean by "rights"? It should be clear already that I define the word more broadly and differently than many who study "human rights." For one thing, I include within my purview property rights, group rights, and even majority rights that are seldom considered by scholars of human rights. For another, I downplay, although by no means omit, the moral component of rights, for reasons discussed later. Instead, in this book I adopt a definition loosely based on the ideas of the legal philosopher Wesley Hohfeld. I define a "right" as the power of one entity, the rights-holder, to enforce a duty on another, the duty-bearer, whether directly or through some institution such as a court.[18] The closely related term "rights claim" is a demand for such a right made by a proponent against an opponent through a rhetorical, legal, political, or military campaign.

These definitions of rights and rights claims are expansive. They cover individual human rights vis-à-vis a government, including the familiar "negative" rights—for instance, to free expression and association, which are realized when states leave individuals alone.[19] These definitions also include "positive" rights, which require states or other entities to provide concrete goods to individuals, such as the right to food or the right to water. Finally, the definition includes group rights, whether those of ethnic, racial, religious, or other minorities—or of majorities or even states—to anything from land for their people to protection for their cultures and territories.

Notwithstanding the scope of this definition, a key point for my purposes is that neither rights claims nor rights are ends in themselves. As Paul Sniderman and his coauthors note, the politics of rights involves "not the existence of support for a particular democratic right or freedom, but rather . . . concrete questions of public policy and constitutional politics."[20] This is a critical point, but it is important to go beyond it: rights and their correlative duties are means of achieving something substantive, whether that be abstract, such as freedom of thought or religion, or material, such as rights to food or shelter. This point is clearest for property rights, which are clearly rights *to* something. Now consider rights that might appear less concrete, such as the right to free expression. In this case, too, the right is inconsequential or at least incomplete without someone saying something— and almost always in the cases that matter most to defining the right, something controversial, hurtful, or offensive to another. Broadly defined rights such as women's rights mean the right *to* equal treatment, among other things. Next consider the right to privacy, which might appear merely to involve the community's leaving people alone. Again, however, being left alone permits the individual to gain something real, such as a contraceptive device or an abortion. In the digital world, the right to privacy provides something equally important if abstract—a zone in which others cannot observe the rights-holder. Reciprocally, the right to privacy imposes a duty on others, whether private or public entities, to stand clear. Finally, it is worth noting that rights provide another abstract but critical end: recognition of the rights bearer as an individual or group. Forcing those in power to grant such recognition may be as important to the rights proponent as attaining material aims.

RIGHTS VERSUS RIGHTS CLAIMS

If rights are means to such ends, the distinction between rights and rights claims recedes in importance. It is true that in legal practice a "vested right" is a right (usually to property) that cannot be taken away. However, in politics rights are seldom if ever irrevocable and self-implementing, automatically providing the entitlement, let alone the objective, they encompass on paper. This is so even for rights embodied in the constitutions of democratic states. In such countries, rights litigation remains a constant feature of larger politico-legal disagreements over shifting conceptions of the substantive goals embodied in particular rights. In these continuing struggles, activists use formal written rights much as they previously voiced rights claims to achieve these goals.

Much political conflict involves the problem of turning a rights claim into a right, usually embodied in a written law. There is no question that the codification of a right is a signal moment. In principle, at least in liberal democracies, it places the enormous power of the state behind enforcement of the duty correlative to the right. But this is never the end of the story. Even after promulgation of rights, rights campaigns continue focusing on three additional matters of critical importance: fighting back against the ostensible new duty-bearer's continuing efforts at reversal; compelling the duty-bearer to implement the novel right, often through pressure on the state to enforce the duty; and shaping the constantly evolving interpretation of the right's definition, contours, and limits. Obviously, there are substantial overlaps among these conceptually distinct but inescapably muddy situations. In recent years in many countries, contending groups have debated whether human rights encompass sexual rights, in particular gay and lesbian rights. Where that question is answered affirmatively with new law, further questions are whether sexual rights encompass the right to same-sex marriage, to adoption by same-sex couples, to rights of transgender people, and more. Given such overlaps, I use the terms "rights" and "rights claims" interchangeably in this book to encompass any of the foregoing attempts to achieve and maintain the underlying goals sought by campaigners.[21]

RIGHTS AND MORALITY

This book's omission of a moral component from its definition of rights should now be even more glaring. In this, the definition used here differs from any number of others, particularly of human rights, such as Ignatieff's quoted earlier, or Micheline Ishay's definition of these rights as "universal," held "equally by everyone . . . simply because they are part of the human species."[22] Similarly absent is any notion that rights are natural or inherent. Rather, my definition follows that of legal realists who argue that the rights available at a particular time and place reflect a transient and conditional balance, pivoting on the political question of who can enforce a duty on another.[23] In this book, I focus on the means by which that fluctuating balance is achieved—in particular, the ways in which political actors use all manner of rights as tools to do so.

Notwithstanding the power of the legal realist perspective, there is a critical moral dimension to rights that legal realists have largely overlooked. Rights gain their tactical usefulness in part from their ability to galvanize constituents and third parties into action, and this in turn hinges on the ethical pull they exert on those audiences. Countless numbers have enlisted in movements and militaries, believing in rights. People have protested, fought, and died in pursuit of rights and, more fundamentally, their substantive goals. Rights claims resonate across national borders and cultural communities. Rights gain acclaim and power because masses of people believe that they and the ends they help realize are good—and right. Yet it is notable that where the rhetoric of rights sounds loudly in a conflict, it resounds on all sides. Adversaries contend over different views of what is right and what their own rights should be. The attraction that one side's claims exercise over its own members leaves the rival movement's constituents cold. We shall see many examples in this book. What this righteous contention shows is that rights' moral dimension is powerful but limited: it may be formidable enough to rouse a particular community, but it is often negligible outside of that community, where other moral visions, rival rights, and contrary goals exercise equal and opposite appeal.

Following this approach, I view such charged terms as "human," "universal," and "inherent" as superfluous to the definition of rights, and even to the definition of human rights, despite being so frequently attached to them. If I am correct, however, this raises the question of the terms' purposes. This will be an important subject for detailed analysis in this book, particularly in chapter 2. The short answer is that these additional terms are rhetorical moves aimed at securing the claimant's underlying goals, most importantly by attracting adherents to the cause through moralistic rights language. Rights' proponents, particularly human rights advocates, may reject such views. After all, they are advocates, and many deeply believe in the goals that these rights help secure. To admit anything different, even if they saw it, would be to call into question the fundamentality of the rights they most revere and reveal them as mere political preferences. However, their deep engagement in activism aimed at achieving those very rights belies this posture. It shows their actual political realism, even if they strategically cloud this with idealist oratory. Notwithstanding advocates' views, this book adopts a legal realist view of all rights, including those claimed to be human.

In adopting this definition, I similarly reject the idea of an a priori hierarchy of rights. Leaving aside the most trivial of rights claims—ones that have failed to generate major political movements—it is hard to prove that certain rights are by nature more important to human thriving than others. This has not stopped political actors from seeking to erect hierarchies of rights. Governments and scholars, especially in the West, have proclaimed civil and political rights more genuine or fundamental than economic, social, and cultural rights, even while Communist and developing states have sought to reverse the ranking.[24] Proponents take a hierarchical view as well: unsurprisingly, they elevate their preferred right to the superior position. Conflict between the right to life and right to choice suggests how controversial activists' rankings are in practice. For the type of analysis I attempt in this book, however, I eschew such a priori hierarchies and instead focus on ones that actually exist in practice (even if I may personally disagree with them). If one right is more fully vindicated than another—and this kind of differentiation is inevitable—it is primarily a matter of the right's having an influential political movement or power-holder behind it. Sometimes this movement is so successful that its goals have been incorporated into the state itself, through constitutional or legal provisions. In such cases, the movement may become almost invisible, its formerly controversial goals so broadly accepted as to be treated as unassailable common sense. Still, it is important to realize that no matter how thick the accretion of political, legal, and rhetorical support for a right, it remains subject to possible change in the future.

To go further, the substantive goals that rights help realize are not necessarily liberating or progressive. Rather, the ends that rights may achieve are open and indeterminate. Adversaries seeking divergent, even contradictory, goals invoke rights. The strong as well as the weak assert rights claims and seek to impose duties on others. Making a similar point about the broader concept of liberty, John Acton stated that it has "two hundred definitions, and . . . this wealth of interpretation has caused more bloodshed than anything, except theology."[25] This point applies as well to human rights, although most who promote them would claim that they have a deeper, moral foundation, one that necessarily protects the individual from the collective and the weak from the powerful. That is one potential way in which "human rights" may be implemented. It is by no means the only one, however, and quite possibly not the most common. In today's world, governments and movements of all political persuasions regularly don the mantle of human rights. Some may proclaim the membership of countries such as Egypt and Saudi Arabia on the UN's Human Rights Council as a perversion of the concept. Yet such perversions are inherent in the structure and vague terminology of rights themselves. As Perugini and Gordon argue, any political cause can be draped in a rights frame, even those that involve outright domination of one group by another.[26] Certainly, those who prefer "liberal" concepts are free to label themselves as the sole upholders of human rights. But they cannot prevent others from using the same terminology to advance contrary aims—nor from seeking to achieve them through the imposition of a duty on another.

The Argument

RIGHTS AS WEAPONS

If the ends that competing rights proponents seek are open, conflicting, and not necessarily liberating, activists of all political persuasions also treat rights as weapons of political conflict. They do so in three broad ways, whether leading insurgent social movements, reformist NGOs, or established states. Before the fray, they mobilize their supporters and sympathizers using righteous *rallying cries* to bolster support. In conflicts, they *deploy* rights against their foes. And those targeted *counter* the blows, using their own rights rhetoric to marshal forces against their attacker. In each of these three aspects, those mounting—or rebuffing—rights use a recurrent set of approaches or repertoires. Table 1.1 and the remainder of this section outline each of these tactics, and later chapters describe them in detail.

Consider rallying cries, the rhetoric that activists use to mobilize their own forces and sympathetic third parties. One such method is to argue that a particular right is *natural* or *human*. Broadening their ambitions, rights proponents proclaim certain rights to be *universal*, applicable everywhere and always. To forestall argument about the rights they promote, they portray them as *apolitical*, as neutral baseline principles that must *remain* immune from the sordid compromises of mere politics. On these foundations, they describe their preferred right as *absolute*, trumping rival interests or

---

TABLE 1.1. Rights Tactics in Political Conflicts

RALLYING CRIES

Proponent mobilizes supporters and third parties by portraying its rights as:

    Human (or natural): Innate or inherent to all

    Universal: Applicable across time, space, and culture

    Absolute: Trumping other interests, concerns, or rights

    Apolitical: Above politics and beyond debate

    Violated: By opponent

DEPLOYMENTS

Proponent uses rights as:

    Camouflage: To hide underlying goals and motives

    Spear: To overturn discrete policy or law

    Dynamite: To undermine or destroy a foe's culture or community

    Blockade: To suppress another subordinate group

    Wedge: To weaken or break a rival coalition

COUNTERS

Opponent uses its own rights as:

    Shield: To protect itself from the proponent

    Parry: To repulse the proponent's rights claims through:

        Denial: Rebutting the proponent's claims that its rights are human, universal, apolitical, and absolute

        Rivalry: Promoting its own rights contrary to the proponent's

        Reversal: Depicting itself as a victim of the proponent's violations

        Repudiation: Rejecting seemingly authoritative decisions against itself

---

community concerns. Today all four of these rhetorical moves are often mistaken for incontrovertible facts. Certainly, activists advertise them as such, and trumpet them from the ramparts. Simultaneously, they depict their rights as *violated*, publicizing or even flaunting their foe's abuses. But too few scholars have examined these pronouncements as tactical devices aimed at mobilization; nor have they critically probed their sources, structures, and effects among aggrieved groups or potential third-party supporters.

Next consider proponents' deployments of rights to weaken their foes and obtain their objectives. Such tactics include the use of rights as *camouflage* to catch foes off-guard, by hiding or legitimating unpalatable ideas; as *spears* to attack specific policies in the hope of poisoning the larger system over the long run; as *dynamite* to blow up entire cultural or social systems immediately; as *blockades* to thwart rival movements; and as *wedges* or crowbars to fracture or smash opposing coalitions. Nor are these multifold uses of rights mere happenstance. Activists carefully consider the most effective ways to use rights in particular political and social contexts, then put one or more of these tactics into action.

Rights' militant side is revealed not only by the activists who invoke them but also by their foes, who work to counter the initial campaign. When attacked, they use a different set of rights as rhetorical *shields* to defend their current status and privileges. In addition, they fight back. Repressive states facing a rights campaign may deploy paramilitaries, guns, and torture. In other societies, force may be exerted less brutally, with police, courts, and prisons playing key roles in the repression of a movement promoting new rights. Just as important, foes respond to a rights movement with rhetorical *parries* involving a contrary set of rights tactics. *Denial* seeks to puncture the original movement's Olympian pretensions to the naturalness, universality, neutrality, and absolutism of its rights. *Rivalry* raises a contrary set of rights, ones favorable to the original opponent. *Reversal* depicts the foe as a virtuous victim of the original rights movement—and the latter as a persecutor. Finally, there is *repudiation*, the rejection not just of claims but of seemingly authoritative judgments about them that go against the foe, whether these occur in courtrooms, elections, or the streets. Notably, just as with the original movement's rallying cries, these countering methods work to mobilize the opponent's own constituents and potential allies. Parrying tactics will seldom convince the original rights proponent that it is wrong, but that is not their purpose. Rather, like the use of righteous rallying cries to mobilize supporters of a movement, countering devices bolster the foe's defenses and ready its own movement for action.

A STRATEGIC VIEW OF THE RISE OF RIGHTS

To return to an earlier point, the effects of the righteous rallying cries, deployments, and countering tactics outlined here hinge in part on rights' moral appeal to a particular community. For centuries, masses of people have been moved to political action because they believed they were fighting for the good—even if others disagreed and were motivated by contrary rights to pursue opposite goals. Recognizing the intertwining of rights' strategic and ethical dimensions therefore opens an alternative perspective on their historical rise, highlighting their utility in political struggle in addition to their moral magnetism. Few historians would dispute rights' dual nature as both ends and means of conflict. But fewer still have explored the latter dimension as itself a key factor in creating what the international lawyer Louis Henkin has called today's "age of rights," or what the political scientist James Ron and his collaborators argue is an increasingly internationalized rights culture. Some, such as the historian Lynn Hunt, argue that rights have risen to prominence through a seemingly unstoppable cultural shift as human empathy for those different from oneself has gradually expanded. Other scholars portray rights as the product of mankind's innate yearning for dignity; all people desire rights and all people will reach for them. International relations specialists highlight the role of enlightened outsiders—NGOs, international organizations, and fellow cosmopolitans—in bringing universal rights to the world's oppressed. Finally, Moyn holds that human rights represent the "last man standing" among a set of ideologies, such as socialism, that have failed to realize human thriving.[27]

I do not directly challenge these historical interpretations. The rise of rights has many causes. Instead, I supplement these accounts by showing that rights have also risen because of their great utility in political conflicts. Although rights are not the only means of making claims, they are highly effective tools to this end. Proponents have therefore found them important to advancing their goals, as I will show by retelling key episodes in the rise of rights from this perspective. The result is a novel way of explaining how we have entered today's "age of rights." This is a story that is primarily strategic. It illuminates how rights arguments have advanced "progress"—but also slowed or prevented it. Of course, strategy is not everything. Contingency and uncertainty swirl around rhetorical conflicts, just as the fog of war enshrouds real battlefields. New issues arise, old ones look different at later times, and foes may turn one's tactics upon oneself. There is only so much that even the most skillful can predict in a context of inevitable reaction from foes, unforeseen actions by third parties, and random occurrences in the world at large. Notwithstanding such limitations, for analysts and activists alike, understanding the strategic uses of rights in politics—both to build a movement and to undermine a foe—is of great importance.

I am not the first to argue that rhetoric, including rights rhetoric, serves as a tool of politics. As E. H. Carr wrote long ago, "The intellectual theories and ethical standards of utopianism, far from being the expression of absolute and a priori principles, are historically conditioned, being both products of circumstances and interests and weapons framed for the furtherance of interests."[28] Daniel Rodgers argues that "keywords" such as "rights" have been "instruments, rallying cries, tools of persuasion . . . often weapons" in American politics since the founding.[29] In his study of political identity, Joseph Margulies calls the nation's ideals "verbal weapons in a continual struggle" over their content, and Michael Kammen has documented similar uses of the related concept of liberty.[30] The same can be said overseas: internationally, the use of rights language has proliferated as a "master frame," proving Tarrow's point that "contentious language that takes hold successfully in one context tends to diffuse to others."[31] However, as the outline of this book's argument should show, I take the analogy between rights and weapons more seriously than others. Conceptually, I provide the first systematic framework for identifying, distinguishing, and understanding the forms that such weaponry can take. Analytically, I propose a set of hypotheses concerning each of these forms, including their most likely users, targets, content, mechanisms, and probabilities of success. Empirically, I provide sustained analyses of varied domestic and international rights conflicts to demonstrate the utility of the concepts and the plausibility of the hypotheses. Nor do I confine myself to the type of rights most frequently analyzed in recent years, human rights, but instead examine the full panoply of rights in a wide variety of contexts.

Caveats

RHETORICAL, NOT PHYSICAL, WEAPONS

Before detailing this argument in later chapters, let me clarify what I am not saying. First, I do not maintain that rights are literally the same as physical weapons or that activists use rights exclusively for cynical or aggressive purposes. Rights claims have resounded through the most significant advances in human history, helping to bring emancipation and freedom to millions. Many proponents have sincerely believed in the slogans they shout. Rights are commonly used for defensive purposes, and the scholarly literature on rights has highlighted such usages.

What I do claim, however, is that rights have an equally important and underanalyzed offensive capacity analogous to certain types of material weapons and aggressive tactics.[32] Because rights are quintessential tools of politics, they can be used by any side to a conflict. As with material weapons, even the mildest application of rights may be perceived by the opponent as belligerent, no matter how much the claimant argues that this is a misperception.[33] This perception will then affect the way in which the foe reacts and the conflict unfolds. Proponents may not always intend to use rights aggressively, but they can easily turn them this way and often do. Even if normative definitions predominate in scholarly works, hostile uses constantly obtrude in practical politics and legal actions. To identify rights only with the defensive or the good misses much that is intrinsic to their actual usages, even if rights proponents often hide the aggressive element. In short, I seek a realistic understanding of how and why rights are deployed as weapons, as well as the effect of such uses on the movement, its foes, and the larger conflict.

By focusing on the aggressive, I do not reject the fact that rights have other aspects or that they enjoy deep moral resonance among those who voice them. Nor do I hold that conflicts over rights boil down to mere struggles for power. The groups at odds with one another seek power for substantive aims, whether material or abstract. They form not out of individuals' will to power but out of shared identities, principles, or conditions, which in turn are shaped by their interactions with others who are different from themselves. All of this underlines again the need for scholars to analyze rights as offensive weapons that are used to advance a movement's goals and undermine its foe's, albeit weapons that gain much of their power from their strong but limited moral appeal.

This raises the issue of whether we can separate rights as ends from rights as means. Clearly, the two are interwoven. Yet it is possible and useful to disentangle them. Most analysts of rights have done so, but turn their eyes to rights as ends. I take a different tack, highlighting proponents' offensive uses of rights as weapons to achieve all manner of political goals. At the same time, I do not neglect the ends that rights are thought to achieve, but examine how they, and their glorious rhetorical casing, may become corroded when rights are used as means.

OTHER FORMS OF CLAIMS-MAKING

Second, I do not believe that people make claims exclusively by asserting rights, nor should they. Some make claims by pleading for their needs to be fulfilled, or they appeal to a foe's sense of morality or responsibility. Others demand justice, equity, or fairness. Still others posit the societal utility of their goals, bargaining for them against other groups with different goals. In many conflicts, protagonists make multiple arguments simultaneously. But these other demands hinge on the foe's goodwill, empathy, or judgment. They do not result in enforceable legal obligations. Rights do. We therefore frequently see efforts to turn these other arguments into rights claims and rights. One example is the quest for economic development. Long seen as a social good, in recent years it has increasingly been framed as a right by a new movement for "rights-based development." Another is the quest for environmental quality, once justified on ethical or utilitarian grounds but now increasingly portrayed by the environmental movement as a right, even a right of nature. In the end, however, these rights claims amount to little more than an effort to transform a political judgment into a legal mandate and a tool for mass mobilization. Whether or not the turn to rights is a wise strategy in any particular struggle, it is common today in a variety of issues.[34]

Of course, even a right seldom provides certainty of enforcement. In many ways, rights are under constant threat. Foes seek to whittle them away, impose contrary rights, or ignore their duties. Sovereign power, dressed in the garb of majority rights, threatens individual rights, particularly in times portrayed as crises. In liberal democracies with working judicial and enforcement mechanisms, however, rights provide greater assurance that a goal will be realized than do other forms of claims-making.

Rights claims are prominent even in realms far removed from such societies, though they are not the only way that claims are made. Rights talk may have reached its zenith in the United States, but it is now internationally recognized. Such recognition encourages groups around the world, even those without long traditions of rights activism, to broadcast their goals and grievances in the form of rights and their violation. In terms used by scholars of contentious politics, rights are both symbolically resonant and modular.[35] They can be used in vastly different cultural settings with similar effects. Ultimately this entails imposing a duty on another entity, but it also involves using rights as tools to achieve the political goal. Today local activists in global backwaters often request support from powerful Western audiences, asserting that their rights are being violated. For these audiences, rights are an intelligible form of claims-making, even if the pleas emanate from alien locales. Or at least they appear understandable: distant appeals often mask a more complex and contrary reality. Just as important, the workings of power are legitimated by such claims, as we see in examples such as the divine right of kings historically or the supposed rights of the community against those even merely suspected of terrorism or crime today. In most societies, alternative forms of claims-making may offer independent bases of political action, but they must in the end be institutionalized as rights to be enforceable and meaningful. For this reason alone, rights are one of the commonest forms of political rhetoric in the contemporary world.

POWER, HIERARCHY, AND RIGHTS

Third, my downplaying of rights' moral dimension does not mean that I personally agree that "might makes right" or accept existing hierarchies of rights. Limits on state and corporate power have been major achievements in human history, even if much remains to be done.[36] They have not been reached through some immanent force in rights or the underlying goals they provide but only through enormous, generations-long efforts to harness countervailing power. Ultimately these efforts have been aimed at imposing a duty on some other entity. In this, rights strategies have played key roles both in advancing movements' agendas and in undermining foes' contrary aims.

On the other hand, those foes typically gained and maintained control using analogous rights tactics. Even if one opposes such power structures, the realities must be acknowledged for the sake of accurate analysis and critique. Doing so does not signal acceptance of the status quo as legitimate, inevitable, or unchanging, but rather emphasizes the inherently political basis on which rights exist, always in a form contingent on maintenance of the current constellation of power. For unfortunate confirmation of this view, one need only consult the recent history of torture in America. The George W. Bush administration implemented it secretly after 9/11, the Obama administration ended it but refused to prosecute its perpetrators, and Donald Trump shouted his belief in it, then successfully nominated CIA director Gina Haspel, who supervised waterboarding and allegedly destroyed evidence about doing so. The supposedly fundamental right to bodily integrity—one typically placed at the apex of the philosophers' rights hierarchy—has fallen victim, to one degree or another, to the right of the community to feel secure. Indeed, the U.S. government has justified torture using rights-based language and what Rebecca Sanders has called "plausible legality" in which "officials seek out legal cover to secure immunity and legitimacy for questionable policies."[37]

SINCERITY AND CYNICISM

From a methodological stance, these points raise the question of whether and how I distinguish between sincere and insincere uses of rights. For the most part, I do not seek to do so and do not believe it is necessary to solve this conundrum. In political conflicts, proponents' motives are mixed: they may believe in their causes, but they are also willing to use their rights instrumentally to achieve their ultimate goals. Sincerity and cynicism are tightly interwoven, but separating them is seldom essential for analytic purposes. True, certain aspects of rights' effectiveness may hinge on an advocate's force of expression or her belief in the right's ethical imperative. Conversely, if rights were seen for what they are—as staple tools for achieving contending activists' conflicting moral visions—they might lose some of their inspirational force. Nonetheless, because both the weak and the strong use rights tactics to restrain others and to empower themselves, revealing rights' workings is fruitful and even potentially freeing. In any case, rights will still retain their critical legal power: crystallizing the entitlements and duties of individuals and groups, including the state itself, in the wake of political mobilization and conflict.

The Plan of the Book

To make this argument, I present a conceptual framework of the "rights as weapons" perspective, then apply it to historical and contemporary cases. In chapter 2, I detail the ways in which leaders of political movements raise rights as rallying cries to mobilize their members and third-party sympathizers. Chapter 3 turns to how foes counter these tactics, and the movements themselves, with their own rights tactics aimed at shielding their interests and parrying the blows against them.

In the next five chapters, I turn to the ways in which proponents use rights to advance their side or weaken their foe. Chapter 4 examines rights' use as camouflage to cover ulterior motives, a tactic common to all manner of conflicts and one that often accompanies the other tactics I examine. The next two chapters consider the invocation of rights in simple conflicts pitting two antagonists against one another. Of course, conflicts are never so simple, because third parties are always available on the sidelines for mobilization. For heuristic purposes, however, it is helpful to examine this barebones scenario before turning to more complex ones. In chapter 5, I examine the common situation in which a weak actor uses rights against a stronger one. I call this a "spear" tactic because the weaker actor uses only a narrow claim against a single policy, typically because he does not have the power or resources to mount a broader campaign. Chapter 6 considers the opposite situation: the use of rights claims by powerful forces to quash weaker groups. This I call rights as "dynamite," because the aims of making such claims are broad, immediate, and explosive: the destruction of key aspects of the foe's social or cultural system—or the foe itself.

Chapters 7 and 8 examine rights tactics in more complex and realistic situations that involve not only two main antagonists but also third parties. In chapter 7, I examine "blockade" tactics: the refusal of a movement seeking its rights to join forces with other deprived groups against a powerful common foe. Instead, the movement appeals to the foe, arguing that a grant of its own rights will act as a bulwark against the rise of the other deprived group. In chapter 8, I analyze how activists use rights as "crowbars," or "wedges," to break third parties away from the rival coalition and, if possible, have them join its own alliance, weakening the foe and advancing the movement's goals.

Each of these five chapters follows a similar format. First, I define the weapon-like usage of rights and its purposes. Then I discuss several issues: the political context in which rights are likely to be used in this particular way; the movements most likely to do so; the foes most likely to be targeted; the rights most easily fashioned to this purpose; the mechanism of their deployment; and the likelihood of success. Next, the chapters illustrate each tactic through detailed analysis of one or more conflicts. (Necessarily, these case studies also pay heed to the mobilizing, countering, and camouflaging tactics conceptualized in chapters 2, 3, and 4.) Admittedly, there is never a perfect fit between the ideal typical concepts I develop and their manifestations in actual cases. However, the empirical studies demonstrate the plausibility of the hypotheses I propose and indicate that viewing rights through the weapons analogy advances our understanding of political conflicts.

Some of the cases I examine in the empirical chapters are historical, such as America's nineteenth-century voting rights movements (chapter 7 on blockade tactics) and twentieth-century civil rights movement (chapter 8 on wedge tactics). Others are contemporary. I examine the use of rights arguments in the nationalist struggles in Northern Ireland and Catalonia (chapter 4 on camouflage tactics), in Italy's disputes over religious symbols (chapter 5 on spear tactics), and in Africa's conflicts over LGBT rights, in America's war in Afghanistan, and in European burqa bans (chapter 6 on dynamite tactics). In addition, I analyze rights claims surrounding the transgender movement (chapter 7 on blockade tactics) and LGBT rights in Israel-Palestine and the United States (chapter 8 on wedge tactics). As support for my argument, I rely on a wide variety of primary and secondary sources, including interviews. (A complete online bibliography, including active citations for unique activist sources, is available at the book's Princeton University Press website.)

My major criterion in selecting this broad range of cases was to choose those cases that best illuminate the particular tactic under discussion. This approach is particularly useful in books such as this one, which propose new hypotheses and theoretical perspectives. Such "plausibility probes" accentuate key conceptual points and critical empirical processes. In addition, given the importance of many of the cases I examine, the approach suggests that this book's perspective has broader analytic value.[38] On the other hand, it cannot show how common these tactics are. Other researchers will use other methods to answer that question. However, as the panoply of cases mentioned in this chapter and the others discussed in depth later should suggest, it seems likely that these aggressive tactics are common if largely overlooked. At minimum, this book should attune analysts to this possibility as they examine a wide variety of rights movements worldwide.

Conclusion

Notwithstanding the moral pull of rights and rights claims—at least for their proponents—rights of all kinds are inescapably political. From this perspective, this book's central questions are: how do rights claimants achieve their goals, and how do they impose corresponding duties on others? Material factors obviously play a key role. Money, bodies, and arms—these have always been central to struggles for rights, and I do not believe that rights arguments displace them. Instead, I argue that the rhetorical and legal force of rights works powerfully, in mutual interaction with material factors. Threats to rights can and do spark violence. Rights conflicts can lead to real wars. As such, rights and rights claims cannot necessarily be seen as secondary to material factors. The rhetoric of rights, violation, and victim—used by all sides—is itself a potent force. As Stuart Scheingold has urged, rights should be treated "like other political resources: money, numbers, status, and so forth."[39] Like them, rights are instruments of politics. Although they are not as easy to measure in concrete terms, rights are equally useful in a broader political strategy to achieve a particular goal—in part, as we shall see, because of the moral fervor that a rights claim, and the charge of violations, can unleash among the abused community and its sympathizers. This plays a key role in mobilizing a movement and sympathizers to the cause. Just as important, the sharp edge of rights claims makes them formidable and multifold tools against opponents.

If we supplement conventional perspectives on rights, what is the payoff? Most important, analyzing rights' unexplored aggressive face directs attention to rights claims' political aspects, which are frequently obscured or blurred when rights are examined from a moral vantage. Notwithstanding the fact that many campaigns aim to correct egregious and undeniable wrongs, there are numerous others whose claims are less clear-cut. Which should triumph: Reproductive rights or the right to life? The right to property or the right to work? The rights of criminal suspects or the rights of victims? The contention and compromises surrounding these and numerous other issues underline their political aspects, despite their obvious moral content.

In addition, rights campaigns involve continuous and critical strategic decisions, not least about the ways in which claims are made. Yet these decisions are shortchanged in heroic accounts of the subjugated dispatching the oppressor. Examining rights' aggressive face simultaneously directs attention to the resistance raised by this aggressiveness. This perspective also counters teleological analyses of rights campaigns that explicitly or implicitly assume the historical inevitability of a past or future right. In fact, rights as ends remain contingent and vulnerable, even in the most rights-conscious of countries. And a major reason why contestation over their implementation, scope, and meaning continues long after they are added to national constitutions, let alone international conventions, is that rights themselves serve as weapons, not only to advance their proponents' interests but also to wound or even destroy their opponents.

PART I

Preparing for Conflict

Rights as Rallying Cries

MOBILIZING SUPPORT

A strategic view of rights directs attention to three ways in which proponents use them. First, they broadcast rights as rallying cries to galvanize supporters and sympathizers. Second, they deploy rights offensively against their foes. And third, foes counter these onslaughts with their own contrary set of rights arguments. Although all three aspects of rights' use are closely linked, interacting and affecting each other, it is helpful to treat them separately for analytic purposes. In this chapter, I theorize about rallying cries—the use of rights within a political movement to mobilize support among the movement's constituents and its potential third-party allies.

In preparation for conflict, proponents assemble political resources: money, matériel, and masses. One critical way of accomplishing this task is to rouse support using rights rhetoric. Declaring their rights in the strongest of terms—not as their claims or even demands, but as their *rights*—political leaders further consecrate them as human, universal, absolute, and apolitical. With these four expressions as rallying cries, activists worry little about the precise definition of each term, instead banking on their vague, overlapping, and inspiring drift. From an analytic standpoint, however, each rallying cry has a distinct meaning and purpose that is important to disentangle and analyze. In examining these different mobilizing terms, I focus on how they strengthen a campaign, helping the claimant achieve his goals by making the right appear more attractive, especially to a movement's own constituents or potential sympathizers. Rallying cries also encourage activism by placing foes on the defensive—or, more accurately, by appearing to do so—in the eyes of movement members. Here I will briefly preview the discussion of how these tactics work. Describing a right as *human* (or, more commonly in the past, *natural*) furnishes it with deep or innate roots. Framing a right as *universal* expands its scope infinitely across time, space, and culture. Viewing a right as *absolute* adds urgency and implies that it eclipses other interests, concerns, or rights. Portraying a right as *apolitical*, by placing it above politics and beyond debate, renders it transcendent. In addition to these four primary rallying cries, there is a closely related fifth: proponents continuously depict their rights as *violated* by their foe, often with good evidence. Because claims of violation are so closely linked to calls for the right itself, however, I integrate my discussion of this theme into discussion of the other four.

Before detailing the principal mobilizing terms, it is important to discuss in greater depth the groups most likely to be influenced by them. To start with the negative, the various rallying cries will leave foes of a campaign unfazed. However compelling the rhetoric surrounding rights, foes will not be convinced by an advocate's assertions of her rights. After all, any rights campaign invariably puts an opponent's status, interests, and projects at risk and threatens to impose new duties or costs and to reduce the foe's freedom of action. Against these powerful inertial forces, the foregoing rhetoric can do little to change the foe's beliefs (although it may provide a clue that conflict is nearing and that the foe should also begin to mobilize). No matter: persuading opponents is not the main reason that leaders of a rights movement sharpen their claims. They do so to weaken foes indirectly—by mobilizing their own supporters, thereby strengthening the movement.

Constituents

To understand how such mobilization works, it is important to distinguish two groups of potential supporters, constituents and third-party allies. The constituents of a movement—for example, those demanding civil, political, or sexual rights within a country—are all those who are currently deprived of what they consider their rights. These aggrieved populations have a direct stake in the outcome of the conflict. Winning or losing can have a major impact on them. Allies do not have such a close relationship to the cause. When a domestic movement achieves its rights, allies will not gain directly, although an ally may benefit indirectly, if only by being able to claim that it had the foresight to pick a winner. Conversely, if a movement fails, allies suffer few if any consequences. Given these differences, it is important to discuss separately the varying effects of righteous rallying cries on constituents and on allies.

For the aggrieved constituents, such rhetoric might seem unnecessary. Wouldn't anyone without rights want to rise and realize them? In many cases, leading members of a group feel their oppression acutely and advocate for their rights early. But the bulk of deprived populations are not activists. For three reasons laid out by John Gaventa, people may remain quiescent even when the deprivation they face seems likely to breed rebellion. The threat or reality of repression plays a role, imposing high costs on resistance. Beyond outright or veiled brutality, institutions may be so stacked against dissent as to make it appear futile. Or in a conformist political climate, certain goals may be inexpressible or possibly even unthinkable.[1]

For activists, however, rallying cries are a good way of mobilizing the aggrieved even in the face of repression. Although words alone are not enough, rights rhetoric plays an important role in conjunction with and contributing to organizational efforts. Shouting for rights can wake the masses, sensitize them to injustices they have long endured, and make them believe in their own power. Just as battlefield commanders scream war cries, proponents use rights rhetoric to mobilize constituencies into action. In turn, mobilization and organization build confidence and strengthen demands. Invariably, cries of rights are mingled with claims of violations— often with good reason as foes clamp down. In some cases too, valid broadcasting of wrongs slides into exaggerated flaunting of the adversary's abuses. However characterized, such publication serves as a flag to inflame grievances, incite enmities, and rally forces. As we shall see, portraying a claimed right as natural or universal can alter expectations about what is deserved. It can also change how individuals see themselves: the abused as inherently having rights and dignity, the deprived as being equal everywhere, and the forgotten as being history-makers.

For many aggrieved groups, righteous rhetoric legitimates claims that may not have been considered previously. To declare "our rights" acceptable, if not compulsory, is advantageous and even necessary, especially in the lead-up to prolonged, high-risk struggle. Such rhetoric helps create what the sociologist Doug McAdam has called "cognitive liberation" among formerly oppressed groups; it was important, for instance, in inspiring grassroots activism in the American civil rights movement. More fundamentally, such claims may foster a sense of group solidarity and identity. Formerly inchoate masses may come to cohere, working together to assert rights for themselves and their group. For instance, long-standing campaigns for LGBT rights by activist groups such as the strategically named Human Rights Campaign helped convince many to come out of the closet and support political action, with major effects in the United States and European countries.[2]

In addition to mobilizing constituents, a movement's righteous rallying cries influence members' views of the foe. Those who trample human, universal, apolitical rights are enemies of the group and of all mankind. Those who reject an absolute right are blind or evil. By generating adverse views—by turning respect for or acceptance of the dominant into disgust and resentment of the tormentor—the rights movement goes well beyond veiled and individualized acts of resistance, such as the foot-dragging or mockery that James C. Scott has shown to be common among oppressed populations. In rights campaigns, there are loud rhetorical blasts about rights deprived and violations committed. They irradiate the political landscape in harsh contours of friend and foe, victim and oppressor. They lift claimants onto the moral heights and consign opponents to the ethical abyss. With these rhetorical effects, they mobilize those already primed for action. This has seldom been described more vividly than by Samuel Johnson, British raconteur and sworn enemy of American independence. Writing in 1775 about the First Continental Congress's promulgation of its Declaration of Rights, Johnson denounced the "dictators of sedition" who "toss[ed] brands among a rabble passively combustible." Although the Declaration's signatories had "shown no great extent or profundity of mind [and] are yet probably wiser than to believe it," Johnson wrote, "they have been taught, by some master of mischief, how to put in motion the engine of political electricity; to attract, by the sounds of liberty and property." Such rhetorical devices are never enough in themselves to explain the electrification of a mass movement. Other factors play major roles, including the organizational structure of the group and the receptivity of the broader political environment. Nonetheless, in the crucial matter of convincing individuals that political action is necessary and feasible, rhetoric that galvanizes a campaign's constituents and vilifies its opponents primes the oppressed to act.[3]

Potential Allies

Beyond the core constituency of the aggrieved group, third parties are an important additional audience. The goal is to turn them into active supporters of the rights movement. This is usually a competitive process, with each side to a conflict simultaneously seeking to convert third parties, albeit in opposing directions. Two groups of potential allies may be distinguished: those inside and those outside a country. In a world of frequent global interactions, of course, this seemingly simple distinction is more complicated and less definite than it first appears. Overlaps are particularly likely in campaigns for new international agreements, in which cross-border networks formulate and promote claims. International champions of new conventions and rights may not themselves be directly aggrieved, but their material, organizational, and psychological commitments to the cause may be as high as those of the populations who stand to benefit more immediately. In this book, however, I focus on nationally oriented rights campaigns, which in any event are necessary to incorporate international agreements into enforceable and enforced domestic law. In such campaigns, the insider-outsider distinction I make is relatively clear: insiders are citizens of a country or organizations incorporated there; outsiders are neither, and their primary interests are found elsewhere.

To begin with outsiders, they will be little affected by a foreign conflict and will know relatively little about it. Why then would an outsider take up a distant rights movement? This has been a focus of much recent scholarship on transnational advocacy networks. Early research on this issue emphasized principled and altruistic reasons for support—shared values and human sympathies. More recent work has supplemented this view, showing that material and organizational factors play a major role in supporters' selection of particular recipients out of the many clamoring for aid. From both perspectives, local activists increase their chances of gaining outside aid by portraying their rights as human and universal.[4]

The other potential support for a national rights movement comes from within the conflictive society itself. Here we may again distinguish two groups: elites who currently enjoy the right being demanded and subordinate groups who lack these rights but whom the rights proponents view as different from themselves. Regarding the first of these, most members of elite groups ignore or suppress claimants and offer little prospect for support. But some of those who presently enjoy rights may be sympathetic to such movements and even receptive to their rallying cries. For example, in the American civil rights movement, the governments and majority-white populations of segregationist Southern states offered little aid. But other whites, especially from the North, were supporters, despite already enjoying the rights being demanded. A few of these sympathizers even lost their lives in high-risk activism, such as the Freedom Summer campaign.

Apart from sympathetic elites, a second domestic audience for rights campaigns is less noted in the scholarly literature: other deprived groups that are viewed by constituents of the rights movement as distinct from themselves because of religious, ethnic, class, or other markers. Members of such groups may be even more excluded or disadvantaged than those who have mobilized. In some cases, rights proponents themselves may have contributed to the out-group's denigration. Nonetheless, in the conflict of the moment, activists may seek support from the other subordinate group, perhaps because it constitutes a large and accessible population—or perhaps out of fear that it will ally with the oppressor against the movement. Of course, there may be factors that cut against seeking support from members of such groups—turbulent past relations, cultural barriers, or outright prejudice, to name a few. In addition, following a hard-nosed strategic logic, rights movements sometimes strive for their own goals by blockading other subordinate groups from achieving similar rights, as discussed in chapter 7. In the movement's effort to win its rights, however, these factors may fall by the wayside in the short-term interest of maximizing support.

To this end, the sweep of rights rhetoric is helpful. Proponents may proclaim rights to be natural or universal with all deliberate vagueness so as to encompass, at least apparently, all who feel themselves deprived. The Indian independence movement offers a good historical example. Dominated by upper-caste Hindus, the Indian National Congress (INC) based its movement on calls for the right to self-determination of the entire Indian nation. It hoped thereby to attract support from Indians regardless of caste, religion, or ethnicity. In India's divided and hierarchical society, this was a formidable task, made harder by British divide-and-rule tactics. The effort narrowly succeeded among Untouchables, who had been historically oppressed by the upper castes, but it failed among many Muslims, helping to spur growth of a separate independence movement, the bloody partition of the subcontinent, and Pakistan's founding simultaneously with India's.

In other cases, the hopeful haze of rights rhetoric may spontaneously attract other subordinate groups hoping to vault their own rights forward. To take a more recent example, the growth of international women's activism in the 1970s encouraged lesbian and then gay groups to promote their own rights at UN women's conferences, even though women's rights advocates did not necessarily support this. Today such rights encompass an expanding number of sexual minorities—eleven according to a recent count—who have moved from their original, largely submerged claims to open demands for recognition and rights.[5]

Rallying Cries

If every political movement has several distinct audiences, all of them may be mobilized to a greater or lesser extent by the righteous rallying cries I next consider. In discussing each, I follow a similar format. I start with a background account of each appeal that is necessarily brief because each could be, and some of them have been, the subject of entire books. However, few such works have analyzed these terms from the angle I take— namely, one that highlights the galvanizing purposes for which activists use them and the inspirational effects they have on susceptible audiences, both movement constituents and third parties.

HUMANIZING AND NATURALIZING

The best-known mobilizing device is the assertion that certain rights are "natural" or "human." Natural rights theory began in the Middle Ages and reached its zenith in eighteenth- and nineteenth-century Europe. In the seventeenth century, the English philosopher John Locke famously wrote about the natural right to "life, liberty, and property." In the American and French Revolutions, natural rights were a rallying cry. Today claims to rights' naturalness are less frequently heard, whereas human rights rhetoric is common. Figure 2.1, an Ngram analysis based on Google Books in English from 1600 through 2008, provides an indication of the trends. The use of the term "natural rights" has slowly declined since the seventeenth and eighteenth centuries, whereas "human rights" rhetoric has grown significantly in recent decades.[6]

Figure 2.1 cannot be taken to mean that human rights have simply come to replace natural rights. Although they have similar purposes and effects, as we shall soon see, the terms have different sources and connotations. Natural rights were rooted in supposedly inherent characteristics of human beings.[7] By contrast, human rights, although based in part on the natural rights tradition, are today grounded in international and domestic legal texts such as the Universal Declaration of Human Rights (UDHR), the International Covenant on Civil and Political Rights (ICCPR), and the International Covenant on Economic, Social, and Cultural Rights (ICESCR). Together, these documents affirm rights and impose corresponding duties. Of course, there is seldom agreement on their interpretation, some rights are observed primarily in the breach, and no overarching enforcement mechanism is available at the international level. Nonetheless, to the extent

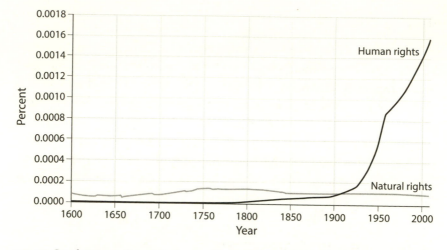

FIG. 2.1. Google Ngram of trends in the use of "natural rights" and "human rights" as a percentage of all two-word phrases used in English, 1600–2008 (case-insensitive; smoothing of 50). *Source*: Google Books, "Ngram Viewer," https://books.google.com/ngrams.

that today's human rights are more than mere words, they have legal texts as their basis.

Still, there are continuities between natural and human rights ideas. Contemporary human rights proponents, longing for more than a merely statutory grounding for their claims, instead reach for other sources. For many, human rights are "the rights one has simply because one is human," "simply in virtue of [one's] humanity," or "reflecting the basic dignity of every person."[8] The UDHR and ICCPR themselves allude to the "inherent dignity of the human person," as a result of which "all human beings are born free and equal in dignity and rights."[9] More generally, as Beitz argues, contemporary human rights are grounded in naturalistic theories.[10] In doing so, proponents seek to base rights on something deeper than dry legal texts or the mundane political compromises that went into them. Indeed, for many enthusiasts, there *must* be such a mystical basis for rights. To root rights merely in the operative clauses of laws and conventions opens the possibility of cultural relativism. It suggests that rights, whether denominated as human or not, are merely political inventions and tools. Yet from a legal standpoint, such high-sounding rhetoric, whether found in preambles or perorations, is surplusage compared to the operative clauses in laws, treaties, and conventions. It does not add doctrinal weight or in itself make rights self-executing. Rather, both the contemporary term "human" and its forerunner "natural" have practical aims—primarily those of mobilizing constituents and third parties.

This has been true for centuries. Even age-old philosophical debates over natural or human rights were far from arcane scholastic exercises. Participants, whatever their intellectual status, were partisans, either openly or covertly, in raging conflicts of their day. This fact is sometimes missed in academic studies of revered philosophical figures. Yet if we move beyond studying ideas alone to examining the reasons why particular thinkers propounded their views and the effects they had at the time, we find this to be the case. Consider John Locke.[11] Far from merely an ivory tower intellectual, Locke was an important if secondary player in England's tumultuous period between the 1660s and 1690s, a time filled with conflict over the constitutional limits of monarchical power and the rights of citizens. In broad stroke, the period pitted a landed gentry and rising middle class associated with a faction that would eventually become the Whig Party against a king intent on aggrandizing power for himself. In addition, a large majority of citizens were propertyless but politicized. Locke's patron, Lord Anthony Ashley Cooper, First Earl of Shaftesbury, was a critic of absolute royal power and "popish plots" to establish it under a Catholic king. He served as lord chancellor and later as lord president of the Privy Council, and he appointed Locke his secretary and adviser. The two may even have worked on certain controversial political tracts together. Locke's most important political ideas—that all men have an equal right to life, liberty, and property; that government is instituted to protect these; and that no one may be arbitrarily deprived of these rights—fit well with the evolving Whig agenda. So did his claim of a natural right to overturn an existing order that failed to meet those goals. The same goes for his less progressive justification of a "class state" in which, as C. B. Macpherson has argued, "the right to control any government . . . is given to the men of estate only," whereas "the obligation to be bound by law and subject to the lawful government is fixed on all men whether or not they have property in the sense of estate." Locke's emphasis on property rights and the right of the propertied to govern thus reflected the political preferences of his landowning faction. It also indicated their fears of the propertyless, whose Leveller and Digger movements had recently threatened exclusive rule by the propertied—and their property itself. As Roger Woolhouse puts it, although Locke's *Two Treatises of Government* are works of political theory, "nevertheless the general thrusts of their arguments, and sometimes their detail, respond to the nature of King

Charles's reign." Or as Mobley writes, "Locke believed the Stuarts were violating the law of nature and wanted to produce an argument that would prompt his readers to resist them," while at the same time maintaining the political power of the propertied classes over the propertyless.[12]

The same is true of today's most revered human rights thinkers. Even if they portray themselves as standing above the fray to defend an incontestable human minimum, their ideas have, and are meant to have, profound political implications. Even the most cloistered of them are well aware of this, and many take an active role in public life if not in politics itself. As in Locke's case, there is every reason to believe that their philosophical ideas reflect their political predilections, and little way to know which came first. All this suggests that politics, more than philosophical reasoning, will drive the realization of any particular vision of rights, let alone which rights might be considered "natural" or "human."

It is also notable that opposing sides use similar "natural" or "human" labels to promote radically different views of politics. This demonstrates the contested nature of the terms. To take one of the best-known such cases, the right to abortion and the right to life vie against each other despite both being labeled as basic human rights. More generally, clashes of rights are ubiquitous in contemporary societies, with the underlying values on which they rest being strongly contested by different political movements. In short, there was deep disagreement about the meaning and content of natural rights yesterday, and there is similar conflict about human rights today. In the political battles to which they have been integral, however, the terms did not need to be consistent, uncontroversial, or precise. A major purpose of using them has been to increase support for the cause among constituents and receptive audiences. Of course, most who voice the ideas have deeply believed in them. Simultaneously, however, they have been proponents of concrete and pressing political objectives. To better reach these, they have used the rhetoric of natural and human rights. Philosophy and rhetoric work in the service of interest and preference.

Why in the midst of historical political conflicts was it so important to use the term *natural* rights? Why is it so common today to speak of *human* rights? How do these terms bring about their mobilizing effects in ways that less freighted terminology, such as "individual" rights, would not? As a preliminary caveat, it is essential to note that in these and other instances where such terms are used, there is a specific historical and cultural context involved. That context, obscure to outsiders or nonspecialists, offers the primary setting within which the terms operate. Nonetheless, it is possible to deduce some of the more general reasons for the popularity and mobilizing potential of these terms in many of these debates. In doing so, I do not argue that this was necessarily the only or even the primary intent of those who yesterday described their preferred rights as natural or today describe them as human. For every political cause, there are multiple motives. In most, sincere belief in the rectitude of the cause is important—but an urge to achieve it is equally compelling.

Whatever the deepest intents of those who naturalize or humanize a rights claim, the terms have practical effects. First, "natural" suggests that God endorses or nature requires the right and that it should therefore be granted. For supporters of the status quo, claiming that it is natural bolsters it further: this is how things have always been because God or nature made it so, now and in the future. For those who seek change, the term suggests the opposite: usurpation. Things are wrong today because they no longer conform to the natural order or God's plan.

Second, for those who rejected such spiritually or religiously rooted views, the term "natural" suggests that something is rational. This is the way things should be, not because of some preordained plan but because simple, unassailable logic demands it. This was generally John Locke's position. He eschewed the idea that the "state of nature" ever existed and instead based his social contract theory on the rational analysis outlined earlier: to what form of government would people reasonably agree in a hypothetical state of nature? For "change agents" such as Locke, the failure of existing institutions to meet their standard of reasonableness provided strong legitimation for restructuring and even revolution. In this view, natural rights may not predate the state or other groups in any provable chronological sense, but they are asserted to be distinct from any such social entities. More important, in a practical sense an individual's human rights are held to surpass the claims of the group. If the state violates one's rights, the individual has rhetorical recourse to higher law and a legitimate basis to rebel.

Third, the term "natural" implies that the right is of such a quality or character to inhere in the subject. It can never be lost. In the medieval and early renaissance worlds, the Great Chain of Being epitomized this view, with members of society assumed to have varying and limited rights within a stable natural order analogous to that of the human body.[13] On the other hand, natural rights claims could, in different times and circumstances, be turned another way. As ideas of human equality gained ground in seventeenth- and eighteenth-century Europe, the claim to naturalness suggested that those who did not enjoy rights had been deprived by force—but could legitimately reclaim their inheritance, their "unalienable rights" in Jefferson's ringing words in the Declaration of Independence. Describing rights as "human" today plays a similar role.

Finally and importantly, describing a right as "natural" or "human" throws those who oppose the movement into a harshly negative light. At best, they behave unnaturally, irrationally, or inhumanely. Ultimately, they are themselves inhuman—monstrous violators. They and their wrongful ways may rightfully be destroyed in the heat of conflict or without the judicial process available to mere human abusers of ordinary law. We see this even today, when those accused of rights abuses are commonly described as "barbarous" and compared to animals or to notorious historical figures such as Adolf Hitler.

Adding "natural" or "human" to rights rhetoric motivates constituents to awaken and outsiders to act in ways that other modifiers would not. Consider this counterfactual suggested by the historian Carl Becker to explain the American colonists' decision to ground the Declaration of Independence in the "Laws of Nature and of Nature's God." As background, in protesting noxious acts of Parliament in the decades prior to 1776, the colonists had cautiously asserted only the "rights of British subjects." Although the natural rights philosophy was a powerful intellectual current of the entire eighteenth century, colonial dissidents had refrained from emphasizing it because they sought to remain within a reformed Great Britain where they would have equal rights with their brothers in the British Isles. Once they opted for American independence, however, the rights of British subjects became irrelevant to the revolutionaries, whereas natural rights suddenly became useful and leaped to the rhetorical fore, not least in the Declaration. As Becker writes: "To have said: 'We hold this truth to be self-evident, that it is a right of British subjects not to be taxed except by their own consent,' would have made no great appeal to mankind. . . . Separation from Great Britain was therefore justified on more general grounds, on the ground of the natural rights of man."[14]

UNIVERSALIZING

If naturalizing bolsters a right by furnishing it with roots, universalizing does so by enlarging its scope, infinitely. This is so even if those who drape rights in the mantle of universality claim merely to be stating a minimalist consensus position. In this view, human rights are a kind of ethical common denominator. As Alison Renteln writes, they are "cross-cultural universals," or as Sumner Twiss puts it, the "expression of a set of overlapping moral expectations to which different cultures hold themselves and others accountable." Such views are not merely academic. As U.S. senator John McCain wrote in critique of a Trump administration that he feared would be reluctant to intervene in countries accused of rights violations, "America didn't invent human rights. Those rights are common to all people: nations, cultures and religions cannot choose to simply opt out of them."[15] Such language, seemingly stating an anthropological verity but seldom rooted in empirical proofs, indicates the mobilizing and sometimes coercive intent of claims to universality.

Like naturalizing, universalizing rhetoric has been used for centuries, famously in the French Revolution's Declaration of the Rights of Man and of the Citizen—itself based in part on the American Declaration of Independence and other similarly expansive declarations of the time. As the historian Lynn Hunt has argued, "despite the controversy provoked by the French Revolution" and its excesses, the Declaration of the Rights of Man inspired movements for rights around the world and "incarnated the promise of universal human rights." However, the Declaration of the Rights of Man did not feature a hallmark of contemporary universality: rights divorced from national laws and the nation itself. The Declaration made rights contingent on citizenship in a state, not citizenship of the world. Article 3 states, "The principle of all sovereignty resides essentially in the nation. No body nor individual may exercise any authority which does not proceed directly from the nation." As Samuel Moyn has argued, truly universalistic claims—those not dependent on state citizenship and protection—were first heard after World War II, with issuance of such documents as the Universal Declaration of Human Rights. Even then, stateless refugees were frequently bereft of a basic "right to have rights," as Hannah Arendt termed it in the 1960s. In Moyn's telling, it was only after 1977, when today's fundamental human rights treaties came into force and the contemporary human rights movement took flight, that truly universalist rhetoric assumed its current prominence. From the strategic standpoint central to this book, however, Hunt's looser concept of universality remains as apt as Moyn's. Even if activists once believed that rights remained dependent on state citizenship and narrowed rights accordingly in practice, claims to universality had important effects on constituents and audiences in political campaigns. Today this is all the more the case.[16]

First, within aggrieved groups, universalist rhetoric provides a powerful psychological boost. It encourages members to present novel demands as normal and acceptable because others elsewhere have achieved them and the group therefore deserves them too. This cosmopolitan perspective creates an incentive to mobilization even among populations whose primary identity has long been local, ethnic, or national. It helps even the most isolated see themselves as part of a common humanity, worthy of these rights themselves. This was evident from the era of the American and French Revolutions, when those excluded in practice from the universalist promise even within their own societies rose up in protest and revolt. Even before the Declaration of Independence, slaves reinterpreted the rights language used by the colonists against the British to demand their own freedom. As the historian Gary Nash has shown, particularly in the North, slaves filed individual lawsuits against their masters demanding freedom. They also petitioned colonial and state legislatures for general emancipations. Most of these early attempts to gain freedom failed, but the mobilizing potential of universalistic rhetoric abided. In the revolution itself, slaves across the colonies seized the opportunity, defecting en masse to the British. Great Britain's Dunmore Proclamation of 1775, freeing all "indented Servants, Negroes, or others" who joined the royalist side, was as much a response to a tide of slave defections as a tactical choice to bolster the Crown's army.[17] Similarly, in the French Revolution the propertyless demanded real equality, in political as well as civil rights, as did women. In each of these cases, the original rights proponents, shocked by subordinates who used the universalist rhetoric for their own purposes, responded forcefully and even violently against the new claimants. The broader point remains, however. Universalist rhetoric can inspire the oppressed to mobilize nationally and internationally, even when the primary audience is a narrow section of a single society.

Strategically minded local activists use universalist rhetoric for a second purpose: to convince outside audiences to identify with and lend support to their causes. Doing so creates a tenuous but real psychological bond with distant strangers, lending believability to demands that might otherwise be misunderstood or ignored. Consider again America's Declaration of Independence. It was not merely a "decent respect to the opinions of mankind" that led the Founding Fathers to publish the "causes which impel[led] them to the separation" from Great Britain. There was also a fervent hope that these "facts . . . submitted to a candid World" would bring allies to their aid. Indeed, "foreign fighters" inspired by the rhetoric of rights soon flocked to the cause, led by such luminaries as the French Marquis de Lafayette and the Polish Tadeusz Kościuszko. And because of rights' universalist aura, those who fought overseas brought the rights fever back to their home countries, spreading it widely.[18]

In turn, such aid may strengthen the local rights movement, as new resources and sometimes troops funnel in. Even without such direct support, asserting a claim as universal adds weight to the underlying political project. All the world, all humanity, is ostensibly behind it. Either way, the balance of forces in the immediate conflict can be shifted through the attractant power of universalist rhetoric. Obviously, this does not change outcomes in every case. Those who might provide assistance often have other reasons—material, strategic, or even moral—not to do so. And opponents may be so strong domestically that even large amounts of external support have little effect. Nonetheless, the purpose of universalist rhetoric is often to help its user gain outside aid.

Today, given the number and breadth of rights conventions and declarations, solutions to any number of social problems can be outfitted as universal rights. This results in a certain homogenization of grievances, clothing all manner of political projects in a uniform of rights. As Ignatieff has written, many local activists today "espouse the universalist language of human rights but actually use it to defend highly particularist causes."[19] Meanwhile, the number of rights continues to balloon, with all manner of problems such as underdevelopment or malnutrition deprecated as the violation of a universal right. No matter: with such framing, local movements may attract foreign allies eager to uphold what appear to be the very rights they support in their distant homes.

This suggests a third effect: even without an oppressed local group expanding its claims, those who currently enjoy rights use universalist rhetoric to justify enlarging the geographic range of their own concerns. By grounding rights in a claim that they stem from a baseline of agreement or overlapping consensus among the world's people, activists need no longer confine their projects to their own national or cultural milieus. Proponents who array themselves in the mantle of universality have no compunction about applying their ideas elsewhere and everywhere. This was evident centuries ago, as the French revolutionaries sought to bring *liberté* and *égalité* to the *fraternité* of European nations, in part through conquest. In the middle of the nineteenth century, campaigns to free the Greeks and other oppressed peoples so that they could enjoy rights within their own new states garnered popular support on a similar basis.[20]

Even more today, the ethos epitomized by the Universal Declaration of Human Rights justifies or rationalizes a spectrum of overseas actions. Those who promote rights' universality feel free to press them into the hands of distant groups who might otherwise have little use for them. Education programs disseminate rights doctrines and strategies to cultures around the world, no matter how diverse these may be. Purveyors of rights identify distant interlocutors, then provide them with practical training in the deployment of rights in local conflicts. The claimed universality of human rights makes them ideal rationales for justifying foreign interventions by powerful states, including military actions. With the universalization of rights, it is seldom enough for a state interested in exercising its power overseas to speak of national interests, ideological allies, or social solidarity. Rights are enlisted as well, making interventions possible anywhere.

Among distant bystanders to conflict, universalism works in two distinct ways. First, it underlies an apparent concern for the well-being of others, regardless of whether less estimable motives also play a role. The 2011 NATO intervention in Libya was justified largely in this way, with claims about the Gaddafi regime's rights violations and genocide, debatable as they were, prompting a bombing campaign and regime change.[21] Earlier, the Kosovo intervention of 1999 had a similarly high-minded rationale. There is also a second, less recognized way in which universalism helps justify overseas interventions: it suggests that violations in faraway places affect or even threaten the home state. The vaguest claim is that because of rights' universality, violations anywhere make abuses more likely everywhere. Neglecting the continuing power of sovereignty and cultural differences, this aspect of universalism suggests that rights crusades should not stop at a country's shores but should—indeed must—extend beyond, if only for the security of rights at home. Nor is the force of such views confined to specific regions, where geographic and cultural nearness might make contagion more plausible.[22]

In recent decades, universalism of this kind has undergirded both international NGO and military campaigns, which increasingly work in tandem. Justifications for humanitarian interventions in poor, weak, and faraway places no longer rest only on succoring hapless victims (if ever they did). They are also grounded in self-interested universalism—the debatable claim that what happens "over there" can hurt us "back here." Listen, for instance, to Amnesty International USA's executive director William Schulz in his book *In Our Own Best Interest: How Defending Human Rights Benefits Us All*. He is advising fellow rights activists about how to make what he calls the "human rights 'sale'" to a skeptical American public: "We need to be unafraid to say, 'Support human rights! They're good for us!' . . . Supporting human rights . . . [has] a profound impact on Americans—politically, economically, environmentally, and in dozens of other ways. Caring about the fate of our 'neighbors' is far more than a matter of conscience. It is in truth a matter of survival—our own survival . . . our health and security."[23]

In other words, violations overseas make problems at home more likely, with all manner of other threats thrown in for good measure. Taking self-interested universalism one step further, U.S. ambassador to the United Nations Samantha Power provided expansive justification for overseas actions such as the 2011 attacks on Libya: "It is now objectively the case that our national interests are increasingly affected not just by what happens between states, but also by how people are treated within states. . . . It is precisely our self-interest that requires us to get better at improving human security in the service of national security."[24]

Finally, universalist rhetoric has the effect of throwing opponents of campaigns on the defensive, at least in the eyes of the movement. It does so because universalists portray themselves not only as supplanting the parochial but also as partaking of the modern and the progressive. This is the case despite universalism's ancient roots in Greek cosmopolitanism, most famously embodied in the dramatist Terence's comedy *The Self-Tormentor*. In his book *Cosmopolitanism: Ethics in a World of Strangers,* the contemporary philosopher Anthony Appiah glowingly describes what he calls the "golden rule of cosmopolitanism." This is expressed by one of the play's main characters, Chremes, who defends his meddling in his neighbor's affairs by saying, "I am human: nothing human is alien to me." However, this seemingly open-minded viewpoint is followed by a less remembered but telling justification for his inquisitiveness: "If you're right, I'll do what you do. If you're wrong, I'll set you straight."[25] As the last sentence indicates, universalism is open to the world in a limited way—only to the extent that the universalist finds the world to his liking, in his interest, or in sync with his understanding of the universal. Otherwise, as judged solely by the universalist, he sees himself as having a mandate to force the other to adopt his advanced and superior ways.[26]

In this view, then, to resist universal rights is to be narrow, parochial, or backward. Given universalism's patina of dynamism and advancement, opponents must be retrograde and in need of outside encouragement or coercion to free them from their hidebound ways. More sharply still, those who violate universal rights are barbarians and savages. This becomes clear from the rhetoric of primitivism sometimes directed against cultural practices such as genital cutting (strategically renamed female genital mutilation) or, increasingly, male circumcision.[27] Notably, even democracies that fail to live up to "universal" rights ideals for their own historical or cultural reasons face similar attacks. European activism against the death penalty in the United States is shot through with such sentiments, with executions frequently denounced as "inhumane" and "incompatible with human dignity and the right to life."[28] Countries such as Norway and Japan face analogous attacks by animal rights activists denouncing them for whaling. Notably, therefore, universalist rhetoric not only calls into question long-standing traditions but rejects policies that have been approved by democratic states. From a tactical standpoint, however, what matters most is that rights proponents paint their opponents as regressive—as brutish foes whose customs and sometimes their whole cultures merit destruction. This seldom shames or convinces the foe, but that is hardly the point. Rather, like the other rallying cries discussed in this chapter, it encourages constituents of the campaign to mobilize in self-righteous indignation against the benighted.

DEPOLITICIZING

In a third type of rallying cry, advocates strive for transcendence: they assert that the rights they seek are above or prior to politics. These apolitical or antipolitical claims are said to represent merely the practical and unobjectionable outgrowth of supreme moral, logical, or philosophical principles—or of the most basic understandings of what is necessary to live as a human being. Neutral and divorced from partisanship, these must be accepted as bedrock truths not subject to sordid political squabbling.

The assertion that rights are apolitical has been part of rights conflicts for centuries. When America's Founding Fathers spoke of "self-evident" and therefore inarguable truths, they were engaging in antipolitics. From a wholly different direction, in 1895, when the reactionary French psychologist Gustave Le Bon worried that the "divine right of kings," which had once enjoyed the "tyrannical and sovereign force of being above discussion," had been replaced by an equally apolitical but dangerous new concept, the "divine right of the masses," he too was alluding to rights as antipolitics. Especially in recent decades, a move to depoliticize rights has become common. In the 1970s and 1980s, dissidents fighting Communism, such as György Konrád and Václav Havel, promoted human rights as antipolitics and its ostensible purveyor, civil society, as nonpolitical. In saying this, they claimed only to want the truth to be spoken in their corrupted societies—and for the state to refrain from repressing it. More recently, listen again to American senator John McCain in his opinion article attacking Trump administration foreign policy: "Human rights exist above the state and beyond history. They cannot be rescinded by one government any more than they can be granted by another. They inhabit the human heart, and from there, though they may be abridged, they can never be extinguished." Senator McCain, with his strong support of overseas military interventions that consumed thousands of lives, might seem an odd purveyor of an antipolitical human rights argument, but he and other politicians are in fact primary exponents of what they hope will be argument-halting ideas.

Human rights lawyers similarly use such approaches in a version of what Judith Shklar called "legalism"—a "quest for the holy grail of perfect, non-political, aloof neutral law and legal decisions." Although ostensibly apolitical, rights claims cannot fail to be political. Dissidents such as Havel clearly recognized this, writing in 1978 that when anyone in a Communist society rejects its lies to instead "live within the truth," he "denies it in principle and threatens it in its entirety." Powerful foes recognize this also, targeting rights claims and their exponents such as Havel for repression.[29]

Indeed, the antipolitics idea is the epitome of politics, necessarily implicating state and societal demands upon individuals, and vice versa. This is true even for the "thinnest" conceptions of human rights, such as Ignatieff's vague view of them as "the minimal conditions for any kind of life at all." It is also true for thicker "negative" definitions, such as that suggested by one of the founders of Human Rights Watch (HRW), Aryeh Neier, who defines rights as "a series of limits on the exercise of power. The state and those holding the power of states are forbidden to interfere with freedom of inquiry or expression. They may not deprive anyone of liberty arbitrarily. They are prohibited from denying each person the right to count equally and to obtain the equal protection of the laws. They are denied the power to inflict cruelty. And they must respect a zone of privacy."[30]

In practice, all such limitations are forged in the crucible of politics, primarily at the national level. Moreover, the results reached in democratic societies remain malleable even if embodied in laws and constitutions. Their current status is contingent on the outcome of inevitable future frays with still-viable opponents who are eager to return to prior power relations.

All the more so, then, is antipolitics an inaccurate, if politically appealing, description of today's burgeoning panoply of negative, positive, and group rights. Their proliferation, although decried by some rights scholars and practitioners as "inflation," is welcomed, not only by the purveyors of new rights but also by their primary guardians, United Nations agencies. In response to the growing crush of new rights, bureaucrats in New York and

Geneva solemnly assert that all human rights are "indivisible."[31] Yet this is simply another antipolitics claim—not for a single right, but for the whole mushrooming mass. More worryingly, "indivisibility talk" masks inevitable competition, both among different rights and among the activist groups promoting even a single one. In the 1970s, Third World activists and developing states used the term in an attempt to raise the status of economic and social rights relative to that of civil and political rights, correctly claiming that the existing hierarchy was highly political. Their hope was that a newly proposed right to development and a New International Economic Order might lead to better terms of trade and more development assistance. But these goals, framed around a claim to indivisibility of all rights, failed in practice even if the right to development has entered the crowded rhetorical field of UN-recognized rights. Ultimately, as in this case, political struggle determines the scope and very existence of any right vis-à-vis others. If a certain set of rights is momentarily above others or even above dispute, it has attained this status only through a movement's long and hard political struggle, and its maintenance is always tenuous. Claims to rights' apolitical nature are certainly made—by those who support the goal that the right seeks to ensure. But these are either unreflective utterances or calculated efforts to improve the right's mobilizing power by draping it in loftiness. Claiming indivisibility for all rights has similarly unrealistic bases and pretensions.

Nonetheless, the frequency of antipolitics rhetoric demonstrates its tactical importance. In political conflicts, claiming to soar above partisanship rather than admitting to one's biases has two main purposes. First, as with other devices for depoliticizing issues, it is meant to halt debate and remove issues from political processes. With their supposed neutrality, rights must be accepted, not opposed. More importantly, they must be accepted in the form and with the effect envisioned by the proponent. As such, claiming antipolitics is a gambit aimed at forestalling debate, silencing opponents, and sweeping the conflict. Of course, those who reject the rhetoric of antipolitics never go quietly. With their own interests, privileges, and rights at risk, they invariably denounce antipolitics as . . . politics. But for constituents of a movement, viewing their rights as beyond dispute can be a powerful catalyst to mobilization. How else to elevate themselves to their proper place? For outside sympathizers as well, transcendent words resonate better than political ones. This is true even if antipolitical claims front for movements aiming to remake whole societies and entire polities.

There is also a second, more cutting edge to antipolitical claims: Those who fail to recognize rights' true nature are partisans. They are compromised by bargaining and concession. They are blinded by power, ideology, interest, superstition, or prejudice. At the extreme, they are perpetrators of war, massacre, and genocide. By contrast, those who portray rights as anti-politics purport to float over the whole dirty business with unobjectionable ethical principles. Even if opponents reject all this, those who stand to benefit and those who sympathize readily accept it. In the name of antipolitics, they do not retreat into apathy. To vanquish the zealots and achieve their own ideal world, they enlist to join the conflict.

ABSOLUTIZING

As a final mobilizing device building on the others, activists lend urgency to their right by absolutizing it—claiming that it must be granted in full, now, and that anything less is violation or abomination. For constituents of the movement and sympathizers, such rhetoric can be compelling, prompting immediate action. Absolutizing therefore serves again, if in a different way, to bolster mobilization. Providing an abstract historical example of such assertions, the German philosopher Immanuel Kant wrote that "there is nothing in all the world so sacred as the rights of others. They are impregnable and inviolable. Woe unto him who infringes those rights, and tramples them underfoot! The right of the other should keep him secure in everything; it is stronger than any bulwark or wall." More recently, Ronald Dworkin popularized a view that rights are "best understood as trumps over some background justification for political decisions that states a goal for the community as a whole." Following this logic, Dworkin holds that "individuals have rights when . . . a collective goal is not a sufficient justification for denying them what they wish, as individuals, to have or to do, or not a sufficient justification for imposing some loss or injury upon them."[32]

Although Dworkin termed his definition merely "formal" and acknowledged that collective goals may negate individual rights, his unvarnished words are reflected in rights campaigns. Absolutist language is common, and activists do not compromise or delimit their maximalist pretensions unless forced to do so. In the heat of conflict, all that matters is that *their* right conquers. As Hopgood has written about human rights, their proponents aim to "trump the day-to-day political process with an unanswerable reference to a superior position of judgment."[33] In reality, of course, rights are never absolute. They always butt up against the rights of others and the needs of communities. Yet time and again in political struggles, activists portray their rights as supreme.

What are their intentions, and what are the effects of absolutism? First, assertions of absolute entitlement encourage total commitment to the cause. Violation generates white-hot outrage. Brandishing such claims, movements can convince their followers that existing principles, whether instituted by a dictatorial regime or a democratic majority, are now suspect. At minimum, absolutist avowals shift the burden of justification from the proponent of a new right to those opposing it, at least in the minds of proponents.

Second, absolutist language is useful for stoking aggression. It creates a zero-sum mentality in which movement constituents are made to fear that any compromise will undermine their cause, identity, or very lives. More sharply still, absolutism reduces incentives to minimize one's own losses. When those losses seemingly mean gains for foes, the sting is doubly strong—and the incentive to instead hurt the foe becomes all the stronger. Such hard-line attitudes help in the first days of political struggle, to fire up one's own constituents with a dose of hostility, even hatred. Ultimately, of course, most political disputes end, at least for a while. Conflicts may even end with all sides viewing the outcome as a win-win situation, particularly when the antagonists come to believe that their desired goals are secure enough to share. But in the early stages of conflict—or of renewed conflict, since "resolved" disputes often flare up again in new guises—galvanizing one's constituents is critical. Even if aggression is submerged, absolutist oratory fires movements with the belief that their goals should be granted forthwith, obviating the need for tedious debate. Kindling such zeal lends a movement strength both to demand immediate results and to stifle moderate efforts at deliberation, negotiation, and compromise.

For their part, however, foes accused of ignoring absolutist dictates scoff at the extremism of rights proponents, writing this off as posturing or delusion (even as the foes also gird for conflict). So rights proponents go beyond rhetoric alone. As a third tactic, they turn to "absolutist" institutions, ones that sidestep the sluggishness and frustrations of ordinary politics, to achieve their goals. As the legal philosopher Hans Kelsen noted: "If one believes in the existence of the absolute, and consequently in absolute values, in the absolute good . . . is it not meaningless to let a majority vote decide what is politically good?"[34] Rights activists heartily agree! Even while slogging through years of mass mobilization, they try to leapfrog their way forward using more efficient means. In liberal societies such as the United States, courts are the key countermajoritarian institution. Judges are empowered to make decisions that resolve competing claims based not on majority sentiment but on vague constitutional principles. They are bounded by rules of procedure, interpretation, and precedent limiting their discretion. But ultimately the country's highest court can interpret the law in strikingly new ways, in effect creating entirely new law. For activists, courts can therefore be a way of achieving maximal goals quickly—although equally judges can block them from doing so.

In most democracies, however, judges reflect at least distantly and indirectly the political preferences of competing sectors of the population. Even as they apply law, interpret statutes, and decide cases, they are not insulated from political currents within their own societies—even if their decisions may contravene the current consensus and instead reflect a prior or possible future one. A major aspect of rights movements and rhetoric therefore is to convert tractable judges and whole judiciaries into institutional sympathizers for their causes. Charles Epp has shown how civil rights decisions in U.S. courts in the 1950s and '60s reflected the growing power of a "support structure" of legal and political activists. Prior decisions establishing separate-but-equal institutions and approving Jim Crow laws were undoubtedly rooted in an earlier constellation of political power. More recently, American courts have again come to reflect the power of a rival support structure, the conservative legal movement, and have restricted affirmative action and even the Voting Rights Act. The furious political battles over U.S. Supreme Court appointments and lower-profile but equally vehement contests over other federal court judges demonstrate the perception and doubtless the reality that the American judiciary moves with larger political currents.[35]

Given the uncertainties of domestic courts, rights activists imbued with the absolutist spirit have sought to establish international courts staffed by fellow believers. There they aspire to bring cases challenging national policies grounded in local political realities. Such challenges are framed as representing widely accepted international norms and are based on the view that these should trump domestic ones. This tendency has reached one of its main goals with the establishment of human rights courts of varying reach and power.[36] By far the most important and powerful of these is the European Court of Human Rights (ECHR). Of similar ambition but different scope is the International Criminal Court (ICC), whose coverage is global, although its jurisdiction is restricted to war crimes and crimes against humanity. Some activists are now calling for establishment of a World Court of Human Rights.[37]

In all these cases, one of the key promises of international courts, at least for proponents, is their absolutist nature—their ability to sweep aside domestic recalcitrance in the name of a higher ideal. Of course, for those courts already established, the reality is rather different. The ECHR has recognized the "subsidiarity principle" and the "margin of appreciation" doctrine, both providing great range for national-level views, particularly in controversial cases. (Chapter 4 discusses one important recent example.) The ICC has thus far prosecuted only alleged violators from weak African states. Whatever the status of these novel institutions, however, for good strategic reasons absolutist rhetoric and methods mark contemporary rights activism.

Conclusion

When political leaders issue righteous rallying cries, they engage in a strategic move aimed at bolstering their own side. To strengthen these cries, activists combine them with vociferous advertising of the foe's violations, abuses that are often real but sometimes embellished to advance the cause. Of course, not every rights movement necessarily uses all of these methods to mobilize support. As in other aspects of a political campaign, decisions about tactics will be subordinated to the overriding purpose of achieving a movement's goals. In some cases, that may mean avoiding some of the rhetorical devices discussed here. Or it may mean embracing them at one point and then rejecting them at a later time.

Notwithstanding these caveats, the rallying cries discussed here are common to political conflicts involving rights claims. With these mechanisms of mobilizing one's own side and discrediting the other understood, it is now time to examine the ways in which foes repel the onslaught—with these same mechanisms aimed at mobilizing their own constituencies and third parties, but also with their own distinctive rights tactics.

3

Rights as Shields and Parries

COUNTERING THREATS

What of the foes of a political movement? How do they react to the righteous rallying cries used to mobilize forces against them? Because of rights' sway and revolutionary potential, opponents vigorously defend themselves. In part they do this by mobilizing their own constituents and allies, using the methods discussed in chapter 2. Beyond rousing their forces, they employ rights as shields. If the foes of a rights movement hold sufficient power themselves, or if they can convince powerful institutions and third parties to support their own rights, such defensive tactics may be sufficient.

In addition, those facing a challenge fight back. Not to do so, and to rely only on protective measures, is to put their own power, status, and rights in jeopardy. Such conflict can involve real warfare. Always it involves the opponent's use of rhetorical devices aimed not only at shielding itself but also at parrying the proponent movement's claims and subverting the movement itself. Four methods distinct from and in addition to those discussed in chapter 2 may be identified: denial, rivalry, reversal, and repudiation. Opponents of a movement usually combine several in the fight to maintain themselves and their rights. Before discussing these tactics, it is important to reiterate that the labels rights "movement" or "proponent" on one side and "opponent" or "foe" on the other are far from perfect in capturing the dynamics of conflict. This is chiefly because "foes" may also be seen as movements (movements that have sometimes captured organs of the state), albeit voicing an opposed set of rights from those used by the proponent. As a result, the original movement is obviously also an opponent in the eyes of the original foe. Notwithstanding the reciprocal aspects of rights conflicts, for clarity's sake in the remainder of this chapter, I retain the terminology of "movement" or "proponent" and "foe" or "opponent" as I focus on the latter.

Shields

When used as shields, rights protect individuals, groups, or whole societies—and the interests, values, and goals they carry with them. Recall from chapter 2, for instance, the way Aryeh Neier defined individual human rights as "a series of limits on the exercise of power." The scholarly literature on rights and especially international human rights has highlighted such defensive uses, as well as the associated methods that NGOs such as Human Rights Watch have long followed. Again in Neier's words, these are: "documenting thoroughly and with great care abuses of human rights by governments and those exercising the power of governments; pointing out the responsibilities of various international actors; comparing the practices that are documented to international standards; and generating pressure on those directly and indirectly culpable to end or alleviate abuses."[1]

Such methods exemplify the use of international human rights as protective shields. Similar methods apply within democratic states where national laws and courts play a larger role. Scholars of political science and international relations have developed elaborate analytic formulations, such as the naming and shaming of violators, to help explain the generation of political pressure to protect the needy. Because of the large literature in this area, I will not discuss rights as shields in detail, except to say that a focus on such tactics, although important, is incomplete.[2] It is critical in studying unprovoked attacks on innocent or defenseless people for whom international or domestic laws provide formal protections. But it is incomplete even in those cases because responses to violations are seldom only defensive. Protecting the vulnerable inevitably means protecting them from someone or something. This in turn requires imposing a duty on those deemed responsible, either a negative duty to stop abusive behavior or an affirmative one to start ameliorative action. A focus on rights as shields is even less helpful and certainly less comprehensive in analyzing broader political conflicts. In these, defensive and offensive tactics are difficult to distinguish, particularly on rhetorical battlefields where all sides simultaneously advance and guard particular visions of society. The question of who started a dispute is always thorny, and groups that are threatened do not sit back and rely only on rhetorical shields to protect themselves. All sides to conflict, even those facing attacks on their rights, will use active measures to enhance their positions, in addition to raising shields.

Parries

Such measures begin with the opponent parrying the proponent's claims about the latter's purported rights and their supposed violations. The broadest goal of parrying tactics is for the foe to drum up sufficient resources and power to preserve its own hard-won rights. As one part of this, the foe galvanizes its constituents and competes for third-party support, using the same set of rhetorical devices employed by the original movement, although with contrary rights as content. Prior to a challenge, the foe may not have openly enunciated a justification for its position—or for the impositions it placed on those now mobilizing against it. Facing few obstacles, the opponent blithely exercised its prerogatives and enjoyed its lifestyle. But with the rising threat from a new movement, the foe will now claim its *right* to continue doing so. As with the original proponent, leaders of the foe will appeal for support to its own constituents and potential allies. Moreover, the foe will lard its appeals with humanizing, universalizing, absolutizing, and de-politicizing rhetoric—but with polar ideological and practical implications. For instance, foes confront the movement's claims to equal rights with assertions about the natural order of hierarchy, which they head, and the necessary duties of people in lower ranks. They parry claims to the universal rights of individuals with assertions of the universal rights of states and communities to live as they or their majorities choose, whether that choice was made through democratic or more passive means. They celebrate the law's apolitical majesty—for upholding the present state of affairs, not some altered future one.

With these and other rhetorical parries, opponents of the original rights movement scare their complacent constituents and sympathetic third parties into action. Just as with the original movement's absolutist rhetoric, opponents stoke zero-sum fears—that rights for the upstart will necessarily erode rights, status, and privileges for "us." This move occurs not only in campaigns where gains and losses are easily measurable, such as in contemporary urban disputes over gentrification, where owners' rights to use of their property run up against tenants' rights to housing or even their "right to the city."[3] Zero-sum arguments also echo where material stakes are not obvious. Arguments that same-sex marriage threatens all marriages are a good example. They may be hard to credit from the outside, but they work to galvanize constituents and like-minded third parties worried about the unpredictable effects of change.

DENIAL

As a first method of parrying the rights proponent's thrusts, opponents deny key aspects of the original rights claim. Initially, they may use passive or concealed methods to do so. They ignore the rights movement and its outlandish contentions for as long as possible, refusing to dignify them. By so doing, they hope to deprive the movement of mobilizational oxygen or strangle its rise covertly. If such methods do not snuff out the movement, the foe will turn to more active denial. Particularly when a new right is being promoted, when it is novel or alien to a society, this denial may start with the very existence of the right itself. Time and again, rights claims are at first scoffed at as nullities. Consider how traditionalist counterrevolutionaries such as Joseph de Maistre or Louis de Bonald denied the "rights of man" in the French Revolution. In de Maistre's view, the abstract concept of "man" did not exist and therefore there could be no such thing as the rights of man. Indeed, enemies of the Revolution went further and denied the very concept of rights. As de Bonald wrote, the "Revolution began by the Declaration of the rights of man and . . . it will only end with the declaration of the rights of God."[4] Today few deny the existence of man or of rights *tout court*, but many deny specific rights, especially those that appear new or to newly threaten long-standing verities. In recent decades, children's rights faced—and among certain governments such as the United States still face—rejection. Claims to animal rights endure the same treatment in many quarters today.

Beyond denial of the right itself, foes criticize proponents' assertions that what they demand is natural, universal, absolute, and apolitical. As noted previously, such assertions are not aimed at convincing opponents but rather at mobilizing constituents and third parties. In turn, it is toward bystanders that the foe directs its denials, hoping to keep them on the sidelines or even have them join its own team. Dripping disdain, foes puncture the movement's pretensions one by one. As indication of these arguments, consider some classic critiques still relevant and influential today. To the claim that rights are natural or human, conservatives such as Burke argued that rights "cannot be settled upon any abstract rule" and that rights exist only in society, not individually. More specifically to the idea that all men naturally have equal rights, Burke retorted that hierarchy and aristocracy are in reality natural to society.[5] Utilitarians such as Jeremy Bentham famously denounced natural rights as "anarchical fallacies," as "simple nonsense: natural and imprescriptible rights, rhetorical nonsense,—nonsense upon stilts." By contrast, he held that rights can only have meaning when they are "the fruits of the law, and of the law alone. There are no rights without law— no rights contrary to the law—no rights anterior to the law."[6] By contrast, natural rights were "invented to cut up law . . . and legal rights"—and, in Bentham's view, to mobilize people to do so: "When a man . . . feels an ardent desire to see [a political caprice] gratified but can give no reason . . . , when he finds it necessary to get the multitude to join with him, . . . he sets up a cry of rights." The core utilitarian argument against absolutist claims is also well known: social utility, the greatest happiness for the greatest number, must trump the claim to individual rights' absolutism. Any legal rights that exist must be either limited or combined with responsibilities that undercut the claim to absolutism. To the idea that rights are apolitical, radicals, such as Marx, have denounced this as pretense, covering up bourgeois domination. And to the claim of universality, critics of diverse political stripes have argued for the importance of social convention, national understandings, and local culture.

As a final aspect of denial—one tied to the fact that those promoting rights invariably link their assertions to claims of concrete violations—foes deny particular abuses. As the sociologist Stanley Cohen has shown, such refutation takes three forms: literal (denying that anything occurred), interpretive (claiming that if something occurred, it was not a violation), and implicatory (arguing that what might appear to be a violation was legally justified and therefore nugatory).[7] Although Cohen applies his framework to states, any group that is accused of abuses is likely to use similar methods in conjunction with the previous forms of denial about the right itself. Consider, for instance, the ways in which Indian police officers who have undergone international human rights training deny that they are engaging in violations when they torture or kill people who are merely suspected of criminality. As Rachel Wahl has shown, the security forces justify such extrajudicial actions—and receive widespread public support for doing so—by claiming that suspects have lost all their rights because they are presumed to have broken the law.[8] Using their own locally grounded understandings of international rights doctrine, fortified by their view that powerful states such as the United States unleash similar practices against suspected terrorists, police view their actions as permissible and even obligatory.

RIVALRY

To understand fully the argument of those accused of such abuses, one must examine a second parrying device found in this and many other cases. India's police forces routinely supplement their denials of abuse by claiming that their actions protect another right that suspects have presumptively violated: the community's right to security. As Wahl's police interviewees believe, "security is a basic right, so the armed forces are protecting basic rights by violating the rights of those who threaten security." In other words, the rights of the community or of potential crime victims are raised against the rights of individual suspects, notwithstanding efforts by India's internationally linked human rights movement to protect the latter. This conception turns dominant liberal conceptions of human rights on their head. Yet it is equally grounded in a rights-based viewpoint, albeit one that assigns the right to the law-abiding majority of society. As Wahl shows, police in India and elsewhere "actively engage rights concepts and negotiate their meaning, using the language and logic of rights to contest the very principles on which rights are premised. . . . They maintain the discourse of rights protectors while still defending the use of torture." The same could well be said for those who supported torture during the Bush administration or targeted killing in the Bush, Obama, and Trump administrations, as Rebecca Sanders has shown, although these cases involve international rather than purely domestic situations. Indeed, local police officers in India point to these cases in justifying their own actions.[9] For those merely suspected of crime or terrorism, the effect is to destroy all individual rights in the name of society's rights.

More generally, most foes of rights campaigns parry them by advancing rival rights. As Sniderman and his coauthors argue, "rights are claims, and claims are contested . . . inevitably and conspicuously evok[ing] counterclaims." The individual rights so dominant today in liberal societies were themselves developed in reaction to other preexisting rights, such as the divine rights of kings. Today as well, the rhetoric of rights is constantly met by what Scheingold calls "negation through competing myths." In the American civil rights struggle, Tarrow has noted, "every expansion of rights to black Americans . . . has triggered a countermovement often couched in the language of rights."[10] This insight should be broadened: rights are forged against other rights. The proponent movement raises new rights against existing rights relished by the foe, even if the latter's justification may no longer be expressly stated. The foe in turn surfaces its own rights and their rationale when it faces threatening new rights claims. As recent examples, the women's rights movement against entrenched male power spurred creation of the men's rights movement, and the LGBT rights movement energized a Christian rights movement.

From this book's perspective, the rise of rival rights is unsurprising. The best way to preserve one's power and privilege is to inculcate a right as an unexceptionable social relationship. If challenged, however, it may be necessary for the foe to make the right explicit again. For foes who previously imposed duties on others through force of habit, suasion of ideology, or barrel of gun, it may become necessary to formulate and foreground rights and their basis. From a chronological standpoint, this occurs as foes begin to fear losing power, or as the broader cultural landscape shifts toward fuller acceptance of the insurgents' rights. Then opponents of the original rights movement find it beneficial to fight right with right—and often with might. In doing so, they do not portray their claims as fresh stratagems to defend against the new rights movement. Rather, they armor them in the mail of tradition, a defense of time-tested if newly burnished rights. For the foe this is not, or not merely, a cynical ploy to protect his own interests. In most cases, the foe believes in his own righteousness. In this, of course, he is no different from the proponent in the conflict, and in some ways the two become mirror images of one another. Both combine strategy and sincerity, using the edge afforded by rights to advance their contrary causes. Both denounce the others' rights claims as illegitimate and insincere. As Daniel Rodgers remarks regarding white Southerners' raising "states' rights, law and order, the rights of private property and free association" against the American civil rights movement: "To their users they were the crux of the issue; to their opponents they were the subterfuges of a 'new racism' that would not admit its name."[11]

In addition to the foe's raising his own rival rights to offset those of the proponent, there is another form of rivalry. Just as the original rights proponent sought to galvanize other weak groups within his own society, the movement's opponent seldom lets this happen without a fight. Rather, the foes of rights campaigns will seek to enlist other subordinate groups for their own defensive purposes—by offering them their rights in a form of divide-and-rule strategies. Consider again the fight over Indian self-determination in the twentieth century. The movement was dominated by high-caste if largely secular Hindus. For their part, the British sought to peel away subaltern groups from the movement, in particular Muslims and Untouchables, dangling before them the prospect of separate rights superior to those on offer from the broader independence movement. In the lead-up to Nigerian independence in 1960, a similar dynamic played out in a territory dominated by three large ethnic groups, the Igbo, Yoruba, and Hausa-Fulani. Many minority groups with smaller populations preferred the limited rights ensured them by British colonialism to the less expansive ones that seemed probable if Nigeria became independent under the domination of the three largest groups.[12] In the competition over allies, the original rights proponent is often at this kind of disadvantage. As the movement strives for unity and strength, it is in a position to offer only its own rights or a strategically expanded version of some hazy composite right. By contrast, foes may have the ability to offer other subordinates their own distinct set of rights. In addition, the powerful are in a better position than movements to offer material incentives to convince weak groups to ally with them rather than with the upstart.

REVERSAL

Even as the foe raises new rights, it also adopts a third, closely related method: proclaiming itself the real victim and the rights proponent the real oppressor.[13] The first of these forms of reversal, the self-construction of victimhood, is well known. Why is victimhood so attractive? As we have seen with respect to the rights proponent, portraying oneself as a victim, even a possible future victim, may create sympathy among third parties. Reversal is particularly powerful when the victim depicts himself as innocent.

The second aspect of reversal—the construction of oppressors—is equally important, if less studied. As conflict mounts, the foe proclaims the original movement the oppressor. Using much the same approach as the original rights proponent, the foe paints the latter as evil. To return to the Indian torture case discussed earlier in this chapter, police and rights activists each promote the idea that the other is ignorant or driven by self-interest.[14] Ultimately, they portray one another as not only violating natural or human rights but as being literally inhuman. However obvious, the aim is important: to delegitimize the movement among potential supporters. Few wish to be accused of bedding down with rights violators. If the foe can persuade the world that the original rights movement is but a persecutor cynically wrapping himself in rights rhetoric, the likelihood of the movement's converting potential allies to actual ones declines.

The upshot of rivalry and reversal is a swirl of competing claims around rights and violations. As the rhetoric flies, "rights races" develop: competing sides propel themselves forward by claiming that theirs is the most fundamental and most important right. There is also "rights-mongering," with both sides waving the other's abuses as a flag to fuel resentment among supporters and sympathizers. For analysts, this can be difficult to parse. For opponents, of course, generating a righteous fog is often a goal in itself. Deliberately enough, it can confuse third parties, blur the sharp lines of conflict that the rights proponent sought to draw, and compel supporters and even constituents to tread carefully or go slowly in lending aid.

REPUDIATION

If the foregoing moves fail, powerful opponents of rights movements may reject seemingly definitive political or legal judgments against them. This is most obvious in the ways that "losers" in rights conflicts fight on. Unless their defeat is total, they have the resources and the will to do so, notwithstanding a specific decision against them. Using their own rights claims, however bruised and battered these may be, they also have a doctrinal basis for continuing the struggle, albeit one that may need reformulation in the changed political circumstances. Beyond denial tactics such as delegitimizing the repugnant decision (and the decision-maker), they will eat away at it through new challenges meant to win back parts or all of their own reduced rights.

Alternatively, the losing side in a national rights conflict may simply refuse to recognize or even abide by the result. To help in such repudiation, it will turn to a more receptive political venue where it may create a parallel structure of laws vindicating its rights (although with varying degrees of authoritativeness). In today's world, this is more possible than it once was, in institutions both above and below state, international, or subnational institutions. To take the first of these, as many scholars have shown, in recent decades the number of international organizations and transnational NGOs has grown significantly. Even if these entities can seldom enforce contrary policies and laws on states, those who have fallen before national rights campaigns frequently search for allies abroad and for sympathetic overseas venues where they can at least vent their grievances. Frequently, as well, those who have failed to block rights movements at home and who consequently find their own rights reduced can find sympathetic audiences overseas. They may even be able to create an international simulacrum of what they have been deprived of in their native country. To take one example at the grandest level of rights, the Unrepresented Nations and Peoples Organization (UNPO), an NGO headquartered in The Hague, offers a kind of alternative United Nations for groups deprived of various forms of self-determination in their own states. In UNPO's cramped spaces and darkened hallways, would-be national flags droop limply. But in its periodic conferences, UNPO's members can air their grievances, make connections with like-minded or similarly deprived groups, and dream of vindicating their rights to self-determination. At the UN itself, certain forums, especially low-level agencies within the sprawling Human Rights Council, permit deprived or abused groups to voice their claims. And in less elevated spheres, there are any number of transnational networks promoting an ideologically diverse spectrum of rights that one or another state violates.

In addition to reaching above the state, groups that find themselves in reduced circumstances because of a contrary movement's triumph in national politics may turn to the subnational level for solace. Outvoted by national majorities, they will seek to elevate the power of subnational units, or at least their own such unit. In the United States, states' rights are a prime example of this form of repudiation. Most famously, in the wake of the Civil War, the prospect of equal rights for blacks, won at huge cost in blood and treasure and seemingly institutionalized by constitutional amendments and related laws, quickly fell by the wayside. Federal fecklessness was partly to blame, but also important was the furious Southern resistance, punctuated by frequent use of force and violence against African Americans. This resistance, most of which was rationalized and implemented through the South's claims to states' rights, left the Civil War's promise unfulfilled for most of a century.

Nor are such tactics dead today. Across the globe, ethnic, religious, and ideological minorities continue to clamor for their own community's rights even after contradictory state laws have been established. Sometimes these rearguard movements go nowhere, eventually dying out. More frequently, they temporarily retreat from public prominence, awaiting an opportune moment to revive themselves. To take one recent example, pro-life activism in the United States suffered a major blow from the 1974 *Roe v. Wade* decision. But it soon began whittling away at reproductive rights, not only at the national level but also through any number of state laws limiting access to abortion. Decades later, the pro-life movement remains a powerful force in American politics, and its long-standing repudiation of the Supreme Court decision may ultimately be vindicated through legal or political means. Likewise, in the case of internationally powerful rights movements, states that fall outside the mainstream will redouble their emphasis on nationalist idioms and reiterate their veneration of domestic politics. Given the continuing strength of sovereignty, this is usually sufficient to allow even international outcasts to continue their preferred ways at home, framed as a right to national sovereignty or cultural preservation.

Conclusion

To counter rights campaigns, opponents turn to rights as well, deploying them against the movement they face. Along with the existing rights they use to shield themselves, backed if possible by institutional and political power, foes deny the original movement's claims, raise their own rival set of rights, and reverse the movement's arguments, claiming themselves as the truly oppressed group. The alleged violator seeks to turn himself into the blameless victim. Finally, if all else fails and the original movement succeeds in gaining its rights, the foe, now portraying itself as a victim, gathers its strength and fights on. Refusing to accept the new status quo as legitimate or permanent, the foe repudiates it instead.

These countering measures and the rallying cries discussed in chapter 2 are used by rival political movements in most conflicts to galvanize their constituents and attract allies. In addition, movements aggressively deploy rights directly against their foes, as the rest of this book will discuss by both conceptualizing those methods and providing case studies of their use. I begin in chapter 4 by considering how activists avail themselves of rights as camouflage in all manner of political conflicts. In chapters 5 and 6, I examine the use of rights as spears and dynamite against opponents. Finally, chapters 7 and 8 focus on situations in which movements fashion rights into blockades and wedges to prevent third parties from joining with the foe.

PART II

Contending with Foes

Rights as Camouflage

MASKING MOTIVES

In July 2010, Spain's autonomous region of Catalonia banned bullfighting. For animal rights activists, this was a major triumph achieved after decades of fruitless criticism, protest, and lobbying. But the ban was more than just a victory for animal rights groups and their recently formed Plataforma Prou (Enough Platform).[1] It was also, if less gloriously, a vehicle for long-standing nationalist conflict between the Catalan minority and the Spanish state dominated by the country's Castilian majority. In 2008, Prou leaders had presented Catalonia's regional government, the Generalitat, with an initiative signed by 180,000 citizens demanding a ban on bullfighting. Under Catalonian law, the regional parliament was required to act, but for years it dawdled. Dominated by politicians who cared little about bulls, it ignored the Prou campaign's repeated calls for a parliamentary vote. Then, in June 2010, Spain's Constitutional Court reached a major decision on an unrelated case challenging Catalonia's Statute of Autonomy (Estatut d'Autonomia de Catalunya). Most importantly, the Court rejected the law's declaration of Catalonia as a politically distinct "nation" within Spain. Days later, an estimated 430,000 people—one-sixth of the region's population—protested on Barcelona's streets. Meanwhile, in the regional parliament, irate Catalan nationalists suddenly seemed to grasp bullfighting's brutality. They took up the stalled Prou initiative and worked together with the animal rights activists they had previously spurned. One month after the

Constitutional Court's slap at Catalan autonomy, parliament voted to safe-guard the bulls.

No doubt some legislators were moved by tender concern for bovine suffering or a real belief in animal rights. But something else was afoot: Catalan politicians, angered by the Constitutional Court decision, had struck back at Spain's Castilian majority, many of whom honor bullfighting as a treasured cultural heritage—*la fiesta nacional* (national festival). In their long-standing conflict with Madrid, the Catalans used the anti-bullfighting initiative and its animal rights impetus as cover for retaliatory urges. Oppos-ing them, Spanish nationalists and bullfighting aficionados sought to un-mask the campaign while also exploiting the relationship between animal rights and Spain's dueling nationalisms in other ways. Nonetheless, the Catalans' camouflaging tactic served its aggressive purposes. Bullfighting was prohibited, pleasing both animal rights activists and Catalan national-ists, albeit for different reasons. Outside Spain, the ban was portrayed largely in animal rights terms, with headlines around the world heralding the end of bullfighting, rather than the latest round in Spain's ongoing nationalist struggle. Weeks later, however, Catalonia's same lawmakers gave cultural heritage status to an equally cruel but indigenous Catalan tradition involving torment of bulls, the *correbous* (flaming bull) spectacle.

In using animal rights to camouflage an attack on Castilian culture, those involved in this Spanish spat employed a tactic that is hardly unique. Diverse political movements around the world find rights of various kinds a useful means of covering up other agendas or tactics. The result is a mixing of mo-tives, goals, and movements, with important but understudied implications for understanding rights. This chapter explores the use of rights as camou-flage by first defining the term and differentiating its forms. I explore key questions about this tactic, including: Which groups are most likely to use rights as camouflage? Which rights or rights movements are best fashioned into camouflage? And how do opponents react to such tactics? In the heart of the chapter, I look at a number of cases in which rights were used as camouflage, with a focus on the Catalonian bullfighting ban.

Finding incontrovertible instances of camouflaging is not easy. It is one of the dark arts of politics—its essence pretense, even subterfuge. Although there is a public side to all camouflaging, concealment is obviously critical to its success, its users hiding their actions and motives. On the other hand, complete secrecy is seldom possible in politics, and so those who camou-flage also seek deniability—ways to claim convincingly that the camouflag-ing imputed to them is not that at all. They will claim that the attribution was in error, the association coincidental, and any fortuitous covering inadvertent. All of this presents a challenge to analysts: it is difficult to be sure that political actors are using camouflage. Nonetheless, in this chapter I theorize about this covert but important concept and provide strong evidence of its use. The chapter also describes the tactic's prevalence and effects—and the consequent need to understand it better.

Camouflage Tactics

DEFINITION AND CONTEXT

Camouflaging occurs when a political actor seeking one goal adopts and promotes a new and distinct rights issue, one that has no direct bearing on the actor's original or dominant aim. The tactic may be used for a number of purposes, but before analyzing them, it is useful to consider its broader bases. Political life is rich with principles, rights, and causes. Yet most political movements focus only on a narrow set of issues, ignoring numerous others. Even for those broadest of political entities, parties and states, certain goals must dominate while others are necessarily shortchanged. These neglected issues may initially appear secondary or irrelevant to the pursuit of core goals. However, for strategically attuned actors, peripheral or unrelated issues may someday prove useful.

Recent scholarship has captured this point by highlighting the coexistence of varied fields or arenas of contention.[2] As conflicts develop and change over time, what once appeared extraneous—as part of a different arena or field—can later serve to advance an actor's cause or undermine the foe's. Such issues therefore are better viewed as resources to be tapped by a strategist when and if needed. Accessing them later is possible because political movements are malleable. Even if most have fundamental goals, they are also able and willing to assume a variety of guises.[3] The key question in deciding whether to don a camouflage of rights is to ask if the tactic helps achieve the movement's deeper concerns. In the context of such strategically rooted plasticity, the ideological emptiness of rights makes them invaluable as camouflage. Movements of varied political character can snatch claims from other arenas, even those that lie outside their central concerns.

THE PURPOSES OF PRETENSE

Camouflaging has three overlapping but distinguishable purposes present to one or another degree when leaders of a movement use the tactic. Camouflaging *masks* the movement's ulterior motives from potential third-party supporters and sometimes even from its own constituents. It *diverts* these audiences from the movement's most contentious goals. And it *decoys* foes into perilous political terrain where the movement holds an advantage.

Rights serve as masks when they conceal the tactician's underlying aims. When might a mask be needed? As social and cultural changes occur within societies, movements can be left behind. Their rhetoric or goals, which were once openly voiced, can shift to being viewed as questionable or illegitimate in broader society. Movement constituents, however, are slow to rethink their underlying interests and beliefs, even if they sense that times have changed. To mobilize these groups without offending newly established sensibilities and earning more enemies, movement leaders avoid terminology that has gone rancid or even turned toxic. To do so, they invent or hijack anodyne rights rhetoric, covering up the retrograde goals they would prefer if they had the power to achieve them. They speak in code, with words that mean one seemingly unobjectionable thing to outsiders but that have another, harsher meaning to initiates and true believers. Rather than openly voicing racist sentiments, for instance, activists may speak of "states' rights" or "majority rights." Using such dog whistle techniques allows movement leaders to show to their constituents that they still sympathize with or seek long-standing goals, even if those goals now lie close to or beyond the political pale.[4] This technique may also reassure those constituents who have grudgingly accepted the broader cultural change that their interests are still recognized, even if *sub nomine*, in the new climate.

Of course, complete concealment is seldom possible. Those who put on a rights mask may be too well known, their goals too familiar, the fit too awkward, for the disguise to deceive. The ever-watchful foes of a movement will be suspicious about the hidden motivations of those mouthing the new rights issue—and will have no compunction about ripping the mask away. Despite such revelations, constituents and sympathizers of the movement will often remain loyal to it for the reasons just noted.

In addition, outsiders to a conflict may be diverted by rights rhetoric into lending their support, ignoring or downplaying what is really driving the movement and what is at stake in the fray. The scholarly literature on the moral hazards of humanitarian intervention has made this point, from a different angle. This controversial but convincing literature shows that certain insurgent groups deliberately inflame conflicts with their authoritarian home states, expecting them to react with harsh repression. When a crackdown ensues, they publicize the resulting human rights violations, hoping thereby to attract third-party support and if possible military intervention. In the late 1990s, for instance, the Kosovo Liberation Army (KLA) used human rights rhetoric and the reality of the Yugoslav government's reactive killings of a small number of Kosovars to deflect attention from its bald secessionist agenda. This paid off handsomely. The United States and its NATO allies came to the Kosovars' rescue with months of aerial bombardment—despite the fact that only years before the United States had denounced the KLA as a terrorist organization. Conducted in the name of human rights, the Kosovo intervention led to Kosovo's separation and later independence.[5]

As this case suggests, a tactician's promotion of a distinct rights issue can serve as a diversion from a movement's contentious core goals. A new and different rights issue can create a fruitful blur: third parties who previously might have been indifferent or even opposed to the movement's aims may rally round or make common cause with it because of the additional one. Even when the original goals retain their centrality to insiders, new rights issues can make it difficult for outsiders in the heat and haze of conflict to recall those underlying motivations. When a conquering army suddenly champions the rights of an oppressed group in the territory it has attacked, camouflaging of this sort is often involved. Diversion also creates ambiguity, making it possible for the tactician to reposition the conflict along new and more productive lines. Promoting a distinct rights issue may associate the movement with a "white knight," a well-regarded, innocuous, or seemingly neutral cause that can launder or improve its reputation. When the anti-immigrant English Defence League unexpectedly evinces concern for the rights of animals slaughtered using ostensibly cruel halal methods, one may suspect that this move has diversionary purposes.[6] Either way, camouflaging can sow confusion or uncertainty that the tactician can exploit to his benefit, attracting new supporters to the cause. Of course, raising new issues for diversionary purposes may also raise the question of what the movement really stands for. But leaders will have little doubt about their main goals, even if the movement's rights rhetoric seems to give it a shiny new face.

Masking and diversion are aimed at a movement's constituents and potential sympathizers. Bolstering itself with support from these audiences, the movement simultaneously weakens its foe. Another aspect of camouflaging, decoying, aims to weaken foes directly by luring them onto treacherous new terrain. In a decoy strategy, a movement pursuing one aim will suddenly champion a distinct set of values or the rights of an unrelated group. The movement portrays these rights as menaced or hurt by the depredations of the foe. The plan is to impel the enemy to expend time and energy in this other fight. The tactician thereby hopes to ensnare or embarrass the rival, at minimum draining its resources, at maximum winning the side event and, perhaps as a consequence, the principal conflict.

The usefulness of rights rhetoric in these masking, diversion, and decoy tactics should be obvious. By suggesting a legal or even constitutional status, rights enjoy an air of neutrality. Their long-standing association with the underdog, despite their equally hoary if less noted utilization by the overlord, lends them apparent validity. Their celebration by varied freedom movements in recent decades gives them a positive, contemporary halo useful even to movements with antithetical ends. Their seeming familiarity, even if they issue from unknown quarters in faraway places, eases their appeal. Reciprocally, for astute political movements, the existence of large reservoirs of rights consciousness among powerful outsiders makes a camouflaging strategy tempting. Raising a shiny new rights screen can keep overseas supporters from penetrating to the less palatable limitations and compromises that mark every movement. Even in the age of the internet, it is difficult to grasp local realities from afar. Outsiders who support the right in the abstract or in their own milieus may therefore be drawn to the fresh exponent, overlooking its deepest intentions. All of this can help a movement achieve its real goals, even if newfound supporters remain transfixed by its surface appeals.

DEALERS IN DECEIT

Who is most likely to engage in camouflaging? Although all kinds of groups utilize this tactic, those most likely to do so have underlying goals or tactics that are either dubious or unacceptable to larger society. In the last two centuries, as principles such as racial equality, social toleration, and religious openness have gained ground, movements that continue to oppose them have been ostracized. Yet these movements or their ideological descendants remain on the political scene, conveniently modifying their goals and tactics, but sharing similar values. If it is politically incorrect to peddle blatant racism or aggressive nationalism, such movements adapt. They paper over their most contentious preferences and their most inflammatory language with the antipolitics of rights. Using seemingly neutral, well accepted, or distinct principles, they lay a patina of respectability over goals or tactics that broader society has recently come to abhor. Not to do so would be to weaken or delegitimate the movement. Doing so makes them appear respectable and contemporary. In one implication of this point, camouflage has become more common as norms of equality and nondiscrimination have gradually gained wider assent. Where opposition to certain groups and identities could previously be voiced openly, today that is no longer possible without dismissal as reactionary. Yet political descendants of yesterday's oppressors remain, moved by pale but real versions of the old ideologies. Updated and prettified with rights claims, these may still be spoken. Such statements do not aim to convince the movement's enemies, who may still denounce them as deplorable. Their primary targets are third parties, who may unwittingly lend support to the rights movement without understanding the background or the stakes.

Groups that portray themselves as liberal but that use violence to achieve their goals are also likely to resort to camouflage. The need to deflect attention from brutal methods compounds the urge to cover up. To garner support for the blood and treasure consumed, a transcendent moral vision is expedient. The image of rights protected or vindicated makes it easy to overlook the price paid. Those unfamiliar with a conflict are often blind to the subterfuge, so captivated by the corona of rights that they ignore the resulting rubble. This has been the case in numerous wars conducted by liberal states.[7] One example discussed at greater length later in this book is the American government's use of women's rights to help justify America's war and occupation in Afghanistan in the decades since 2001.

WHICH RIGHTS? PICKING A DISGUISE

Which types of rights are most suitable as camouflage? Political actors are opportunistic and seize on all manner of rights depending on the circumstances. Nonetheless, the rights that make good camouflage at particular junctures have several characteristics in common. First, the right must be one that enjoys some support among the movement constituents and potential allies who are the main audiences for camouflaging. This does not mean that all members of a society must support the right, nor even a majority. But if a significant segment does, this gives the camouflager's move surface validity. Second, the right must be readily available at the time of a conflict, meaning that differences over it must be a part—albeit a minor part (at least initially)—of the disagreement between the main parties. A right that is not touched upon in any aspect of the conflict will not be useful for camouflage.

Beyond these basic propositions, there are a few corollaries. Expansive rights that are widely acknowledged (if still disputed) in a particular society are suitable as camouflage. They can easily encompass most who seek to camouflage their motivations, and they do not draw attention to themselves as novel or unfamiliar. Already, of course, it will come as a surprise that certain movements abruptly voice support for a new and distinct cause. To distract from this shift, broader and more conventional rights make superior camouflage. This may be one reason that white nationalists have become new champions of free speech in a number of liberal democracies. Of course, in the United States the Constitution's First Amendment does permit them to voice hateful ideas. But if direct intimidation of minorities and open incitement to violence are central to their "free expression," this suggests that the right is being used at least in part for camouflage.

RIGHTS GUARDIANS AND SUCCESSFUL CAMOUFLAGING

Related factors explain when camouflaging is most likely to succeed—that is, when it goes undetected or is convincingly denied by the user. Reactions by a right's self-appointed guardian are most important. "Guardians" are preexisting organizations that promote a right or, more accurately, particular interpretations of a right and that enjoy stellar reputations among wider audiences sympathetic to those interpretations. Typically there is more than one such guardian, and all of them claim to interpret the right—often in contrary ways—and compete with one another to convince multiple audiences. Self-appointed guardians, both national and international, are common in many societies. In the United States, for instance, such groups as the American Civil Liberties Union (ACLU) and the National Rifle Association (NRA) seek to serve this function for the First and Second Amendments to the Constitution. Of course, these organizations' sway is confined to audiences that share their interpretation of each right; other audiences may disagree, but the organizations nonetheless exercise considerable authority in their own circle. Internationally, groups such as Human Rights Watch and Amnesty International act as guardians for human rights writ large, even though there are other, less prominent groups that disagree with them over the meaning of particular rights.

How a prominent guardian reacts to the unexpected invocation of "its" right by a questionable new actor is a key factor in whether the latter's camouflaging will succeed. On the one hand, the guardian may ignore this move, hoping that it will pass unnoticed and that neither the right nor the guardian will be tainted by the strange-bedfellows linkage. This response is unlikely, however, because the movement camouflaging itself acts openly, publicizing the newly adopted right to conceal or legitimate its real aims. As public awareness grows, the guardian will face pressure to take a stand on this association. In many cases, particularly when the camouflager is seen as unacceptable to broader society, the guardian will reject the unwanted arriviste. The exploitation of a revered right by a disreputable political movement can easily sully the reputation of the right, and guardians will work hard to prevent this. If the guardian repeatedly shouts that its favored right is being misappropriated, camouflaging loses its effect.

On the other hand, for some guardians certain groups may not be so reprehensible or alien that rejecting their use of the right is an option. The ACLU certainly opposes Nazism, but the free speech principles raised by white nationalist marches are at the heart of its mission. The ACLU has therefore reluctantly represented such groups. Still, in 2017 it adopted a policy of rejecting representation for groups that carry arms and otherwise engage in intimidation in their protests, suggesting the organization's suspicions that white nationalists are using speech rights as camouflage.[8]

In other circumstances, guardians publicly embrace a newfound but suspect adherent, especially when the latter is a powerful political actor and the guardian believes that the association will advance its own goals. When, as mentioned earlier, women's rights were unfurled by the U.S. government to justify the Afghanistan War—diverting attention from the war's enormous human toll—rights groups in the United States welcomed this embrace of their cause. In expressing their belief that the war would bolster women's rights in Afghanistan and at home, even though many Afghan women opposed it, these U.S. groups reinforced the government's camouflaging.[9]

This raises the question of how a movement's opponent will react to camouflaging. The tactic will not fool a foe. He will easily recognize his antagonist and seek to unmask him. The harder task is inducing third parties less versed in the issues to see through the screen. Because political motives are so often mixed, the foe may find it difficult to demonstrate convincingly that the initial movement is camouflaging its real purposes. Of course, the foe may appeal to the guardian—or lash out at it, depending on the latter's response. If a tactician has chosen his righteous camouflage wisely, however, the guardian may act as a kind of human shield. If the guardian is a renowned organization or sympathetic figure, the foe may be reluctant to criticize (at least openly), fearing that the resulting damage may be counterproductive. At minimum, the foe will need to differentiate the movement's alleged misuse of a revered right from its own support for the right's authentic meaning.

CLUES TO CAMOUFLAGING

Before analyzing examples of camouflage, it is useful to touch again on the question of sincerity. How can analysts know whether a political actor is using a rights claim sincerely or cynically as camouflage? As I have suggested earlier, this question matters less than it first appears. We can examine a conflict and draw conclusions about the effects of a particular tactic even if we can never be certain of its user's heart. It is also true that in most cases motives are multiple. Nonetheless, in the specific instance of camouflaging, there are clues to real intentions—or at least to those playing the major role. A document or speech may urge that a rights argument be used as a means of advancing some other agenda. For obvious reasons, however, such statements will usually be secret, their disclosure rare. Absent direct proof, close study of a case may reveal circumstantial evidence suggesting that camouflaging is occurring. For example, by examining political movements over time, analysts may find that they start or stop using rights arguments at moments unrelated to ongoing debates about the right itself. This hints at inspirations other than sincere belief.

Consider Denmark's 2005 Muhammad cartoons controversy. Prior to the cartoons' publication in 2005 as a legitimate instance of journalistic satire, how often did right-wing anti-immigrant movements in Europe celebrate free speech? If the answer is seldom, this suggests that camouflaging was part of their motivation for citing the right when praising the cartoons. Associating themselves with a right they had previously disregarded could not only divert attention from their anti-Muslim animus but also raise their status more generally. By contrast, the journalists who published the cartoons and had long defended free speech, whether or not it gave offense, would not be engaging in camouflage.[10]

From the other side in the cartoons controversy, Egypt and other secular authoritarian countries in the Middle East raised the right "to be protected against the denigration of 'religious figures.' "[11] As Jyette Klausen shows, this newly invented right and the larger Muslim mobilization against the cartoons had a variety of ulterior motives, not least an effort by these states to counter America's "Freedom Agenda," itself ostensibly aimed at democratizing the Middle East. Attacking the agenda directly was tricky for authoritarian leaders who received large amounts of U.S. government support for their military and police forces. Mobilizing the public against the Freedom Agenda was risky too because such protests could easily be directed against regimes so dependent on Western support. On the other hand, demanding protections against denigration or defamation of religion could camouflage the deeper motive of weakening a Freedom Agenda in which freedom of expression featured prominently. Such putative rights could also be used to mobilize citizens exclusively against the West, reducing the danger of blowback against authoritarian rulers.[12]

Another clue that camouflaging may be at work comes from contradictions in the invocation of a right. If political leaders urge unlimited adherence in one breath and limits in another, one may suspect camouflaging and not merely hypocrisy. Consider the French government responses to the *Charlie Hebdo* murders in January 2015. These heinous crimes immediately elicited vociferous defenses of free speech and the right to ridicule. Little, it was said, more directly threatened French and Western values than attacks on those engaging in offensive speech, such as the murdered writers and artists. Yet weeks later French officials had no compunction about prosecuting citizens, including comedians, whose Facebook posts or drunken outbursts ostensibly condoned, but did not incite, terrorism.[13] Camouflage was certainly not the only reason that the French defended freedom of speech after the *Charlie Hebdo* killings. Belief in the right clearly predominated in the outpourings after the murders. There are also obvious differences between killing an offensive speaker and jailing him. But the timing and selective application of the right raises suspicions that some of the vehement defenses of free speech were less than wholehearted, covering up for anti-Muslim sentiments. From an analytic standpoint, close comparative analysis in highly contentious situations can suggest or reveal camouflaging.

Camouflage in Nationalist Conflicts

Camouflaging occurs in other types of conflicts as well. Nationalist struggles offer many instances. Although the exact patterns vary, group efforts to gain greater self-determination are usually at the heart of these uses of camouflage. Precisely what that right means—its scope, boundaries, and usages—is often unclear, however. The association of nationalism with racism, xenophobia, and violence in many parts of the world has given open expression of such sentiments an unsavory reputation. In this context, other rights can act as screens, and many nationalists have adopted them to cover up, supplement, or legitimate their agendas. "Rightsifying" their claims, they transform them into forms palatable to distant audiences and potential supporters.[14] As we have seen, rightsifying can work because rights have the appearance of universalism and neutrality—even when used by parochial

interests. More important, beyond one's own society, rights act as transla-
tors, albeit unreliable ones: they allow people far from the site of conflict to
"know," usually in simplistic terms, what seems to be at stake. Outsiders
assume that they understand the claim even if the specific form it takes, the
particular event it celebrates, or the intense feelings it arouses are alien to
them. In reality, it may be difficult for them to grasp or even to hear the
underlying identity claims, which will be framed in a language internal to
the group and referencing events, personalities, and dates vital to cultural
insiders but obscure to outsiders. A *right* to such an identity—or as more
frequently framed, to manifest that identity—through freedom of expression, religious freedom, or freedom of association resonates around the
liberal world, even when the substance behind it is aggressive or illiberal.

It is doubtless true, as Marc Howard Ross has argued, that such usages
of rights are secondary to the cultural contestation at the heart of ethnic and
national conflicts. The controversies are "not fundamentally about freedom
of speech or religion or protection from intimidation, but about the threatened identities of people."[15] Nonetheless, rights claims are a key instrument
in such conflicts. They are a vehicle for advancing ethnic identities and protecting them against threats. Rights are used in this way not only by minority
and indigenous groups but also by majorities claiming that they seek only
to shield their distinctive way of life.[16] Yet such claims provide cover for attacks on minority or "foreign" groups. In some cases, righteous camouflage
works to attract outside support and affect the character and outcome of
nationalist conflicts.

In addition to the Kosovo case noted previously, consider Northern Ireland. Although violence has declined in recent years, disputes between Irish
Republicans and Unionists continue—for instance, with regard to the long-
standing practice of parading.[17] In the context of a decades-old conflict that
has taken thousands of lives, marches by activists from one community have
long been viewed as provocative by the other. Indeed, in past years the
parades themselves frequently sparked violence. On the one hand, as stated
by the British government's Parades Commission (which is charged with
refereeing disputes), "there is still a perception amongst many Nationalists
that some Loyal Order parades are simply triumphalist displays by anti-
Catholic organisations." On the other hand, the commission also notes,
"there is a perception amongst many Unionists that the smaller number of
republican parades . . . are a glorification of terrorist organisations."[18]

One of the most inflammatory of these marches occurs in the town of
Portadown, where Protestant Unionists have long sought to march through

neighborhoods and on streets that in recent times have become predominantly Catholic. To deal with the turmoil there and elsewhere, the British government has tried many tactics, including banning, moving, or regulating the parades. In response, the Portadown Orangemen, like other Protestant Loyalists in Northern Ireland, have in recent decades framed their parades in terms of the abstract and widely accepted rights to free expression and cultural identity. Their website includes a "civil rights" menu discussing their toleration—so different from their Catholic opponents', in this telling—as well as their devotion to a long cosmopolitan tradition of rights. According to the Orangemen, the parades "are not offensive, are not political and are not staged purely to annoy members of the Roman Catholic community, as some commentators would have people believe." Instead, the parades are an expression of Protestant identity, and as such Protestants have a basic right to them: "The Orangemen of Portadown are engaged in a campaign for 'Civil and Religious liberty' for all the citizens of Northern Ireland both Roman Catholic and Protestant. . . . Like Martin Luther King we have taken the stand we have on behalf of all the people of Northern Ireland, Protestant and Catholic, who have had enough of terrorist-enforced segregation, of being ordered around by sectarian IRA and UVF gunmen and bombers."[19]

It is unclear how many Portadown Catholics are swayed by this rights rhetoric, despite the website's claim that "many in the Catholic community have written to Orangemen to express their support for the right of Orangemen to express their culture and heritage." Much of the violent conflict in prior years occurred in confrontations between paraders and those protesting the parades. But the point of this rhetoric is not to convince opponents. Rather, it helps muddy the waters, giving the Orangemen a legitimate and widely recognized basis, in rights, for their underlying cultural claims. Few other rhetorical strategies would have such power. The ease with which the Orangemen invoke Martin Luther King suggests a considered effort to maximize this appeal and create righteous resonance. Such rhetoric also raises absolutist pretensions, at least among their own constituents. This is true even though the Parades Commission emphasizes that "there is a right to parade, as there is a right to protest," but that "these rights are not absolute." For the Orangemen themselves, however, absolutist language stokes passion. As their "civil rights" webpage concludes: "Here we stand—We can do no other."[20]

In this case, it seems clear that many Orangemen ardently believe in their right to march. It is less clear to what degree they support freedom of expression more generally. Rather, the right serves, at least in part, as a screen for promoting their primary interest: preserving their community and its traditions against a perceived Catholic threat. Their protestations that they do this for "all the citizens of Northern Ireland" and "not . . . purely to annoy" Catholics ring hollow given the raucous and offensive way in which many marches have unfolded. As Ross has written, in nationalist conflicts, the "expression of [cultural] differences in moralistic rights language means it is especially difficult to devise pragmatic solutions since rights are hard to compromise and hurting an opponent often becomes more important than minimizing one's own losses."[21]

Animal Rights in the Catalonian Conflict

The Catalonian bullfighting ban, which introduced this chapter, offers another example of the use of rights as camouflage, one that is worth examining in detail. The status of Catalonia in relation to Spain has been an important issue for centuries. The region's rights to self-determination and cultural expression have been primary focuses, with the skirmish over bullfighting playing a relatively small role. Yet despite its apparent idiosyncrasy, the case illuminates how adaptable nationalist politicians exploit rights that extend well beyond those of their own communities to advance their cause and hurt their foes. Detailed examination of this case is useful because, compared to other cases in which one may suspect camouflaging, the evidence is strong despite the tactic's covert nature. Finally, the case illuminates the ways in which other players (such as animal rights activists and defenders of bullfighting) employ intersecting rights claims, using them as camouflage for their own purposes. In the following pages, I first set the context for the case within the contested nationalisms of Spain and the more recent history of animal rights. Next, I show how key players dealt with the camouflaging opportunities presented by the campaign to ban bullfighting. Finally, I examine the consequences of rights camouflaging in the case.

CATALONIA AND SPAIN

Catalonia is a region of northeastern Spain with a distinct language and culture, as well as a history that includes long periods of self-rule.[22] The region, once part of the independent kingdom of Catalonia-Aragon, was forcefully incorporated into Spain in 1716. In the decades that followed, Spanish authorities suppressed Catalan language, customs, and autonomy.

When the region led Spain's industrialization in the late nineteenth century, Catalan culture flourished more openly again. In the early twentieth century, Catalonia enjoyed brief periods of autonomy within Spain. Then, in the Spanish Civil War, the region staunchly defended the Republican government. When the Republicans lost the war, the military regime of General Francisco Franco ended regional autonomy and outlawed the Catalan language and cultural practices. Franco sought to dissolve the Catalans and other Spanish minorities into a single nationality dominated by Madrid. As part of this cultural onslaught, the government built or improved bullrings, particularly in Spain's peripheral regions, and promoted bullfighting at home and abroad as *la fiesta nacional*. Although it was not as objectionable to Catalans as the policies that suppressed their language, the broader effort at cultural homogenization sparked resentment in the region.

With the end of dictatorship and the rise of democracy in 1975, the Catalans renewed their quest for self-government and cultural rights. In 1979, Spain promulgated Catalonia's "Statute of Autonomy," recognizing the region as an "autonomous community" with distinct "nationality," a regional government (the Generalitat), and significant autonomy. (Spain has sixteen similar statutes for its other autonomous communities.) Primarily under the leadership of a moderate nationalist coalition known as Convergence and Union (CiU), the Catalonian government slowly enlarged linguistic, legal, and political autonomy over the ensuing decades. In 2005, a new coalition, the left-wing Tripartito, won power.[23] With support from its allies in Spain's Socialist government, it held a regional referendum to declare Catalonia a "nation" within Spain and to enhance the status of the Catalan language. The referendum passed, and an amended Statute of Autonomy came into force in 2006.

However, at the regional and national levels, Spain's other major party, the conservative People's Party (Partido Popular), challenged the amendments in the Spanish Constitutional Court. On June 28, 2010, after four years of litigation, the Court reached a 6–4 decision. Although this decision upheld most of the Statute's 233 articles, it found fourteen key provisions unconstitutional, including the Statute's designation of Catalonia as a "nation" and Catalan as the preferred language in the region. As noted previously, the Court decision immediately sparked protests in Catalonia and deepened conflict between Catalonia and the central government, soon to be led by the People's Party. The bullfighting ban was a small but telling part of this larger dispute, which reached a climax in October 2017 with a contested referendum on independence. Unauthorized by the Spanish government, the regional referendum passed overwhelmingly but with a turnout of only 43 percent of eligible voters. When the Generalitat declared independence, the Spanish government immediately suspended the regional government.[24]

BULLFIGHTING BACKGROUND

For aficionados, bullfighting, *la corrida de toros*, is a unique form of cultural expression, extolled by artists and intellectuals as the supreme contest of man and nature.[25] In Spain and other Latin countries, matadors have long enjoyed celebrity status, with museums honoring the best fighters as well as the fiercest bulls. Although most closely associated with the Castilian heartland, bullfighting thrived in Catalonia (and southern France) for many centuries. The practice is said to have originated in the area, there is a regional bullfighting association, and some of Spain's greatest matadors trained in Catalonia. In the early twentieth century, Barcelona is said to have had three major bullrings, more than any other city in Spain, although this is disputed by Catalan activists.[26] In rural Catalonia, traditional "spectacles" involving men and bulls are common.

In recent decades, however, bullfighting has dwindled in popularity across Spain, especially in Catalonia. By the late 2000s, only a single bullring remained in Catalonia, although bullfighting was still popular there. To stem the decline nationwide, the Spanish government strongly promotes bullfighting as central to Spanish culture. The government subsidizes the bullfighting industry, sponsors bullfights on television, and teaches children to appreciate the art of *tauromaquia*. The country's animal cruelty laws include special exclusions for the bulls and horses used—and injured or killed—in bullrings. A powerful bullfighting lobby is active not only in Spain but also in Portugal, France, and the European Union, as well as in Latin American countries. This lobby fights hard to preserve its livelihood and love, wrapped in the mantle of Spanish culture and tradition. As one bull breeder stated, "This is a part of life, a part of our nation, like flamenco dancing. If you take away the bulls, you take away everything. It is a thing that is very much ours."[27]

For animal rights activists, however, Spain's continued glorification of cruelty has long been an affront, and many have organized against it. In 1985, Spain's Association for the Defense of Animal Rights (ADDA) declared it a "horrible massacre, it's barbarous, it's obsolete, from the times when people were burned at the stake." In the 1990s, ADDA helped lead a national campaign with the slogan "Torture is neither art nor culture," with activists declaring bullfighting a "barbarity" and labeling it the "national shame." As one stated in a 1994 interview: "Animals, as well as human beings, have the right to a dignified life and a painless death."[28] Over many years of campaigning, Spain's anti-bullfighting groups achieved some successes, especially in Catalonia. In 1988, the region prohibited construction of new bullrings. In 1992, when the Olympics were held in Barcelona, the local government symbolically proclaimed itself an "anti-bullfighting city," even though the practice continued there. Meanwhile, European institutions such as the European Parliament investigated the practice as animal cruelty.

The rise in activism may have contributed to bullfighting's slow decline. Nevertheless, the suffering and death remained in public view in bullrings and the media every week across Spain, celebrated and supported by the national government. In addition, some of the victories won by animal rights campaigners had glaring gaps. For instance, a 2003 campaign in Catalonia resulted in a strong Animal Protection Law declaring animals "physically and psychologically sensitive."[29] Yet the bullfighting lobby again secured an exemption, and bulls and horses continued to be allowed to bleed and die in the rings of Barcelona.

STRATEGIES OF THE PROU CAMPAIGN

In early 2008, a coalition of eleven Spanish and international animal rights groups began a major new campaign, the Plataforma Prou, to abolish bullfighting worldwide. Its first, highly symbolic target was the custom's heartland, Spain. Explaining its philosophy and application to bulls, the Prou campaign's website stated: "We are not asking for the rights of animals to become equal to those of people, but neither do we accept that animals are reduced to objects or things. . . . Bullfighting in our culture ratifies the notion that an animal is a thing, an object which can be used to entertain us without taking into account its suffering, without showing it any respect."[30]

The campaign set in motion a series of strategic maneuvers involving multiple uses of rights rhetoric, much of it to conceal other agendas. Animal rights groups, keen to pass the ban, subtly appealed to Catalan nationalist sentiments to move their campaign forward. The nationalists in turn vented their anger over Spain's Constitutional Court decision and broader Castilian domination under the guise of animal protection. Both groups' chief foes, the bullfighting lobby and its political backers in the People's Party, draped their support of bullfighting in the rhetoric of free expression, workers' rights, and even animal rights themselves. Unraveling this contest helps reveal the varied ways in which rights can be used as camouflage.

Prou leaders, who served as self-selected guardians for the rights of bulls, had a strong strategic vision that informed every aspect of the campaign.[31] To start, it is important to note that the animal rights groups that formed the Prou campaign did not target bullfighting primarily because of the degree of its cruelty or the number of animals involved. Other practices, such as factory farming, were arguably worse, as activists admitted. More importantly, the unique nature of *la corrida de toros* as a publicly celebrated spectacle of cruelty raised the possibility that victory in this arena would be a dramatic and perhaps catalytic step toward improving society's treatment of all animals.

With regard to the venue for its campaign, Prou strategists opted for a regional, rather than national or European, approach because Spain's autonomous communities control animal welfare and cultural practices. Catalonia was the obvious region to target. Barcelona was home to a cadre of experienced activists, many of whom helped pass the 2003 Animal Protection Law, a legal landmark despite its gaps. Regional laws provided several mechanisms for citizen initiatives, including the one ultimately chosen: the Popular Legislative Initiative (ILP), which would compel the Catalonian parliament to vote on a proposed law if a sufficient number of citizen signatures (50,000) were obtained within a 120-day period. In addition, the Prou campaign chose a propitious moment in the context of Catalonian politics: the Tripartito coalition included a Green party, making it appear more susceptible than earlier governments to an animal rights campaign.

Most important, the Prou campaign was keenly aware of the opportunities but also the difficulties posed by Catalan nationalism. Catalonia's antipathy toward Castilian culture and resulting coolness toward bullfighting relative to the Spanish heartland could only help the cause. Yet key strategists worried that an open appeal to nationalism would backfire, inflaming antiseparatist sentiment in other parts of Spain and harming their initiative. Thus, the Prou campaign carefully avoided overt nationalist appeals. It also resisted allying with the region's nationalist politicians *qua* nationalists, instead seeking support across the political spectrum. In the words of a Prou leader, Leonardo Anselmi, "we didn't want nationalist votes."[32] As we shall see, the Prou campaign even struck back against opponents who sought to tar it with the Catalan nationalist brush.

Yet the Prou's strategists could not help but be attentive to the conflict dividing Catalonia and the rest of Spain, in which bullfighting had played a small but long-standing role. Choosing to target Catalonia rather than other regions was an acknowledgment of that reality. Beyond that, the Prou campaign subtly appealed to Catalan nationalist sentiments. For one thing, leaders of the campaign highlighted Catalan conceptions of their nation as distinct from and more advanced than the rest of Spain. Cultivating this view, the Prou website spoke of Catalonia as a "pioneer" in animal rights for passing its "avant-guard [*sic*]" law prohibiting new bullrings in 1988.[33] It praised Catalonia for "accept[ing] the evidence that bulls are capable of suffering" and concurring that humans "share many aspects of our neurological and emotional make-up" with bulls. Also praiseworthy: Catalonia, like many places "with long democratic histories"—but presumably unlike greater Spain—"rejects mankind as having absolute rights over animals allowing them to treat animals with violence and aggression." More cuttingly, the Prou campaign stated that those signing the initiative "are not, nor want to be barbarians or savages, preserving ancestral traditions based on inflicting pain and death on peaceful herbivores." On this basis, the Prou campaign demanded that the Catalonian government recognize the "concerns of our Catalan society" by passing the proposed ban. Associating the campaign with global trends toward better treatment of animals, the Prou campaign reached out to European and international celebrities. At the top of the campaign's website was a shifting set of photographs and pleas from cultural luminaries. Among those gracing the website were South African Nobel Literature laureate J. M. Coetzee, British comedian Ricky Gervais, and American *Baywatch* star Pamela Anderson. In sum, Prou leaders had a finely tuned ear for rhetoric and linkages that might effectively, if deniably, rouse nationalist feelings among some Catalans. As the head of the Catalan Studies Institute of Barcelona put it in supporting the ban: "The issue is a moral one. . . . Are we a modern nation, or are we going back to the Middle Ages?"[34]

In another example of the Prou strategists' alert treatment of Catalan nationalism, they opted for a narrower ban than many animal rights activists would have preferred. The Prou campaign did not seek to overturn the 2003 Animal Protection Law's provision that, at the behest of the bullfighting lobby, excluded bulls. Instead, it only sought to ban bullfighting. This seemingly small distinction was crucial. Ending the exclusion in full would have meant outlawing several lesser-known, indigenous Catalan customs involving cruelty to bulls. The most prominent of these is the *correbous* (flaming bull), in which flares and fireworks are attached to a bull's horns, maddening and blinding it while onlookers torment it. The *correbous* is practiced in small towns and rural areas of Catalonia and nearby parts of other regions. Trying to ban it would have placed the Prou campaign in direct opposition to Catalan culture and nationalism. By contrast, seeking to abolish only the more "alien" *corrida de toros* made it less likely that nationalist politicians would oppose the initiative—and more likely that they would take up the Prou cause themselves. Although other considerations played a role, espe- cially the fact that bullfighting is better known than the *correbous* across Spain and internationally, the Prou campaign opted to ignore the cruelty of the *correbous* in large part because of the nationalist dynamic.[35]

As might be expected, this decision to narrow the campaign's focus was contentious. Purist supporters of animal rights, unaware of or unmoved by the Prou leadership's calculations, were incensed. But for the strategically minded Prou leaders, the nationalist dynamic required a campaign more surgical and concealed than they might have preferred. The initiative cam- paign and the proposed ban therefore called only for the prohibition of bull- fighting, defined by its occurrence in a bullring and by the wounding or kill- ing of bulls using special bullfighting apparatus. Indigenous traditions such as the *correbous* would remain unaffected. Indeed, as we shall see, just weeks after passage of the bullfighting ban, the *correbous* gained legal recognition from the regional government—with the Prou campaign's endorsement, further proof of its subtle use of Catalan nationalism to further its cause.

CATALAN NATIONALIST SMOKESCREENS

Turning to the Catalan nationalists' handling of the Prou initiative in the regional parliament, the timing, vote, and circumstances of the ban strongly suggest that these politicians used animal rights to camouflage their real, nationalist motivations. Before showing this, the following procedural back- ground is of note: The Prou campaign submitted the text of its initiative to a parliamentary committee in the summer of 2008. By early 2009, it had gathered, certified, and submitted 180,000 signatures to parliament. For over a year afterwards, however, the initiative languished in the Catalonian parliament, despite laws requiring that a parliamentary vote be held. The ruling Tripartito coalition was divided over a bullfighting ban: the Greens supported it and the Socialists were opposed, but neither party felt strongly enough about the measure to risk breaking the coalition over it.[36] Opposi- tion from the bullfighting lobby also contributed to the inertia. Only after more than a year of pressure did the Catalonian parliament agree to hold hearings on the initiative. Televised over several days in the spring of 2010,

ILP supporters and opponents testified in starkly contrasting terms: about the horrors, or beauties, of the bullring; about the virtues, or vices, of animal rights; and about the motives, or subterfuges, of the other side.[37] But the hearings did not lead to a vote on the ILP either.

Then, on June 28, 2010, the Constitutional Court issued its ruling on the Statute of Autonomy. Suddenly, Catalan nationalists became much more enamored of the initiative, and the ruling Tripartito coalition quickly scheduled a vote. Weeks later, on July 28, the Catalonian parliament voted sixty-eight to fifty-five in favor of the ban, with nine abstentions. Although the tally was close, Catalan nationalists from a variety of parties, however uninterested in the initiative at first, became major supporters. It is always difficult to determine legislators' real motivations, especially because balloting was secret. But inspection of the party votes is indicative of the role played by nationalist anger wrapped in animal rights garb. The strongest support for the ban came from the CiU, the opposition coalition composed of long-standing Catalan nationalist parties. Thirty-two of its forty-five members approved the ban, with six abstaining, after coalition leader Artur Mas granted members a "free vote," allowing them to vote their conscience—or political instincts—rather than any party line.[38] (I discuss his rationale for the free vote later.) Among the ruling Tripartito coalition, all twenty-one members of the staunchly Catalan Republican Left Party voted for it, as did the twelve members of the Green Party. However, members of the third coalition partner, the non-nationalist Socialists, whose sister party governed all of Spain at the time, voted against the ban, thirty-one to three, with three abstentions. Joining the Socialists in opposition were regional parties associated with Spain's other main party, the conservative People's Party.

To summarize, members of Catalan nationalist parties overwhelmingly voted for the ban, whereas those from other parties, even including Socialist members of the Tripartito coalition government, opposed it. On this submerged but real nationalist base, and energized by the Spanish Constitutional Court's ruling against the Catalonian Autonomy Statute, the Prou campaign won a major victory as the bullfighting ban passed and was implemented on January 1, 2012. As one CiU deputy admitted, "Some of our people . . . back[ed] the ban on the basis that if they are going to sink our charter, we will sink their bulls."[39]

Further evidence that nationalism, not compassion for bulls, led to the ban came two months after the first parliamentary vote. The Catalonian parliament was considering a new bill about the region's indigenous forms of bull torment, most notably the *correbous*. But this bill did not follow the ban's seemingly humane inclinations to reduce bovine suffering. On the contrary, it proposed cultural heritage status for "flaming bull" festivals and similar Catalan traditions of cruelty to bulls. How did the regional parliament vote? By 114–14, it voted in favor of the *correbous*. Once again, nationalist politicians both inside and outside the ruling coalition, most notably the CiU, led the charge—but this time it was *against* the bulls. Only the Greens stood consistently in opposition to bullfighting, the flaming bull, and the other cruel customs.[40]

Gallingly for strict animal rights activists, the Prou campaign, in line with its earlier strategy, supported the new law enshrining the *correbous*'s august cultural status. For this, the campaign was excoriated. An ADDA press release complained that the *correbous* vote was "hasty and anomalous, . . . shielding clear examples of physical and psychological animal abuse." Prou leaders defended themselves by saying that the pain and injury inflicted on the flaming bulls would now at least be regulated, leading over time to stricter rules. More important, as Prou leader Anselmi put it in an interview with me, "we depended on the CiU to win our vote [for the bullfighting ban]. The CiU was in favor of the *correbous*. We decided that we were in favor of the *correbous* law also."[41]

Leaving aside the Prou campaign's strategic calculations, the twin votes on the *corrida de toros* and the *correbous* are further evidence that Catalan nationalists used the rights of bulls as camouflage for very different aims: exacting revenge for the Constitutional Court ruling, and ridding Catalonia of a tradition seen by many as central to Castilian identity. Granting the *correbous* cultural heritage status in Catalonia only heightened the sting. As one nationalist later stated in explaining the different votes, the bullfighting "tradition is Andalusian, not Catalan."[42] In Spain itself, of course, this camouflaging could be little more than a diversion because the Catalan nationalist agenda is so well known. Beyond Spain, however, the tactic was more effective in masking ulterior motives. Many in the international media portrayed the vote as a major advance for animal rights. International animal activists were even less likely to mention the nationalist angle, particularly because they sought to leverage the victory into bans on bullfighting and broader advances on animal rights worldwide.[43] Yet it is far from certain whether the ban would have passed without the nationalist anger unleashed by the Constitutional Court decision or the broader history of cultural conflict in the region. Meanwhile, the cover provided by animal rights and the Prou campaign allowed Catalan nationalists to flaunt their moral superiority over their old Castilian foes.

PARRYING THE PROU CAMPAIGN

However, opponents of the ban and of Catalan nationalism wasted little time in revealing what they claimed to be the real basis for the Prou campaign. Just as interestingly, they adopted the broader countering and parrying strategies outlined in chapter 3, camouflaging their own goals with other rights. Loosely organized as the Plataforma para la Defensa de La Fiesta (Bullfighting Defense Platform), opponents included members of Spain's bullfighting industry—ranchers, bullring owners, and bullfighters—as well as aficionados from the media, academia, and society around Spain. The opposition also included some of the most conservative leaders of the People's Party. Staunchly defending a unified Spain, they viewed bullfighting as one of the country's most important cultural markers.

Denying and unmasking. Long before the Catalonian parliament passed the ban, one of the Bullfighting Defense Platform's strategies against the Prou campaign had been denial: charging that animal rights were a sham concealing a crude nationalist agenda ultimately aimed at dismembering Spain. One aim of this accusation was to lure the Prou campaign into publicly allying with Catalan nationalism—or at least to create the impression of a strong association—thereby sullying the animal rights activists' ethical arguments. Leading these attacks was the powerful president of the Autonomous Community of Madrid, Esperanza Aguirre. She repeatedly criticized the Prou initiative as "anti-Spanish" and as identity politics in which the Catalans were cynically using animal rights to advance separatism. Simultaneously, she disparaged the Prou campaign as a patsy for unscrupulous nationalists. When the ban passed, she denounced it as an "attempt to break Catalonia's ties with Spain."[44] At minimum, making these accusations might embarrass and weaken the Prou campaign in Catalonia. In the rest of Spain, making such an argument about the troublesome Catalans might shore up bullfighting—and score points in the larger conflict between center and periphery. If the Catalans took the bait and revealed the bullfighting ban to be little more than nationalist pique, they would undermine their own cause.

How did Catalan nationalists respond to these strategies? For his part, longtime CiU leader Artur Mas refused to be decoyed by the accusations. He dismissed Aguirre's assertions with a bullfighting metaphor: his party would not "enter the trap" she had set by making the vote a matter of nationalism.[45] Rather, it would be a matter of principle for which coalition members were given the free vote noted earlier. Of course, coalition members might still vote based on Catalan nationalist sentiment, but the CiU could not be accused of having demanded this, even if its leaders no doubt expected it. Other Catalan parties took similar stances. In the event, the vote did not follow strict party lines. A few members of the Catalan nationalist parties, presumably aficionados themselves or representing areas where bullfighting remained popular, opposed the ban.

The Prou campaign went further in its denials of Aguirre's assertions that its campaign was an instrument of Catalan nationalism.[46] On the one hand, it blamed Aguirre's "provocation" for making "it almost obligatory for all Catalonian nationalists to vote in favor of abolition." On the other hand, the Prou campaign publicly urged any parliament members who might support the ban for reasons of nationalism *not* to do so and instead to abstain from voting. According to a Prou press release, if Catalonia abolished bullfighting as a matter of "identity," only the bulls would benefit. By contrast, if it did so "on moral principles, then Catalonia and its people will also be among the winners"—by being able to "show pride in their own moral progression." Such statements explicitly rejected nationalist appeals. But by suggesting that Catalonia was ethically advanced, in implied contrast to the rest of Spain, it also subtly appealed to regional chauvinism.

Rival rights. To return to the Bullfighting Defense campaign, beyond its denial strategies, it raised its own set of rival rights—to artistic expression, cultural preservation, and economic sustenance. In this portrayal, bullfighting was not brutal but aesthetic. According to the celebrity Catalan bullfighter Serafín Marín, "It is not a cruel show. It is a show that creates art: where you get feelings and a fight between a bull and person, where the person or the bull can lose their life."[47] As another argument, defenders of bullfighting portrayed it as a profound expression of Spanish culture and tradition. The president of the International Bullfighting Association (AIT) told me in an interview: "Human beings have the right to access their own and other cultures; it's natural and fundamental. You can't deny this right because you'd be limiting citizens' freedoms. If you prohibit kids from going to bullfights, you're prohibiting their cultural development and prevent them from passing down the cultural heritage to other generations."

On the other hand, in his view, "animalism" and its animus against bullfighting represented "Anglo-Saxon cultural imperialism," which he characterized as harboring "antipathy" toward "the cultural, ideological, and religious traditions of the Mediterranean peoples."[48] In a similar vein, a French philosopher published a book providing fifty humanistic and ethical reasons to defend *la corrida*.[49] Promoters even touted their respect for the bulls and the environment in which they were raised. Ending *la corrida* would mean that the fierce *toros de lidia* (fighting bulls) that fought in Spain's bullrings would no longer be born and raised to roam free on the wild Spanish plains. Nor would they have their moment of glory in the bullring, finding either an honored death or, in rare cases of true fortitude, a possible reprieve followed by a lifetime of studding. Instead, if bullfighting were abolished, the bulls would suffer the violations and indignities of livestock—penned, fattened, slaughtered, and butchered for market.[50]

Far from meriting abolition as a barbaric "national shame" or a waste of taxpayer money, bullfighting therefore had a strong claim to admiration and support, according to the Bullfighting Defense campaign. Acting preemptively months before the Catalonian parliamentary vote, Espontanea Aguirre pushed through a policy designating bullfighting as a *bien de interes cultural* (BIC) (a good of cultural interest) in the Madrid autonomous region, under a Spanish law protecting the country's historical heritage. At a press conference, posing with a pink matador's cape, she said: "Bullfighting is an art that merits protection and that has been part of Spanish and Mediterranean culture since time immemorial. Goya, Picasso, García Lorca and outside our country, Hemingway and Orson Welles have been inspired by bullfighting as art."[51] In short order, other centers of bullfighting, such as Valencia and Murcia, passed similar BICs. Following the model of the Catalonian legislative initiative and ban, the bullfighting lobby promoted a contrary initiative across all Spain to give cultural heritage status to bullfighting. In 2013, after the initiative garnered 590,000 signatures, the Spanish parliament, under a People's Party government, declared bullfighting part of the Historical Cultural Heritage (Patrimonio Histórico Cultural) of Spain, making regional bans harder.[52]

The Spanish bullfighting lobby went further, seeking international protection by calling on UNESCO to declare bullfighting part of the world's "Intangible Cultural Heritage in Need of Urgent Safeguarding." International bullfighting groups had been attempting this since 2004, when the Convention for the Safeguarding of the Intangible Cultural Heritage, grounded in international human rights treaties, came into effect. They immediately seized this opportunity to shore up the tradition's cultural and material base. In the words of AIT president Williams Cardenas, bullfighting was both part of "universal human culture, which people from all over the world can view and then accept or reject," and in need of protection and subsidization against the forces of globalization.[53]

Reversal: Bullfighters as victims. For aficionados and matadors, however, it was not just that their art encapsulated a critical set of rival rights that must be preserved. More important, failing to do so would violate these and other rights. Reversing the logic of the Prou campaign and Catalan nationalists, defenders of *la fiesta nacional* portrayed themselves as victims. Attempts to ban *la corrida* would gut the most fundamental rights: the rights to freedom of expression and to preservation of one's culture. Through tears at a Barcelona rally held when the ban was first approved, master matador Serafín Marín declared: "This is dictatorship." For Fernando Masedo, president of the International Federation of Bullfighting Schools, which aims to educate a new generation of matadors, "It is an attack on liberty. People are free to go or not go to the bullring." Esperanza Aguirre denounced it as disgusting ("*casposa*") and as "liberticide."[54] The fact that bullfighting involved the public suffering and death of bulls was not an argument against but for bullfighting. As the AIT's Cardenas said, "Bullfighting is a fight that represents men against nature; it's very old. Death is no longer part of city life; people avoid it. But death is still a part of bullfighting and without it, the whole sense of *corridas* would change."[55] In the flurry of competing rights claims, defenders of bullfighting also raised violations of the right to work because the bullfighting industry in Catalonia ostensibly employed thousands, directly or indirectly.

To the strategies of rivalry and reversal, the Prou campaign and other animal rights groups made several ripostes. For one, they argued that morality and aesthetics change over time. Stale and barbaric traditions should be abandoned, not perpetuated. Certainly, modern states or UNESCO should not be granting them cultural heritage status (which Spanish and international animal rights groups such as CAS International fought fiercely against). As one campaign was tellingly titled, "Torture Is Not Culture."[56] Nor was being a *taurino*, a bullfighting fan, an inherent identity. Instead, it was a mere interest, restrictions on which were permissible within a democratic country. Promoters of the ban also dismissed the freedom of expression claim, denouncing it as camouflage. It was exaggerated, ignored the gore of the bullring, and masked the underlying material interests of the bullfighting industry. Whatever the merits of the rival rights arguments, the Catalonian parliament sided with the Prou campaign. Only in regard to the claims of economic rights violations did the final bill prohibiting bullfighting show deference: it included subsidies to ease hardships among Catalonians whose livelihood would be affected by bullfighting's demise.

Repudiating the ban. Notwithstanding this accommodation, the Catalonian branch of the conservative national People's Party took one final step against the ban, repudiating it through a court challenge. The litigation took years, during which relations between Catalonia and the central government deteriorated, sparked in part by the 2010 Constitutional Court ruling. Finally, in late 2016, that same court overturned the Catalonian ban, 8–3. The decision held that Catalonia had no power to prohibit a practice that was part of the entire country's cultural patrimony. At best, a regional government could regulate bullfighting and the treatment of bulls.

Responses from the opposing sides were predictable. The PP and the bullfighting lobby applauded the decision. As Catalan matador Marín exulted: "I am no longer illegal. I am free again."[57] Animal rights activists condemned the decision, with the head of Humane Society International's Europe division sounding some of the same themes of the initiative campaign: "Taunting and killing bulls for entertainment is a brutal anachronism that the Catalan Parliament quite rightly voted to ban six years ago. For the Constitutional Court to overturn the ban is morally retrograde. This decision flies in the face of the clear wishes of Catalan citizens and politicians who, we are sure, will robustly defend their right to outlaw such animal cruelty."[58]

Catalan politicians viewed the ruling through a different lens. As regional official Lluís Salvadó stated, "It's obvious the Constitutional Court never loses an opportunity to attack the legitimacy of the Parliament" of Catalonia. In the words of Catalonian government minister Josep Rull, making no secret of his nationalist views, "The government of Catalonia will make every effort for bullfights not to return to our country. We want a country where it is not possible to make a public spectacle of death and suffering to an animal. This is what we decided at the time in Catalonia and is unalterable for us."[59]

The ultimate outcome is unclear, particularly as the region's nationalist politics has become more contentious. Animal rights groups may appeal to a European court, although the prospects for reversal are poor. On the other hand, the lone remaining bullring, Barcelona's privately owned Monumental, is slated for conversion to a shopping mall. And the city's mayor, Ada Colau, has vowed to "work to ensure the ruling has no effects; we will do everything possible . . . whatever the Constitutional Court says."[60]

Conclusion

Whether Mayor Colau's repudiation of the Constitutional Court will stick is unclear. But the Catalonian cases, and the others discussed more briefly in this chapter, illustrate how rights are used as camouflage by all manner of political movements. This strategy does not always succeed. Indeed, it may be that analysts can study only cases that have failed enough for the screening to be recognized. Even in those circumstances, camouflaging can serve important purposes. Using rights as camouflage can divert a foe's attention and suck away resources, even if it does not completely mask underlying motives. The intersection of diverse rights claims that makes camouflaging possible creates opportunities for political movements. The Prou campaign's careful navigation and subtle exploitation of Spain's nationalist minefield, always in a deniable way, illustrates this point. Catalan nationalists' clumsier usages nonetheless show that having one set of rights cover for other motives is common, not least in nationalist conflicts. One could say the same for many of the rights claims unleashed by defenders of bullfighting against the ban.

From a scholarly perspective, the concepts and cases discussed in this chapter underline an additional point: if rights can act as camouflage for any political movement, their supposedly unique moral value must be questioned. If guardians of rights such as the Prou campaign accept the instrumentalization of their right by completely different political forces, the purity of rights comes into question. From the standpoint of the movement whose right is being "used," there may well be good strategic reasons to accede to this camouflaging. Whether or not this is the case, the ease with which rights can be turned into camouflage for ulterior purposes suggests that analysts should view rights as political tools at least as much as promoters of rights view them as transcendent ethical principles. Underlining these points, the following chapters illustrate how various political actors use rights in ways analogous to specific weapons, often in association with camouflage tactics.

Rights as Spears

OVERTURNING LAWS

For years, two Italian schoolboys, Dataico and Sami Albertin, had outspokenly proclaimed their atheism. In a country where Catholicism is the majority religion, the brothers' teenage peers had responded with harassment and abuse. Nor had the boys found refuge in their public-school classrooms in the country's conservative Veneto region. There, as in all Italian public schools, crucifixes hung from the walls, required by government decree. In 2002, the boys' mother, Soile Lautsi, had had enough. She demanded that the authorities stop the mistreatment and remove the crucifixes as a matter of basic human rights under Italian and European laws: the boys' right to freedom of belief, and the parents' right to educate their children according to those beliefs. Italian education officials were at first unmoved and successfully fought the lawsuit. But in 2009, after years of administrative proceedings and litigation, the European Court of Human Rights (ECHR) unanimously agreed with Ms. Lautsi. In its decision, the ECHR held that crucifixes in classrooms constituted a rights violation and ordered their removal across the country.

In response, Italian pundits and politicians, who had earlier ignored the lawsuit, erupted in fury, attacking the family and decrying the decision. As indicated by the outsize reaction, the *Lautsi* case was about more than protecting the Albertin boys. The case had been orchestrated by Italy's Union of Rational Atheists and Agnostics (UAAR), a group of only a few hundred active members that for decades has condemned what they see as the Catholic Church's undue influence in Italian society. This activism, however, had fallen flat. The vast majority of Italians were indifferent to the UAAR's claims, and few had even heard of the group. In the *Lautsi* case, the UAAR used rights arguments to attack the crucifix in the courts. Even if the group had no luck attracting popular support and no means of fighting the Church's power directly, the UAAR saw this narrow legal thrust as a way to rid schools of the noxious religious symbol. In the long term, the UAAR believed, it might also reduce religion's sway in Italy and Europe more broadly. The ECHR's unexpectedly expansive ruling seemed to portend exactly that. In the end, however, the UAAR's dream crumbled. In the months after the ruling, the European Court came under enormous political pressure from politicians, faith groups, and religiously conservative governments across Europe. Then, in a 2011 decision, the ECHR Grand Chamber, its highest appellate body, overturned the prior ruling, keeping the crucifixes nailed to Italian school walls. Still, the UAAR's case and the angry responses it provoked illustrate another common rights tactic: the use of rights as finely targeted spears aimed at specific policies.

This chapter begins by theorizing about the tactic, including its purposes, users, targets, and likelihood of success. I then show how it works in practice, analyzing the political and legal mobilization around the *Lautsi* case. This was one of the most significant court cases concerning religious freedom in modern European history. I begin by examining the considerations that went into the UAAR's decision to bring the case. I examine the rhetorical and legal conflict that arose after the litigation began, particularly after the shocking ECHR decision against the crucifix. In this, we shall see how the Italian government and its conservative religious allies used many of the countering and parrying tactics discussed in earlier chapters, this time against a rights-as-spears tactic.

Spear Tactics

DEFINITION, PURPOSES, AND ACTORS

In the spear tactic, activists use rights arguments to undermine a single policy or law. Typically, this is part of a larger plan to advance a movement's overall interests and values. The hallmark of the tactic, however, is its precision. It targets only a particular policy, sometimes only in a single locale. Why would a movement take such a narrow approach, rather than one aiming to change broader society more directly? Usually, the decision is made out of necessity: there is no better choice given the power dynamics of the conflict. Movements adopt spear tactics when they are relatively weak groups and their main foes are powerful or dominant entities. Indeed, an individual person may play a key role, serving as a "test case" for the rights proponent's larger goal. In situations of unequal power, it is seldom possible for weak groups to achieve maximal goals immediately or directly, because they do not have the resources or capacity. Such groups cannot hope to achieve victory through majoritarian politics. Nor is a frontal assault on the entire body of offending institutions likely to succeed.

In such constrained circumstances, a narrowly targeted tactic holds greater promise. For one thing, such an approach may weaken or end a state policy that permits a particularly egregious violation, possibly with broader consequences over time. The successful use of a spear tactic may increase the foe's vulnerability, making other advances easier and more effective. Demonstrating a foe's weakness may convince more of one's own constituents and sympathizers to join the campaign. A phalanx of rights activists can be effective more quickly than a single one.

For the tactic to deliver more than a pinprick, however—for it to have any chance of achieving the ultimate goals sought—it must fix on a policy important to a foe's social, cultural, or political power. Such laws are not necessarily those causing the greatest direct or immediate harm to the oppressed group; those may be too well protected for the spear tactic to work. Instead, groups using the tactic will single out key policies that hold together the larger structure of oppression, the destruction of which holds the greatest promise of bringing down the rest of the edifice in the long term. Sometimes the policies have great material weight, buttressing the existing system of authority by means of their social or economic effects. Other times, they play an important symbolic role; shattering such policies can electrify society, throwing the status quo into question and making distant goals appear realizable. Indeed, activists using spear tactics usually have reformist aims. They envision their own inclusion in the larger society, albeit a society that may be changed significantly by their full presence, rather than the wholesale destruction of a targeted community (the goal, by contrast, of the dynamite strategies discussed in the next chapter).

LITIGATION AND PROTEST

Where do movements mount spear tactics? As the weaker party to a conflict, they have limited chances in majoritarian institutions such as democratically elected legislatures or executives. Instead, they favor two broadly defined venues. First, activists use countermajoritarian institutions such as courts. Second, if they have sufficient numbers of constituents and supporters, they may employ non-institutional tactics such as street protests. Often they use both strategies simultaneously.[1]

To take the first of these, rights-based litigation using judicial institutions is an important means by which weak groups pursue their goals and will be the focus of this chapter. (Of course, powerful groups also use cause litigation, but always as a matter of choice, not necessity, and usually as part of a well-financed strategy to influence broader politics.) A classic case is *Brown v. Board of Education*, a crucial part of the larger American civil rights movement. For a more recent landmark example, consider the American LGBT movement and its struggle for same-sex marriage. In the 2000s, the movement had tried, but in most cases failed, to win marriage equality in majoritarian institutions such as state legislatures and statewide referenda. Most of the victories for same-sex marriage occurred through state court decisions using rights-based challenges, as in Massachusetts in 2003 and Hawaii in 1991. After the movement's most prominent referendum failure, the defeat of California's Proposition 8 in 2008, leaders of the movement opted for a constitutional challenge. Some national LGBT advocates believed that the majority culture was not ready for this move, but a narrowly tailored case in a countermajoritarian setting eventually, if barely, paid off with the Supreme Court's 5–4 *Obergefell v. Hodges* decision legalizing same-sex marriage in 2015.

Not just any court will do for litigation-based spear tactics. Whenever possible, plaintiffs will act against the chosen policy in the venue with the highest impact on the entire society—or at least will try to appeal to such a top national court. However, rights litigants are not necessarily looking for the most hospitable courtrooms, at least not initially. In certain settings they may seek to *lose* in a lower administrative unit so that they have the option to appeal to a higher, more visible, and more influential one. In this vein, it is important to recognize that domestic courts are staffed with judges who generally subscribe to the national consensus on political, social, and cultural issues. It is no surprise, then, that it took sixty years for the *Brown* court to overturn the earlier separate-but-equal decision in *Plessy v. Ferguson*.

Today, however, domestic courts may not be the final arbiter for those who believe their rights to be violated. International courts are now available, and countermajoritarian impulses are at their zenith in these venues. The judges, raised and trained in other countries, are likely to interpret national laws and international principles differently than domestic judges would. In recent years, such courts have multiplied in number and are increasingly open to individual plaintiffs, including those chosen for cause litigation.[2] In Europe, the ECHR is a prime example: its power to overturn national laws makes it a tempting venue for all manner of politically weak groups seeking their own rights. It retains this attraction despite the rise of decision-making principles constraining its power. Most notable is the "margin of appreciation" doctrine, which requires the court to respect certain national practices that might otherwise be seen as violating European concepts of human rights.[3]

The second form of the spear tactic is non-institutionalized protest. This may seem very different than rights-based litigation, but the two are unified by the fact that movements facing hostile and powerful majoritarian institutions often use them. Public protest serves several purposes. For one thing, it can swell the size of the movement even further. On this basis, it can generate social pressure that may help achieve its underlying goals, initially an end to specific policies and later, as the movement grows, broader reforms. Attracting large numbers to the streets can help convince other constituents that it is safe to join the movement. Activists with this goal may demonstrate in places that are secure from counterprotests or use government-approved tactics that are unlikely to provoke a state crackdown. On the other hand, as Doug McAdam has shown, protesters may seek out venues where they know they will face open resistance or even violence. Or they may refuse to play by government rules, courting police overreaction. Media attention will be greater in the resulting fray than in more restrained protest and will sometimes galvanize constituents and attract broader support from powerful third parties.[4] Whether on the streets or in the courts, rights proponents using a spear tactic willingly, if warily, enter the lion's den to maximize the chances of attention and effect.

How do foes react to these tactics? In the case of litigation, precisely because activists depend on countermajoritarian institutions, foes will not only fight in court, but also oppose judicial decisions politically, with majoritarian arguments such as states' rights or the rights of the nation. Reactions to court cases, both domestic and international, are likely to emphasize repudiation—threats to the legitimacy or even existence of the countermajoritarian institution that the rights activist is using. For its part, protest will be countered by calls for the majority to be able to enjoy its rights, not least to an ordered existence in its own society—and by crackdowns to restore order.

PINPRICK OR DEATHBLOW?

When is the spear tactic likely to succeed? Notwithstanding my focus on litigation in this chapter, it is usually part of a broader rights movement that uses other strategies as well. As other scholars have shown, the interaction between rights movement and rights litigation is important to success.[5] Broader societal pressure from such a movement is a key factor in whether the tactic works and, even more importantly, whether the movement prevails. Reciprocally, victory in specific litigation or mass protest can help galvanize a movement. If the rights proponent does not have a large movement behind it, however, a spear tactic is only likely to succeed in an institution that is insulated from majoritarian pressures and strong enough to enforce an unpopular decision.

Still, powerful opponents find ways to narrow, differentiate, disregard, or otherwise avoid the consequences of such decisions. This holds with even greater force for the decisions of international courts. Most important, as noted earlier, foes stress the illegitimacy of distant institutions when they reach judgments in favor of unpopular litigants against the majority will. Democratically elected politicians may threaten to abandon countermajoritarian institutions entirely if they make the "wrong decision," pressuring these bodies to conform to popular demands. International human rights courts, most of which are relatively new and weak, are particularly likely to be targeted by such threats. Such institutions are perceived as distant from the societies that bear the effects of their decisions. With little independent power to bolster them, it is therefore likely that courts, both domestic and international, will develop rules minimizing the likelihood of clashes between their decisions in favor of rights-based litigants and the views of majorities. Such rules, combined with repudiation threats by powerful states or majorities, reduce the chances of success for spear tactics, especially litigation divorced from large movements.

To illuminate these points, Italy's controversy over the crucifix makes an excellent case. Unlike many other instances involving a spear tactic, the *Lautsi* case was not part of a major social movement. Undoubtedly, this is one of the reasons that the tactic ultimately failed. But the UAAR's crusade against the crucifix, the reaction it provoked, and the victory it nearly won, all with only negligible political mobilization in its favor, make it a good case for examining the particulars of the tactic. Like other failed rights litigation, such as *Plessy v. Ferguson*, the *Lautsi* case has much to teach us, both about the spear tactic in its juridical form and about the politico-legal countering strategies used by opponents.[6] Moreover, the case involves both national and international courts. By contrast, the well-studied *Brown v. Board of Education* case was part of a much broader and long-standing civil rights movement based in America. Similarly, the *Obergefell* case was part of a long-term LGBT movement that slowly changed American attitudes about homosexuality, rights, and ultimately same-sex marriage. In the *Lautsi* case, on the other hand, a legal strategy dominated, combining national and international elements by both proponents and opponents.

Italy's Atheists versus School Crucifixes

BACKGROUND TO THE *LAUTSI* LITIGATION

Roman Catholicism was Italy's state religion until 1985, when a concordat to the Lateran Pacts with the Vatican made the country a secular nation. For decades after World War II, the country's politics had also been dominated by the Catholic-affiliated Christian Democracy Party (DC). In 1994, however, the DC collapsed, and since then no major party has had such close ties to the Church. Nonetheless, the Church remains influential in Italian politics and society. The Italian Constitution guarantees that "all religious denominations are equally free before the law," but Catholicism enjoys a special relationship with the state, with the two entities considered "independent and sovereign, each within its own sphere."[7]

The Church and Italy's other state-recognized religions receive state support through the *otto per mille*, a tax of 0.008 percent of annual income either distributed to the leadership of the religion designated by each taxpayer or, if the taxpayer chooses none, divided among the religious groups in proportion to the overall designations of the population. More directly pertinent to this chapter, the 1985 revision to the Lateran Pacts recognized "the value of the religious culture" and "the principles of the Catholic Church [as] part of the historical heritage of the Italian people."[8] On this basis, the revision requires the teaching of Catholicism in public schools, although it permits students to study their own religion or opt out completely based on "the freedom of conscience and educational responsibility of the parents."[9] Since 1924, Italian public schools have hung crucifixes in classrooms, as mandated by two royal decrees issued during the early years of Benito Mussolini's rule.[10] The decrees were never passed by the Italian parliament and therefore never became a formal part of Italian law. Nevertheless, the decrees remained in operation, and schools across Italy generally displayed crucifixes on classroom walls.

That this classroom fixture went unremarked by most Italians was unsurprising given that 83 percent of Italians consider themselves Christian and 76 percent Roman Catholic.[11] Even though the country has secularized since the 1970s—a period marked by declining church attendance and the legalization of divorce and abortion—only about 6 percent of Italians call themselves atheists or agnostics. Even among the latter, few have complained about classroom crucifixes. The UAAR, however, has been openly critical for decades.

The UAAR was founded in 1986 in Padua to protect the rights of atheists and agnostics. The *otto per mille* and classroom crucifixes have been two of its main bête noires. For years, the UAAR's dues-paying membership has been tiny in number. In the mid-2010s, the group consisted of no more than about fourteen thousand followers, according to the group's leader, Raffaele Carcano.[12] The minuscule extent of its membership has strongly shaped its political tactics. With so few people supporting its program, the group has been met with indifference, even hostility, by Italian political parties across the ideological spectrum. Its complaints about Catholicism's overreach in Italy and the Church's animus against "atheism and different ways of life" have gone unheeded.[13] Even the Socialist and Communist parties have shied away from championing the UAAR's goals, seeing no political gains to be made from catering to such marginal views. As some of their members griped, "most political leaders are keen to accept [the Catholic Church's] requests disrespectful of rights and liberties, lives and personal stories, beliefs and choices of millions of [Italian] citizens."[14]

Confronted with the dead end of majoritarian political processes, the UAAR has long opted for spear tactics. Because of the group's small constituency, it has avoided public protest and has instead used judicial institutions to fight specific politics. As the UAAR's president explained: "Our strategy is often to bring a case in court to affirm a right. When you have politics against you, you have to resort to court." There, the group has been able to initiate actions to advance rights that the vast majority of Italians care little about or even oppose. In doing so, the UAAR's aim has been to mount test cases with potentially catalytic effects, in which a favorable decision for an individual member might galvanize broader change that the group could not achieve through democratic politics.

These rights tactics began in 1990 with a lawsuit challenging the *otto per mille* tax payment. The UAAR unsuccessfully claimed that it violated freedom of conscience because citizens could designate only religious, not secular, organizations for their tax payments. For years the UAAR has also objected to classroom crucifixes. In one case, a teacher and UAAR member in Perugia faced disciplinary action for removing a crucifix from her classroom. Her administrative challenge to the proceeding failed, and the crucifix was replaced. In another case, a local electoral official was prosecuted for refusing to serve at his polling station—located, like many, in a public school—because a crucifix hung on its walls. In an indication of the small number of Italians willing to raise such challenges, the defendant was the husband of the teacher who had earlier removed the classroom crucifix. In 2000, the Court of Cassation, Italy's highest criminal and civil court, exonerated him, holding that the crucifix violated his freedom of conscience and the principle of secularism.[15] However, this ruling had no effect beyond polling stations. Across Italy, students continued to attend schools under the shadow of the crucifix.

ALTERING ITALY BY LAWSUIT

In 2002, the UAAR decided to challenge the crucifix again, this time using the rights of children and parents. As with most spear tactics, the UAAR's goal was not simply to allow a single child to attend a classroom free of a crucifix. Rather, the UAAR hoped that a court case might transform the educational experience of all Italian schoolchildren and reduce the role of the Catholic Church in Italian life. As the UAAR's president stated, "When starting the case . . . , we did not believe we could change the culture. It is easier to change the law. And we think if we change the law, then culture will follow. If we gain the right, society will change." Exactly what might follow in terms of church-state relations the UAAR has not specified, although UAAR leader Carcano pointed to the Netherlands and Belgium, where both religious and secular groups are granted equal state recognition (and funding), as preferred prototypes.[16] Whatever the new church-state system that might emerge, the UAAR hoped to do far more than simply protect vulnerable children. Its aims were offensive and expansive, with reduction of the Church's role in society the main aspiration. In the UAAR's view, a rights-based legal challenge to the crucifix might cut the Church down to the status of any other civil society organization, religious or nonreligious.

To achieve these weighty goals despite having such little political power, the UAAR followed the approach outlined earlier in this chapter. First, it chose its plaintiff carefully, looking for people who could weather a long contest and the expected counterattacks. In a country with a low birth rate, particularly among the secular, the UAAR needed someone with school-age children. Predicting the harassment the children would face, it sought secondary school students able to understand the case and withstand the pressure.[17] Second, the UAAR studiously selected the venue for its action. Its goal, like that of other litigants employing such tactics to turn a marginal cause into a broad societal reform, was to *lose* the case at the local level and elevate it to a national court on appeal. Victory at a local school board would have been pointless, affecting only a single district. By contrast, a loss would mean the chance to appeal to a court and gain a judicial decision with wider effect. According to UAAR leader Carcano, the group ultimately hoped to receive a positive decision from Italy's Constitutional Court. The result would have been a dramatic change in Italian law and, if such a ruling had been enforced, a change in practice in all of Italy's schools.

Following this logic, the UAAR avoided Italy's "red" regions, Emilia-Romagna and Tuscany, where it had a good chance of prevailing at a local school board. Instead, the UAAR opted for the Veneto, a more conservative area where Catholics tend to be more observant. One of the group's earliest and most loyal members, Massimo Albertin, a doctor, lived there with his wife, Soile Lautsi, and two sons, ages eleven and thirteen at the time. Albertin served on the board of governors for his sons' school in Abano Terme, where crucifixes hung in every classroom. To avoid immediate rejection of the action based on conflict of interest, the UAAR turned to Albertin's wife, Soile Lautsi, who agreed to be the nominal plaintiff. Lautsi was a Finnish-born Italian national who had lived in Italy for over a decade.

Finally, the UAAR sharpened its claims, portraying them as universal, absolute, and apolitical. As the parents of the Albertin boys stated, "We profoundly believe that respect for the rights of individuals . . . is a universal value that must be defended—always and in every circumstance, without if's, and's or but's."[18] Following this view, the plaintiffs rejected any compromise with the crucifix (for instance, negotiating for it to be hung only in certain public school rooms but not in others). Instead, they sought its total and permanent elimination. Their rationale: in a secular state, the rights of parents and children supersede any "personal or political convenience." Individual rights must transcend partisan debate and contrary national practices. They are above politics, enjoying near-sacred status. For the UAAR, victory would guarantee a value they saw as patently universal—the state's complete religious neutrality in public schools. These absolutist claims appealed little to most Italians, but they attracted support from a small number of secularists in Italy and other European countries. When the case reached its conclusion in the ECHR, the claims also drew support from international human rights organizations such as Human Rights Watch and the International Commission of Jurists, both of which filed amicus curiae briefs.

The case had begun with little fanfare years before, on April 22, 2002, when Soile Lautsi asked the governors of the local school to remove the crucifix and other religious symbols from her sons' classrooms. As the UAAR had hoped, the board rejected the request a month later by a vote of 10–2. In July 2002, Lautsi appealed against the Ministry of Education to the Veneto Administrative Court. Revealing the broad implications of the UAAR's litigation plan, she complained that the decision violated the principle of secularism, enshrined in Italy's Constitution through Articles 3 (individual equality) and 19 (religious freedom) and in Article 9 of the European Convention on Human Rights, as well as the principle of impartiality of public authorities (Article 97 of the Constitution).[19]

ITALY STRIKES BACK

These arguments reverberated beyond the single school, implicating Italy's long-standing approaches to national identity, secularism, and church-state relations. Unsurprisingly, then, the UAAR faced opposition. Early on, this came from outside the countermajoritarian sanctuary of the courts, from a key government ministry. In October 2002, the minister of education issued an administrative order that for the first time in decades explicitly required all schools to "ensure the presence of crucifixes in classrooms" in conformity with the Mussolini-era governmental decrees. Justifying the move, the ministry condemned many of the UAAR's arguments, although without mentioning the *Lautsi* case. In the government's newly enunciated view, the crucifix was a symbol of Italy's national identity. Parrying the UAAR's efforts to universalize its rights arguments, the Ministry proclaimed that the crucifix was a symbol that "does not refer to a specific creed but constitutes only an expression of Christian civilization and culture, and that . . . therefore forms part of the universal heritage of mankind."[20] As a result, the order suggested, the Lautsi-Albertin family could not claim a rights violation because the crucifix did not offend freedom of conscience, "religious pluralism," or the "objectives of multicultural education."

The UAAR, of course, vehemently disagreed, but to no avail. As a result, in the short term, crucifixes probably became more, not less, prevalent in

Italian classrooms. By launching the case, the group had provoked stronger government notice and enforcement of a requirement that in practice for decades had been obeyed primarily at the discretion of local schools. Such strong reactions are a constant risk in using spear tactics because majoritarian institutions have the power to react forcefully, in the name of the political or cultural majority, when challenged.

All the more now rode on a decision in the *Lautsi* case, and with majoritarian institutions against them, the UAAR continued the lawsuit. In early 2004, the Veneto Administrative Court, noting the gravity of the issues, referred the case directly to Italy's Constitutional Court, the country's top court for such matters. At the end of the year, however, the Court sent the case back to the administrative tribunal, stating that its jurisdiction covered only the constitutionality of Italian laws, not Mussolini-era royal decrees such as the one requiring crucifixes. In March 2005, the Veneto Administrative Court issued a far-reaching verdict dismissing the case. First, the court held that "the principle of the secular nature of the State [is] now part of the legal heritage of Europe and the western democracies." Although this point might seem to help the plaintiffs, the court disagreed that classroom crucifixes offended secularism. For one thing, the court ruled that, as the government had argued, the crucifix was "a symbol of [Italy's] historical and cultural development, and therefore of the identity of our people." In the court's majoritarian view, the rights of individual citizens must fall before the right of the nation to maintain its identity, an identity in which Christianity and secularism were entwined.

As the court stated in a remarkable passage: "The link between Christianity and liberty implies a logical historical coherence which is not immediately obvious . . . partly because in the constantly changing relations between the States and Churches of Europe it is much easier to see the numerous attempts by the Churches to meddle in matters of State, and vice versa, just like the frequent occasions on which Christian ideals have been abandoned, though officially proclaimed, in the quest for power, or on which governments and religious authorities have clashed, sometimes violently." In addition, the court held that, as an admitted emblem of Catholic values, the crucifix symbolized . . . secularism: "With the benefit of hindsight, it is easy to identify in the constant central core of Christian faith, despite the inquisition, despite anti-Semitism and despite the crusades, the principles of human dignity, tolerance and freedom, including religious freedom, and therefore, in the last analysis, the foundations of the secular State."

Summing up, the court held that the crucifix was not only a symbol of national identity but also "a symbol of a value system: liberty, equality, human dignity and religious toleration, and accordingly also of the secular nature of the State—principles which underpin our Constitution."[21] For the Lautsi-Albertins, this meant that the nation's secular identity, as embodied in the crucifix, must trump their individual rights to freedom of conscience. By contrast, they had argued that their rights and Italian secularism itself could only be vindicated by the crucifix's ejection. In effect, the decision preserved not only crucifixes in the classroom and the policies requiring them, but also the intertwining of religion and the Italian state that the UAAR had sought to undermine through its lawsuit.

As such, the decision was hardly news in the Italian media; it was simply business as usual. To the UAAR, however, it was laughable to claim that crucifixes in classrooms demonstrate to children the state's secular identity. Lautsi therefore appealed the decision to Italy's supreme administrative court, the Consiglio di Stato. In April 2006, that court adopted much of the Veneto tribunal's decision, holding that the crucifix is "a symbol capable of reflecting the remarkable sources of the civil values . . . which define secularism in the State's present legal order."[22] With this decision against it, the UAAR's litigation tactic appeared to have failed. The group had exhausted all Italian judicial institutions and found them as unresponsive as the country's legislators.

But the UAAR was not broken. The plaintiffs continued to believe that fundamental principles, both Italian and international, demanded that the state be neutral and remove all crucifixes. With a return visit to the Constitutional Court impossible, their only choice for continuing the action was the European Court of Human Rights. The ECHR will hear applications from individuals claiming that their civil and political rights under the European Convention of Human Rights have been breached. As such, ECHR rulings can affect the laws and policies of all forty-seven state members of the Council of Europe, with a total population of more than 800 million people. The court has therefore become an attractive venue for rights-based litigation. Even though the UAAR had not initially contemplated an ECHR appeal, it soon realized that a positive ruling there could have greater significance than the ruling of an Italian court. It could upend church-state relations not only in Italy but also across Europe, establishing a new reign of secularism in the many states where religion still assumed pride of place. The UAAR, eager to achieve this expansive goal, hired new lawyers versed in ECHR principles and procedures.

LOWERING THE CROSS: *LAUTSI I*

In its appeal to the ECHR, the UAAR argued that classroom crucifixes violated the European Convention's principle that "the State shall respect the right of parents to ensure . . . education and teaching in conformity with their own religious and philosophical convictions."[23] The plaintiffs also maintained that the cross infringed on the rights to freedom of religion or belief.[24] Of course, behind these claims of individual rights violations still lurked the UAAR's broader offensive purposes—to change law, education, and ultimately church-state relations across Europe.

The ECHR's ruling of November 3, 2009 (*Lautsi I*) threatened exactly such far-reaching consequences, although the court framed its decision as one relating to the rights of parents and children. In essence, the court adopted much of the UAAR's argument, including its view on the universal and absolute nature of the human rights at issue in the case. The seven-member court unanimously held that the state had an obligation to "refrain from imposing beliefs, even indirectly, in places where persons are dependent on it or in places where they are particularly vulnerable," such as schools. Because the crucifix has strong religious content, even if it might also have other connotations, its presence would mean that the "school environment" would be "marked by a particular religion." This could be "emotionally disturbing" to certain students, particularly those with minority beliefs. Under European human rights law, therefore, students in public schools needed to be provided "negative freedom of religion," including the absence not only of religious services and education but also of religious symbols.

In this key respect, the ECHR adopted the UAAR's countermajoritarian arguments about the importance of individuals' rights over the community's. Neither the beliefs of the majority of other parents, nor the political compromises with religious political parties that might have explained the crucifix requirement, nor the claim that Italy's distinctive national identity was intertwined with the Catholic Church, could outweigh these concerns. In sweeping terms, the court held: "The compulsory display of a symbol of a particular faith in the exercise of public authority in relation to specific situations subject to governmental supervision, particularly in classrooms, restricts the right of parents to educate their children in conformity with their convictions and the right of schoolchildren to believe or not believe."[25] In effect, the court consigned crucifixes—and by implication, religion more generally—to the private sphere. It also awarded the plaintiffs 5,000 euros in nonpunitive damages.

BLESSING *LAUTSI I*

For the UAAR, the court's decision was a momentous victory. As UAAR president Carcano recalled about the halcyon days after the court's ruling: "We thought we could change Italy's [national culture]; after the first ECHR decision we thought we were on the way to changing this country." Nor were supporters of the ruling in any mood to limit the scope of their victory. Universalizing the decision, they exulted in the fact that it would exert influence across Europe in all Council of Europe countries governed by ECHR decisions. They confidently predicted that the logic of the ruling would be upheld in an expected appeal by the government of Italy. And they embraced the case as a prelude to removal of all religious symbols from all public institutions across Europe. As one supporter of the case enthused: "The notion that the state should refrain from imposing beliefs in places where individuals are dependent on it is, to various extents, valid for all public institutions. . . . Denominational neutrality is relevant whenever citizens' presence on the premises of some state institution is compulsory irrespective of religion."[26]

Others, such as the European Humanist Federation, extended the absolutist stance of the *Lautsi I* ruling to a host of other issues: "Majorities . . . have no right to remove the human rights of even one individual contrary to the law and the Convention. . . . So-called group rights are an automatic denial of the human rights of individuals within those groups—especially individuals who think for themselves and question group norms—and those who customarily suffer oppression, such as women, gays, Roma and other ethnic minorities."[27] Providing backhanded support to these expansive possibilities was one of the UAAR's international NGO foes, the powerful American religious advocacy group, Alliance Defending Freedom (ADF; formerly Alliance Defense Fund). Assessing the threat posed by the first *Lautsi* decision, ADF lawyers later wrote that "it would be illegal under the European Convention on Human Rights to have religious symbols in any state institution anywhere in Europe. That would . . . set a dangerous example for the rest of the world." Even more broadly, it would mean that all European "nation[s] must forsake and discontinue how [they] handle . . . millennia-old traditions."[28]

DAMNING *LAUTSI I*: PARRYING TACTICS

As already indicated, the Italian government reacted to the court's decision with rage directed at the Lautsi-Albertin family, the UAAR, and the ECHR. As the defense minister Ignazio La Russa repeatedly shouted on Italian television: "Death to those people and those international institutions that don't count for anything."[29] A like-minded mayor and parliament member demanded that "Wanted" signs of the atheist family be placed on billboards around the country.[30] Although other critics were not so extreme, harsh condemnation came from across the political spectrum, including leaders of Italy's Communist Party. Only the small Radicali Italiani Party supported the verdict—and their offices were promptly painted with crosses.

Nor was the shock confined to Italy. Twenty governments from religiously conservative states established an alliance to fight back. At its core were members of the European People's Party (EPP), a conservative European-wide party founded in 1976 and active in the European Parliament and the Parliamentary Assembly of the Council of Europe (PACE), the legislative arm of the Council of Europe. The EPP's PACE chairman at the time was the Italian parliamentarian Luca Volontè.[31] An observant Catholic, he had previously worked with two powerful American legal organizations active in litigation on religious rights in Europe: the ADF and the European Centre for Law and Justice, partner to the American Center for Law and Justice (ACLJ). These two groups provided international legal firepower to the defense of the crucifix, submitting legal memoranda to the court and representing members of the European Parliament from the many nations that intervened in the appeal. To argue before the ECHR Grand Chamber, a group of state opponents of *Lautsi I* turned to a well-known lawyer and New York University School of Law professor, Joseph Weiler, who wore a yarmulke while presenting his case. Their goal, as Volontè told me in an interview, was "to give to the judges the opinion that [this was] not only [an] Italian, not only [a] Catholic question, but was [a] more comprehensive decision about freedom of religion in the public square."[32]

In reviling the *Lautsi I* decision, the crucifix coalition used a number of parrying tactics common to foes facing spear and other rights tactics. They denied that the Albertin children or their mother had suffered any rights violation. They raised a rival set of rights that they claimed should trump the family's. They portrayed millions of believing Italians and the Italian state itself as potential victims of the *Lautsi I* decision. And they openly threatened to repudiate and disobey the decision if it was not overturned.

Denial. To deny the ruling, supporters of the crucifix used a number of methods. Most simply, they rejected the idea that the crucifix's presence in classrooms had caused any violation. Cardinal Giovanni Battista Re, for instance, was dumbfounded because the crucifix was "an image that cannot but be the emblem of a universally shared humanity . . . that teaches us to learn to love . . . and to respect . . . even those who belong to a different culture or religion. How could someone not share such a symbol?"[33] Denial was also directed at the expansive claims in the *Lautsi I* decision and the UAAR's legal briefs regarding the allegedly universal and apolitical aspects of the human rights proclaimed there. On the contrary, according to the supporters of the crucifix, the court's *Lautsi* decision reflected little more than the parochial, secular beliefs of the judges, influenced by states with very different church-state traditions, such as France or the United States. Nor was state neutrality toward religion a transcendent and apolitical position, according to the crucifix's defenders. Rather, it was highly political and, worse yet, represented the partisan politics of cultures foreign to Italy. The fact that an international, rather than domestic, court issued the ruling, and that Soile Lautsi was Finnish-born, added fuel to the argument that the *Lautsi I* decision was the narrow-minded imposition of an alien court, not the embodiment of universal rights.

Rivalry: Rights of nations. Against the UAAR's rights claims and their view that "nations . . . hold no rights," the crucifix's defenders marshaled rival rights.[34] After their initial shock at the ECHR's ruling, members of the coalition came to see the appeal as an "opportunity to reaffirm human values" and to work together for common goals. First, the coalition urged respect for the rights of majorities to preserve their national traditions of church-state relations, no matter how varied those might be on the continent. In this view, the right of a group to maintain long-standing national practices (such as religious symbols in classrooms) should trump the right of individuals to avoid their effects. More generally, the coalition sought to "enlighten the court that this case was not only a specific case between a family in Italy and the Italian state, but also [that] around many Parliaments in Europe, it was considered a real chance to reaffirm the freedom of Church in the public square." In doing so, however, the coalition was careful not to "use the brand of Catholics or Evangelicals," which might have connoted too narrow a concern. Rather, they grounded their arguments in universalism—in "reason, expertise, but enlightened by our faith." In this way, they could "work with many different religions . . . in the same direction."

Second, and more basically, the pro-crucifix coalition argued for the rights of sovereign European states to determine their own national policies regarding religion in public institutions. There was no European consensus on such matters, with variation ranging from countries with established state churches such as England to those such as France espousing *laïcité* (strict separation of church and state). For these reasons, the coalition argued, European nations should have the right to choose their own religious practices. As part of this, the crucifix's defenders challenged the UAAR's claims to rights' supra-political and absolutist nature. National decision-making in democratic societies, they contended, should be preserved as a basic tenet. This would allow for political conflict and bargaining that might gradually change a state's relationship with its religious communities. But, according to the religious conservatives, by altering this relationship through judicial edict and proclaiming certain rights transcendent and absolute, the UAAR undermined the fundamental right of states to determine their own futures.

Reversal: Victims of rights. As another line of argument, foes of *Lautsi I* portrayed themselves and their majority coreligionists as victims. ECLJ head Grégor Puppinck, for instance, characterized the "strategic alliance between Catholics and Orthodox" galvanized by the *Lautsi I* decision as "defend[ing] together the Christian tradition against secularism, liberalism and relativism prevailing in Europe."[35] Volontè stated that in a Europe with "common Christian roots," the decision was a profound threat to Christian ways of life.[36] Worse yet, this threat was mounted by proponents of a "militant secularism . . . no less dangerous than Marxism."[37] In the Grand Chamber's oral arguments, Italy's counsel associated the plaintiffs' goal of religious neutrality in the public square with imposition of state atheism, a source of some of the twentieth century's gravest human rights violations, he pointedly claimed. For defenders of the crucifix such as Puppinck, the case was "emblematic of a desire to secularize and . . . de-Christianize" Europe, to "question . . . the legitimacy of the visible presence of Christ in the schools." All of this, according to defenders of the cross, was done in the name of a false "neutrality" toward religion. In their view, the injection of rights-based neutrality into Italian society was anything but apolitical. It displaced society's traditional religious underpinnings with a new "cultural model in which the absence of values (neutrality) and relativism (pluralism) are values in themselves"—values that would exercise a "philosophical monopoly" in public space.

As noted previously, although the UAAR framed its goals in different terms, it hoped that its litigation against the crucifix would shift Italy's cultural and political landscape toward such "neutrality." But for defenders of the crucifix, such as the ECLJ's Puppinck, "religion is by nature a social phenomenon" and "a State and its people necessarily have an identity," an identity that includes "a religious dimension."[38] To claim, as the plaintiffs and the *Lautsi I* court did, that "society must . . . renounce its religious identity in order to be democratic" would be to destroy Italy's historically rooted identity. More abstractly, it would be a rejection of the "religious dimension of a collective identity and the social dimension of religion." Again, for the UAAR this was exactly the point, and a beneficent one at that. But for those at the tip of the rights spear, it was a mortal menace.

In addition to portraying themselves as victims, foes of *Lautsi I* fingered the culprit—not just the UAAR but also, and more interestingly for this book's argument, the tactic it had used. Puppinck, for instance, argued the following: Rights are grounded in a belief that the individual conscience is paramount and universal, creating an "adversarial" rather than "complementary" relationship between the individual and society. This creates "a protesting mindset of 'my rights' against those of the society as a whole" under which "the right of Miss Lautsi's children not to [be] compelled to see symbols of Christ should trump the will of the people of Italy . . . without any compromise being possible." As noted previously, the UAAR did take this absolutist stance, and the *Lautsi I* court had adopted it.[39] Most gallingly for defenders of the crucifix, the UAAR had used religious rights against religion itself. As Puppinck wrote: "Religious freedom, which was designed to protect society from the atheistic state, became *in fine* an instrument of the social de-legitimization of religion and the removal of religion from the public sphere to the private life of people as *individuals* (i.e., religious 'privatization')."

Repudiation: ECHR in peril. Although the *Lautsi* case had focused on a particular family and a narrow policy, the ECHR's 2009 ruling upped the ante. Of course, the case had never been only about rights violations against the Lautsi-Albertins. Rather, the UAAR's spearlike litigation had been a tactic born of the small group's political isolation, with the hope that toppling the Mussolini-era decree would spur broad social change in Italy. With the initial ECHR ruling, the case had potential to remake church-state relations across the continent. The ECHR, at the UAAR's instance, had asserted that it could decide on any member country's policy regarding religious symbols in public institutions—and by implication other fundamental matters. Debate over the ECHR's power vis-à-vis states had been an undercurrent in its jurisprudence and in European politics previously. In the aftermath of *Lautsi*, this debate roared back with an explicit threat against the ECHR itself. Because *Lautsi I* had such major implications, Italy and the religiously conservative nations that joined with it in the appeal openly stated that they would defy the ruling and repudiate the Court if it was not reversed.

To understand this, some background information is helpful. In earlier cases, the ECHR had largely adhered to the idea that it played a subsidiary role in disputes, with national courts and political systems playing the primary role. In a number of cases, the court had held that it had to grant countries a "margin of appreciation" with respect to certain national practices that might otherwise appear to violate international rights standards.[40] According to this doctrine, "each society is entitled to [a] certain latitude in resolving the inherent conflict between individual rights and national interests or among different moral convictions."[41] But this doctrine had never been accepted by human rights absolutists. For example, in a 1997 ECHR case about the release of medical records in a Finnish criminal proceeding, dissenting judge Jan de Meyer denounced the "margin of appreciation," urging that "this hackneyed phrase and . . . the relativism it implies" be "banish[ed]." In de Meyer's expansive view, "where human rights are concerned, there is no room for a margin of appreciation which would enable the States to decide what is acceptable and what is not. On that subject the boundary not to be overstepped must be as clear and precise as possible. It is for the Court, not each State individually, to decide that issue. . . . The empty phrases concerning the State's margin of appreciation . . . , as wrong in principle as . . . pointless in practice, should be abandoned without delay."[42]

In *Lautsi I*, the ECHR omitted consideration of the margin of appreciation, abandoning the doctrine as completely as de Meyer had urged in his thunderous dissent years earlier. For the Italian government, this represented a blatant power grab by an unelected international court. The fact that a foreign-born plaintiff had brought the *Lautsi* case bolstered the view that the sovereignty of Italy and other Council of Europe states was at stake. For Joseph Weiler, another peril was the Americanization of European law—namely, the replacement of the ECHR's existing subsidiary role in European jurisprudence with a new supreme role, one reminiscent of the U.S. Supreme Court. As ECLJ leader Grégor Puppinck later wrote: "Those who want the European Court to overstep its jurisdiction . . .—in a very medieval way—long to see it set up as a new spiritual authority above the States: a theocracy of the atheistic religion of human rights[,] . . . the functional equivalent of an ultimate oracle of a new magisterium, which specifically applies directly to States, not only in civil matters but also in moral and religious matters."[43] Central to this pernicious development, according to an ADF lawyer, was the role of rights: "The principle of tolerance and non-discrimination was developed as a shield but is now all too often being used as a sword to defeat the fundamental freedoms of religion and expression. Tolerance is slowly becoming totalitarianism."[44]

This outcome Italy and her state and nonstate allies could not tolerate. Top officials, starting with Prime Minister Silvio Berlusconi, announced that they would not enforce any order to remove crucifixes. The Moscow Patriarch stated that the Russian Orthodox Church would work with the Roman Catholic Church to "inform the world and European communities of its categorical rejection of such judgments and stimulate the condemnation of the European Court of Human Rights' practices in various domains."[45] Nor was the Patriarch alone in this sentiment, as the number of amicus briefs by supporters of the Italian position attested. If so many states rejected the ECHR's ruling and lax view of the margin of appreciation, the legitimacy and even the future of the ECHR itself was clearly at stake in the appeal.

RALLYING FOR SECULARISM

Against these overwhelming political threats, the UAAR, along with new-found allies among international human rights organizations, offered rights-based retorts. Their lawyers urged that the Grand Chamber accept the earlier decision, reminding the court that they were not arguing for state atheism but for individual rights. The Lautsi-Albertin family merely wanted neutrality so that all students, particularly those with minority beliefs, could enjoy freedom of conscience from a "despotism of the majority" and "publicity material" for the country's dominant religion.[46] They admitted that removing crucifixes would eliminate "part of Italian cultural identity" from schools. However, they found this acceptable, because the crucifix did more than infringe upon their own rights: it was "incompatible with the foundations of western political thought, the principles of the liberal State and a pluralist, open democracy."[47]

Politically, the UAAR coordinated with overseas allies. No states came to its aid—unsurprising, given that *Lautsi I* threatened aspects of state sovereignty. But the European Humanist Federation and a group of sympathetic law professors did rally to the cause, although the court rejected participation by these would-be amici curiae. Several respected international human rights organizations also took up the charge and were accepted. Of particular note was an amicus brief filed by Human Rights Watch, Interights, and the International Commission of Jurists—three of the world's most prominent human rights organizations. Its core argument was supported by references to international and national jurisprudence, particularly from the United States, where displays of crosses in schools have repeatedly been found unconstitutional. Echoing the universalism and absolutism of the plaintiffs' claims, the brief argued that, in the public schools of a "multireligious, pluralist society," the rights to freedom of religion and freedom of belief and the right to education required "state neutrality between beliefs." States must "not endorse or favour any particular religious belief" because the "officially-sanctioned and uncritical display of religious symbols . . . offends the principle of state neutrality."[48] Unsurprisingly, these NGOs also tacitly supported the ECHR's role as absolute human rights arbiter. Only such an international court could stand above myriad national traditions and local cultures, offering opinions about which of these met universal human rights standards. From the perspective of these NGOs, a neutral and supreme legal institution, above state interest and political debate, was as important as a neutral public square for the preservation of rights. They rejected the legal and political arguments of Italy's defenders that in the country's historical context religious neutrality was itself biased and that nations had the right to make their own democratic decisions on such issues.

CRUCIFIX RESURRECTED: *LAUTSI II*

The Grand Chamber, aware of the political forces ranged against it, began its analysis from a different starting point than the judges in *Lautsi I*: the margin of appreciation rather than the rights of individuals. In taking this approach, the court adopted the majoritarian principles urged by Italy and its intervenors, making the outcome predictable. According to the court, the European Convention on Human Rights gives its members "a wide margin of appreciation," particularly in questions about maintaining traditions for which there is no European consensus on a practice.[49] Nor did the plaintiffs claim that any active "indoctrination" occurred.[50] The court admitted that a classroom crucifix "undoubtedly refers to Christianity" and "confer[s] on the country's majority religion preponderant visibility in the school environment." But the court stated that the crucifix was an "essentially passive symbol."[51] Hence, they ruled, Italy's classroom crucifixes did not violate the parents' or the children's rights to education in accordance with their religious and philosophical beliefs. In effect, the right of the Italian state to display the symbol of its majority religion to all its schoolchildren trumped the individual rights of the Albertin boys and their mother—no matter how loudly they declared that their own individual rights should instead trump those of the majority.

Italy and the crucifix coalition reacted with joy and relief. Crosses remained proudly posted in classrooms. The right of states to protect their own traditions and beliefs stood, even against contrary rights that came clothed in universal, absolute, and apolitical garb. The ambitions for ECHR power suggested in the first ruling had been smothered. A generous margin of appreciation was afforded European states, even in core issues of international human rights.[52] To gain further assurance that nothing similar can happen again, members of the European People's Party at the Parliamentary Assembly for the Council of Europe have since taken further steps. They pay closer attention to appointments of ECHR judges, aiming to reject those whom they deem "inexpert" or "prejudiced." As Volontè stated in an interview, "It is the only way . . . to defend yourself [from] any attacks." As a further measure against European secularists, the religious conservatives have intensified their international cooperation. They do so both by "defend[ing] our opinion about human values and human rights, and [by] find[ing] any possibility through judgment by the court or reporting in the Parliamentary Assembly to propose or improve our point of view about human values."[53] As Volontè concluded, it is "politically very important that our so-called enemies [know] that we are working in the same way [as them], jointly, and sometimes it is not so obvious that they can win everything. . . . The best prize for us is to know that they know that something has changed and that many people have rediscovered their courage."[54]

For the UAAR and its allies, the *Lautsi II* decision was a major defeat, one suggesting that the quick prospect for radical change offered by a rights spear would need to be rethought. In a context where no significant political movement or party backed the group's position, the tactic was easily halted, even if an international court, divorced from Italian politics and society, had initially taken it up. The result of this miscalculation has been problematic for the UAAR's agenda. As its leader acknowledged in an interview, "the reversal is a big obstacle, stating that every country can make rules at home, despite human rights. For me this is absurd. This is an enormous problem because every appeal to the European Court on religious issues can be dismissed immediately because there is margin of appreciation. This is a problem for us and for all secular organizations in Europe."[55]

Conclusion

In one sense, the *Lautsi* case could be seen in conventional terms—as a defensive action by a victim of rights violations. The Lautsi-Albertins certainly portrayed themselves that way. They were using the shield of Italian and European rights laws to protect their children and themselves against the overawing political power of the state and the cultural weight of the Church. But the legal and political fights provoked by the *Lautsi* case also reveal important aspects of rights' employment as spears. The UAAR's goals were far larger and more aggressive than simply protecting the rights of the Albertin boys and their mother. At minimum, the group sought similar safeguards for all Italians and Europeans. In the long term, they hoped to undercut the Church's role in Italian society and to remake church-state relations across Europe. Yet they had little political power to achieve any of these goals. For this reason, a narrowly gauged tactic was their only choice, their hope being that ejection of crucifixes from Italian classrooms would be one small but catalytic step forward. Where majoritarian political and social institutions are hostile, activists apply rights narrowly, in spearlike jabs. They choose their venues carefully, favoring countermajoritarian institutions such as courts. If domestic courts are hostile, they resort to international institutions, especially courts, where countermajoritarian impulses are at their zenith.

Even so, where rights' litigants do not have politics on their side, chances of success are slim, as the *Lautsi* case shows. If the UAAR followed a classic minority strategy in raising its challenge to the ECHR, the Italian state followed the classic majority strategy. It activated the public bully pulpit, broached democratic values, and stressed majority rights. It rapidly attracted its own coalition of states and NGOs anxious to save the crucifix. To do so, the coalition adopted emblematic parrying tactics. It denied the UAAR's claims by referencing the limits of individual rights. It raised a rival set of rights—those of society and the majority. And it expanded the sphere of conflict beyond the courts to political settings where majorities ruled. It reversed roles with the Lautsi-Albertins, portraying traditional societies as victims of an aggressive secularism. In this view, Catholicism was under threat in its homeland, and Europe faced imminent "de-Christianization." Meanwhile, the crucifix coalition convincingly threatened repudiation of the ECHR itself. Key members of this coalition, starting with Italy and including at least twenty other states, had the power to carry out these threats. Whatever the merits of the two sides' arguments, the ECHR judges had to be cognizant of the peril in which this placed their court.

Judicial institutions are sometimes viewed as neutral forums for nonviolent conflict resolution in democratic societies. But in critical cases such as *Lautsi*, a top court's institutional interest in self-preservation comes into play. Indeed, as much as savoring its victory over the UAAR the powerful crucifix coalition celebrated its weakening of the ECHR, the countermajoritarian institution that the far weaker UAAR had vainly hoped would vindicate its spear tactic. In the next chapter, we focus further on the powerful, analyzing the rights tactics that they deploy to restrict or crush weaker groups.

6

Rights as Dynamite
DESTROYING CULTURES

In January 2014, Nigeria adopted a harsh new law criminalizing same-sex marriage and strengthening punishments against homosexuality. Marriages would be punished by fourteen years in jail, "amorous relationships" with those of the same sex by ten years, and membership in LGBT organizations by ten years. In passing the Same Sex Marriage (Prohibition) Bill, the Nigerian legislature repeatedly invoked the supposed evils of homosexuality, the purported threat that it posed to the country, and the right of the nation to protect itself. To justify passage of the law, Nigerian senate president David Mark stated: "We are a sovereign nation and we have the right to decide. . . . Same-sex marriage is against our . . . culture and tradition and against our beliefs." These views spanned the country's political parties and its diverse ethnic and religious groups, and the new law passed by an overwhelming vote. The debate around the bill also revealed a deeper, more aggressive aim: to use the rights of the majority to extirpate Nigerian homosexuality. As Senator Baba-Ahmed Yusuf Datti urged, LGBT "elements in society should be killed." In this way, the justifications around the bill resembled those given in similar debates in other African states, where openly LGBT populations are tiny in number, politically weak, and yet harshly treated as a matter of majority right. In Uganda, the 2014 Anti-Homosexuality Act imposing life imprisonment for the "offence of homosexuality" was defended by appealing to the rights of the nation and its religiously traditional majority.[1]

This kind of rights tactic, where a dominant group deploys the rights of the sovereign nation, its culture, tradition, and beliefs against a weaker group, is far from unusual. For centuries and in numerous settings, the powerful have used rights as "dynamite"—to attack minority communities, to subordinate them as permanent second-class citizens, or even to destroy them. They do so in the name of majority rights, states' rights, or sovereign rights. For liberal human rights NGOs, of course, such rights are nonliberal, or not rights at all, but merely excuses for imposing majority tyranny. Importantly, however, it is not only such group rights that are used as dynamite. At times, even individual rights are invoked by the powerful against weaker communities. One need look no further than the international controversy surrounding policies toward gays and lesbians in African states. The United States, the United Kingdom, and other powerful entities have insisted that African countries provide rights to LGBT populations and have cut development aid to far weaker countries that have passed laws similar to Nigeria's, such as Uganda and Malawi. No matter how appropriate these demands and cutoffs appear to Western liberal audiences, from the perspective of many Africans, they are coercive and imperialistic, aiming to erode national autonomy and shatter traditional societies that have their own conceptions of rights and duties. Nor are such critiques exclusive to conservative governmental or religious leaders. They are widely shared in African societies. As we shall see, even African LGBT organizations have called for Western states to "review . . . decision[s] to cut aid to countries that do not protect LGBTI rights," calling them a threat to "national state sovereignty."[2]

In this chapter, I analyze how the powerful may use both group and individual rights to dominate the weak.[3] To argue that liberal individual rights are used by the powerful against the weak is, of course, contrary to the conventional way of viewing them. But I hope to show that liberal rights are in fact sometimes employed this way, even if this is by no means their only use. I begin by defining rights' usage as dynamite and developing propositions about related issues. Next, I analyze several important cases, demonstrating the analytic utility of the perspective. These include France's 2010 ban on the full veil justified in part by women's rights, the recent controversy over LGBT rights in African countries such as Nigeria, and the U.S. war in Afghanistan, again justified in part by women's rights.

Dynamite Tactics

DEFINITION AND PURPOSES

What is the dynamite tactic, and when can we say that rights are being used for "explosive" purposes? An initial comparison to the spear tactic is helpful. As detailed in chapter 5, a movement using the spear tactic brings a narrowly framed rights challenge against a single policy, with the hope that this will precipitate broader societal change and, in the long run, inclusion of the movement's constituency in a reformed society. By contrast, the hallmark of the dynamite tactic is the use of rights arguments in a direct and immediate attempt to undermine or destroy a targeted culture or community, often by forcing alteration in key values, ideas, or institutions. Whatever its rationale, the dynamite tactic resembles the large-scale use of coercion or violence against an entire community. Physical force is often deployed as well, as I will show in discussing women's rights and the Afghanistan War. In the latter case, as in others involving physical violence, those who use rights as dynamite may not own up to their radical effects. Outside observers sympathetic to such uses may not be so coy, however, about acknowledging what is happening. Consider, for instance, Council on Foreign Relations fellow Max Boot. In the early days of the Iraq War and the early years of the Afghanistan War, he urged the United States to embrace an imperial role by "imposing the rule of law, property rights, free speech and other guarantees, at gunpoint if need be."[4] Even without such an open linkage between rights and force, rights rhetoric provides rationalization and cover for military incursions overseas. With rights' generally positive connotations, their invocation in such cases suggests that little untoward is happening or that the high price of war is worth it.

In domestic politics, majoritarian institutions such as executives and legislatures are usually the instigators of dynamite tactics. In recent decades, for instance, European countries have passed laws that claim to protect majority populations and dominant cultures from immigrants and their different cultures. Their effect and intent, however, is at minimum to restrict the rights of minority communities and place them in a subordinate position with regard to the exercise of certain rights, and at maximum to drive them away. Well-known examples include veil bans in France, Catalonia, and elsewhere; minaret prohibitions in Switzerland; and a variety of culturally based limitations on immigration across the continent. These have not only been promoted by nationalist and nativist movements but also embraced by mainstream politicians and institutions. Grounded in a scarcely concealed idea of cultural nationalism and superiority, positing a sharp dichotomy between the rights-respecting West and rights-violating others, these policies have diverted resources and attention away from continuing if different rights violations in the West.[5]

In other parts of the world, indigenous cultural majorities have long used rights claims to elevate themselves over other groups. In Malaysia and Indonesia, for instance, *bumiputera* policies restrict minority groups portrayed as "migrants" from access equal to that of "native" populations to jobs, educational opportunities, and governmental offices. This is true even though ancestors of the "migrants" have lived in these countries for generations. Similarly, in Nigeria and India, "sons of the soil" policies legalize discrimination against fellow citizens from different parts of the same countries who are of different ethnic or religious groups.[6] Although such policies may not aim to destroy migrant groups, they reduce their life chances and create a form of second-class citizenship relative to the population that portrays itself as "native."

What unifies these varied usages of rights as dynamite is their rationale: to protect the user against a supposedly existential threat. The more that a group, whether rightly or wrongly, perceives itself or its culture to face such a threat, the more likely it will be to invoke its right to survive as a group or a nation. Notably, of course, such perceptions can be wrong and are subject to a variety of well-known biases. Thus, even objectively small threats may be the basis for outsize reactions, undertaken in the name of the community's right to survive. When using rights in such destructive ways, threat inflation is a common means of rationalization.

DYNAMITE USERS

Which groups are most likely to use rights as dynamite? More than anything, using rights explosively requires political clout. Although weak groups may long to use rights in a similar way, they lack the sway or resources to do so. Powerful groups, on the other hand, may prohibit or limit the rights of minorities. They assert states' or majority rights, placing a democratic imprimatur on their explosive goals, and use institutions of government to bar or reject minority groups as their sovereign right. Exerting material force along with their rights claims, they cajole, push, or compel the weak into conformity, or at least quiescence. In domestic contexts, force may be implicit, although police power will ultimately enforce it. Internationally, dynamite rights tactics are tied more closely to overt coercion or violence, whether through boycotts, sanctions, attacks, or invasions.

If dynamite is a tool of the powerful, it is worth reiterating that it is not only powerful illiberal forces that use it, as might well be expected, but under certain circumstances liberal organizations and states as well. As the political philosopher John Gray and others have written, liberalism seeks to impose a substantive, and not only procedural, vision of politics. Gray notes that "the liberal discourse of rights and personal autonomy is deployed in a continuing conflict to gain and hold power by communities and ways of life having highly diverse values."[7] Despite frequent claims of liberalism's tolerance of difference, certain types of difference are just as frequently not tolerated. This is justified by arguing that liberal societies need not tolerate the illiberal or the intolerant because they pose a threat to liberalism itself—or at least to the culture of a particular liberal state. However, defining what and who is "intolerant" is highly political. To take just one example, in the US debate over same-sex marriage and opt-out provisions for companies that claim a right not to supply various services to such weddings, both sides trade bitter charges of intolerance.

DYNAMITE TARGETS

Identifying the materially powerful as the groups most likely to implement dynamite tactics also identifies the targets: weaker groups. Of course, determining who is weaker and who is stronger is always a relative matter, as between the two primary players. Those best able to use the dynamite tactic, however, are always weightier in political or material terms—usually significantly so—than their targets. On the other hand, there is a "nesting doll" aspect to the use of these tactics, particularly in today's world where domestic conflicts are so frequently internationalized. The LGBT rights controversy introducing this chapter presents an example. At the national level, Nigeria and other states in sub-Saharan Africa use majority cultural attitudes and rights as a basis for their harsh laws. The dominant thereby target vulnerable individuals and weak communities within their own societies. At the international level, however, Western states and international organizations condition development aid to African countries on whether they provide rights to LGBT people or cancel laws punishing them. In this context, powerful states belabor weaker ones, albeit in the name of even weaker groups facing repression within those states. These burdens that the strong place on the weak—members of minority groups in one case, poor states in another—are not equivalent. But there is no question that governments and broader populations in African countries view themselves as under attack by powerful outsiders.

VICTIMS AT HOME

Given the destructive intentions of dynamite tactics, when dominant groups use them they do so in the name of what they portray as a dire threat either to themselves or to others. To take the first of these, it may seem strange that a powerful entity would frame itself as a victim—as enduring or facing major danger from a weaker group. However, the claim has been made frequently, as the long history of fear-induced pogroms, genocides, and wars makes clear. Within European states, the recent cultural protection measures for majorities noted earlier exemplify this. They are justified by the claim that if nothing is done, the majority culture itself will be eroded or even destroyed. Sometimes the dominant community believes this sincerely and invokes a basic right to cultural self-defense, a right that often blends into offensive tactics against those portrayed as imminent threats.[8]

One would thus expect that, when using rights as dynamite, a dominant group will portray itself as a victim or prospective victim. One would also expect dominant groups to use recurrent themes to make this claim and justify their aggressive right to self-defense: the threat will be depicted as alien, as large or at least growing, and as inexorable—unless drastic measures are taken to stem or quash it. From an empirical standpoint, we might question the veracity, significance, or objectivity of such claims. Overblown threats are a mainstay of dynamite tactics. Politically, however, facts are secondary. If movements or leaders can convince their majority constituents that they are victims or potential victims, the use of rights as dynamite becomes possible for group protection. Moreover, as Donald Horowitz has shown, fears that a culture will be extinguished go hand in hand with worries that individual members of the culture will be extirpated. Dynamite tactics respond to those anxieties with the promise that the threat will be neutralized.[9]

VICARIOUS DYNAMITING

The powerful forces that use rights as dynamite sometimes do so vicariously, on behalf of faraway others, as Western states have recently used gay rights for LGBT populations in Africa. They depict the members of these groups as victims who are unable to protect themselves against the enemies they face. Distant minorities are more easily depicted as victims than the powerful groups using dynamite tactics on their own behalf at home. Many minorities really are subordinated and repressed in their home societies, even if they may be taking actions on their own to change this. In addition, the situation of far-off communities is less understood, and their ability to defend themselves less apparent, than the position of powerful groups attempting to transmute themselves into victims at home. Still, the themes already noted run throughout this framing of others as victims and the vicarious invocation of rights as dynamite against the tormentor. These motifs are necessary because, when powerful outsiders help distant victims, oppressors often begin portraying themselves as the aggrieved party to a broader conflict. As a result, international interventions against palpably weaker foes require constant justification, and the rights of obscure victims of such foes serve this function well.

Notably, however, in using rights as dynamite, there is a significant possibility of unintended consequences—what in military parlance is euphemistically termed "collateral damage." Although the powerful may claim that they act for the victims, the use of rights as dynamite may harm those it claims to protect. How do the latter communities respond to such outside support, with all its attendant risks? In some cases, they react positively. Leaders of repressed groups often seek external aid, publicizing the abuses against them to attract international assistance.

UNGRATEFUL VICTIMS

It is a fallacy, however, to assume that every threatened community wants its rights vindicated by outsiders or that internationally prominent advocates necessarily speak for such communities. Such views may be intimated by foreign states or NGOs seeking to intervene not only for principled reasons but also in pursuit of their own political, ideological, or organizational aims.[10] However, external rights campaigns sometimes face rejection by victim groups, who may even reject their typecasting as "victims."

What explains these varying reactions? The most important factor is whether members of the latter group believe that they will become unintended casualties of the vicarious use of rights as dynamite on their behalf. Put another way, victim communities will weigh the costs and benefits of the tactic for themselves alone. Because the tactic exerts its effects where the victims live, the costs may be high for them, another reason that some needy communities reject outside interventions done in their names. By contrast, powerful intervenors will always consider broader costs and benefits—to themselves or to a notional "international community"—as well as those to the victims. Because they are outsiders, the intervenors' direct costs will usually be low relative to those borne by populations in the locale where rights (and force) are actually used. Outsiders may also benefit psychologically, organizationally, or materially from interventions on foreign soil. Conversely, and contrary to the beliefs of would-be intervenors, external support does not invariably improve a local group's situation and standing. Frequently, the opposite is true, particularly if intervention has fundamental and explosive goals such as changing a culture or a regime using rights in conjunction with force to upend existing power relations.

Whether a group assigned an identity as victim will support vicarious rights tactics hinges on a number of factors, including the victim group's assessment of the magnitude and duration of outside pressure; the likely reaction of the foe, whether to disregard the intervention or, more commonly, to lash out at the victim group; and therefore the extent to which a dynamite tactic will help the group, given the larger dynamics of the conflict. If the victim community believes that external rights promotion will make little difference to the conflict's outcome, it may reject such a tactic even if ostensibly undertaken by the powerful on its behalf. Further, if the victim community believes that such interventions will hurt more than help them, or create a backlash that hardens the foe's attitudes, it is likely to reject the intervention and even the designation as "victim." However, even if victims reject explosive rights tactics, there is no guarantee that the powerful group using them for its own extraneous reasons will abide by this preference.

As a final twist, victim communities are often divided about whether a powerful outsider's explosive rights activism will or will not help them. Personal or organizational factors may cloud judgment, especially if the outsider offers material incentives only to certain local interlocutors. In such a case, those directly receiving support will more likely approve the outsider's explosive use of rights, whereas members of the community who do not receive such incentives will oppose it. Given the radical effects of rights dynamiting, the possibility of collateral harms, and the likelihood of differential incentives, divisions within victim communities about the wisdom of the tactic are common.

THE RIGHT RIGHTS

Which rights are most likely to be promoted through the use of this tactic? When dominant groups use rights as dynamite, they will choose rights their own community endorses. Such rights are generally those that preserve or fortify the dominant culture, way of life, or power structure. More specifically, the powerful will select the right most capable of undermining the minority group they perceive as a threat. In this sense, dynamite users are opportunistic. They will choose whatever majority right or majority-supported right serves their purpose at a particular moment.

But are majority rights truly "rights"? Or is it the case that rights, or at least human rights, can only be asserted *against* a majority? For activists such as Human Rights Watch president Kenneth Roth, "human rights exist to protect people from government abuse and neglect. Rights limit what a state can do and impose obligations for how a state must act."[11] Roth is correct that human rights are typically defined this way by liberal NGOs such as his. As we have seen, however, the modifier "human" is primarily a mobilizational tool; "individual" would be a more objective way to describe these rights. Moreover, any limits on state power are themselves possible only because they were established and are maintained through the exercise of countervailing power. Using the definition in this book, majority rights are rights also. There is a long and infamous history of states' rights, majority rights, and sovereign rights being used against individuals. And controversial as they are, such rights are today gaining political prominence and philosophical justification.[12] Nor is it the case that these uses of the term "rights" can simply be dismissed as cynical misuses. Rights' capacity to be filled with any political goal makes them just as much a majority as a minority tool—a weapon of both the strong and the weak. Roth wrote his words in a 2017 essay decrying a "rising tide of populism in the name of a perceived majority" that "threatens to reverse the accomplishments of the modern human rights movement."[13] However, even if majority rights are not classified as human rights, majority rights share the same mechanism of action, although the rights-holders, the duty-bearers, and, most crucially, the implications for individual lives are reversed.

OVERT OR COVERT EXPLOSIVES?

As shown elsewhere in this book, other rights tactics are often carried out secretly, with the activist camouflaging his motives or efforts. However, when those using rights as dynamite align themselves with the will of the majority, as in domestic contexts, secrecy is less likely. There is little need for it because majoritarian rights enjoy sufficient legitimacy to justify the imposition of duties on minorities or individuals, particularly if those targeted are portrayed as alien or threatening. This is true even in liberal states, where the rights of minorities have long been celebrated. Increasingly, as Liav Orgad has shown with regard to liberal European states, majority populations openly assert their rights, threatening the constitutional or legal protections of minorities. Similarly, as Rachel Wahl found in examining the use of torture and extrajudicial execution of suspected criminals by the Indian police, authorities are more than willing to discuss their actions openly, portraying them as vindicating the community's bedrock right to security.[14]

Internationally, however, where dominant states employ dynamite tactics to impose their views on weaker ones, there can be no majority will. Lacking such legitimation, the powerful are less likely to voice their incendiary aims explicitly. To do so would be to usurp the majority desires of the targeted society. The powerful will not necessarily avoid dynamite tactics overseas, but they will conceal their full aims in doing so. They will profess that they are using the right surgically, that they seek only to help vulnerable victims, and that they do not have broader aims—for example, altering or eliminating the target's broader way of life.

An obvious reason for this obfuscation is that seldom has the majority of the population in a target state agreed to this imposition. They may oppose even the purportedly limited goals that are proclaimed openly, or they may fear the violent means necessary to fight for them. Another, less obvious reason for concealment of ultimate motives is that citizens of intervening states will be less likely to accept a campaign that expressly calls for the wholesale transformation of a foreign society, but more likely to accept a narrowly tailored effort to end one egregious practice.[15] The former smacks of crusade, conquest, and colonization, the latter of an urgent but narrow campaign. If cultural destruction and new nation-building are openly attempted, they are likely to be justified on other grounds, such as the security of the home state.

Before leaving this discussion of the mechanisms by which dynamite campaigns proceed, a brief methodological point is worth raising. When the tactic is covert, how are analysts to determine whether it is actually being used? In such cases, evidence might include: objective assessment of the effects of the campaign; the rights proponent's unguarded statements of his intents; or the contemporaneous views of knowledgeable third parties, especially the victims or beneficiaries on whose behalf dynamite rights campaigns are launched (with or without their consent). With regard to the latter, in certain cases such "victims" will denounce rights campaigns as destructive or counterproductive—a good indicator that rights are being used explosively.

As a final source of evidence about whether dynamite tactics are being used covertly, analysts should consider the perceptions of the accused violators—the targets of a rights campaign. If targets believe that the rights used against them threaten their basic values and institutions, these views should not be automatically dismissed but should at least be noted. Skeptics might retort that the views of violators are at best misperceptions and at worst lies—the exaggerated, incorrect, or motivated views of oppressors who seek to maintain their oppressive ways. As international relations scholars have long argued, however, perceptions and misperceptions are difficult to distinguish, and both influence behavior.[16] If a state, for example, declares that its deployment of antiballistic missiles is purely defensive, other states may view the move as offensive and consider preemptive war as a response. Similarly, if the target of a rights campaign could reasonably believe that the asserted rights threaten its way of life directly or indirectly, this viewpoint should be considered—even if campaigners and analysts believe that the cultural or political practices in question are plainly wrong. At minimum, the target's views, regardless of their validity, will strongly affect its reaction and therefore the conflict as a whole.

SUCCESS AT HOME AND ABROAD

Will the dynamite tactic succeed, undermining the community against which it is directed? As with many of the conceptual points so far discussed, we should distinguish the domestic use of majority rights from the international use of other rights for similarly explosive purposes. In domestic cases, success will hinge on the stability of majority power. If it is stable, the tactic will probably succeed, especially if intractable groups may ultimately be expelled from the society. If there are shifting majorities with regard to a particular issue, however, success is less certain.

Internationally, success is less likely in all circumstances because those using rights as explosives are outsiders. True, rights campaigns, especially those eschewing military force, are relatively cheap for strong states or movements to implement. Furthermore, the powerful may be responding to the urgings of their own constituencies—for example, NGO lobbyists or solidarity movements—motivated by a mix of humanitarian and material concerns. Still, even the most powerful will face difficulties and uncertainties when using dynamite tactics overseas. Over the long periods necessary to dismantle a targeted society, those seeking to impose rights on the recalcitrant often lose enthusiasm or resources. Intervenors, not citizens of the target state, are most likely to face expulsion or to leave voluntarily. Even "weak" targets have unrecognized reservoirs of strength when it comes to upholding their own beliefs and institutions in their home territories. This is especially the case when the rights thrust on them as human, universal, and apolitical are instead perceived as alien, parochial, and threatening.

Domestic Dynamite: France's Veil Ban

Domestically, the rights of states and nations have long been used against minority communities. When such rights undermine key cultural markers or social identities—or even the group itself—they may be considered explosive in nature. France's 2010 law prohibiting full veils in public is a case in point. Although sometimes considered extreme, it exemplifies how surprising coalitions of nationalists and feminists have recently pushed liberal states to enact a wide variety of policies against minorities, particularly Muslims, whose treatment of women they consider wrong and threatening.[17] The law is based on an interlocking set of individual and group rights: the rights of women and, more fundamentally, the rights of the French nation. Proponents' invocation of the "rights of the nation" underlines the power dynamics at play. So does the far weaker target of the law. No more than about 1,900 French women wore the full veil, according to a 2009 government report, which termed the practice "marginal."[18]

VIGOROUS VICTIMS

Nonetheless, as expected from this chapter's conceptualization of rights as dynamite, the law was portrayed as defensive, and those it defended were styled as victims or future victims in need of protection. The commission of the French National Assembly that recommended the ban identified two victims: the French state, and wearers of the veil themselves. With regard to the first, the commission declared: "The wearing of the full veil is a challenge to our republic. This is unacceptable." The fact that so few women wore the full veil and even fewer expressly challenged the republic in doing so did not matter. As Jean-François Copé, president of the ruling party, the Union for a Popular Movement (UPM), wrote in *Le Figaro*: "The issue is not how many women wear the burqa. There are principles at stake: extremists are putting the republic to the test by promoting a practice that they know is contrary to the basic principles of our country."[19]

What were the basic French principles so threatened that the full veil needed to be expelled from the public sphere? One that underlay the new law was *laïcité*, France's century-old practice of strict church-state separation, including the exclusion of religious symbols from public institutions. Until 2010, the principle, which stems from a 1905 law, had not been extended to the entirety of public space, nor had it been directed solely at Muslims. (In 2004, it had been used to justify a prohibition on the wearing of conspicuous religious garb, including headscarves, crucifixes, or kippahs, in public schools, courtrooms, and similar institutions.) In 2010, the French parliamentary commission recommending the broader ban stated that the wearing of the veil by some women menaced the modern French state's three founding principles: *liberté*, *égalité*, and *fraternité*.

First, the commission held that wearing the veil was coercive, infringing on *liberté*: it was the "ambulatory expression of a denial of liberty that touches a specific category of the population: women."[20] Second, the commission argued that the veil symbolized women's "subservience" and "constitute[d] a negation of the principle of equality." The veil was "a regression of the rights and the dignity of the woman in our society[,] . . . a form of sexual apartheid with on one side the world of men that is open and on the other side the world of women, constrained and closed[,] . . . a uniform that reduces the woman to anonymity, [and erases] the woman in her specificity. . . . It takes her away from the public place."

In these arguments, the commission highlighted the other victim, Muslim women "compelled" to wear the full veil by custom or force. For Muslim women, the ban would be a boon, according to the commission. They would escape the compulsions of religion for the freedom and equality of the public square. Yet many Muslim women loudly differed from the official view, denying that they were victims of the veil. Rather, they claimed that they wore it freely and proudly as an expression of their religion and identity. The veil allowed them to enter the public sphere in privacy, whereas a ban would keep them at home, undermining their equality. Most importantly, in their view, the ban undermined the practice of Islam in France and ultimately Islam itself. These views echo the findings of scholars who have found that many Muslim women do not need or desire Western liberals to "save" them from the veil, nor do they necessarily believe that gender relations are more advanced in Western cultures such as France.[21] In sum, and as this chapter's view of rights would expect, certain "victims" rejected the policy that the French state offered ostensibly on their behalf.

As a third argument, the National Assembly commission held that the full veil violated the principle of *fraternité* because it created one-sided public interactions favoring Muslim women. The wearer could see others while remaining unseen. Her unveiled interlocutors could not see her face, the "mirror of the soul." But this argument raises contradictions. On the one hand, the female veil wearer is pitied as a victim of coercion and subordination. On the other, she is feared as gaining an unfair advantage over others—or, as UPM president Copé stated, she is an "extremist" (or coerced by one), with all the negative connotations that term now carries. However, the commission disregarded the contradictions. For fraternity among all citizens, it ordered the veil's prohibition.

NATIONAL IDENTITY AND MAJORITY RIGHTS

In promoting the ban, government officials usually stated these three "basic principles" of the French republic in positive and practical terms. Their beneficent aim was to assimilate Muslims to French ways of life, particularly to women's freedom and equality. But such goals necessarily had negative consequences: punishment for those who failed to conform to the majority view, and ultimately cessation of this important cultural practice, at least in the public sphere.[22] The rapporteur of the National Assembly commission, Éric Raoult, openly stated as much: "We want to fight Islamic fundamentalism. And the veil is a manifestation of that fundamentalism." The fact that the term "fundamentalism" is notoriously difficult to define and that many nonviolent Muslim women wear veils raises major questions about exactly what is being "fought" by the law. Indeed, the goal of the ban is broader—to erase cultural practices and whole communities different from the French mainstream. As the political scientist Olivier Roy has written: "Very clearly, everything connected to an open (but not necessarily ostentatious) affirmation of Islam is considered the harbinger of a dangerous fundamentalism." Whether or not the veil portended "a dangerous fundamentalism" mattered little. Critical were the rights of the nation and the majority. In this, French citizens heartily agreed with the prohibition. Public opinion polls showed overwhelming approval, 82 percent, with only 17 percent disapproving, and the ban passed the French Senate by a vote of 246–1 and the National Assembly by 335–1.[23]

Skeptics might claim that the French veil ban is an easy case for finding explosive domestic uses of majority rights, given the unusual French concept of *laïcité*. In fact, however, *laïcité* simply makes the use of rights in France more transparent than in other countries. Similar cultural defense policies have become common in Western liberal democracies and are justified as a way of preserving national identities. But current French debates on these issues are about more than just identity. "National identities" are notoriously difficult to define, making it easy for majorities to assert them against those portrayed as threatening. It is difficult to know which came first: a deep-seated national identity or an apparent threat to it in the form of new migrants.[24] This is particularly true when such rights have explosive effects on minority cultures—and are intended to do so.

The heart of the matter is the conflict between the rights of the nation or the majority and the rights of its own minorities. The French government sees the principles discussed earlier as fundamental to "our society's values," as justice minister Michèle Alliot-Marie stated.[25] This view places a duty on all French citizens to abide by them. In the current historical context, and for a variety of political reasons in France, wearing a veil is seen as rejecting liberty, equality, and fraternity. As a result, the small minority of Muslims who don the full veil must, according to opponents, be punished, even if they wear them voluntarily and declare their support of the nation's abstract values. More generally, opponents of the veil believe that the practice, and the broader submission of women that it supposedly symbolizes, must be abolished.

International Dynamite: Cultural versus LGBT Rights in African Countries

Internationally in recent decades, women's rights, and more recently LGBT rights, have served as explosives.[26] Some of the world's most powerful liberal democracies have used them in this way. Their targets are countries that treat women and minorities poorly, unequally, or violently (although geostrategic allies seldom face strong criticism). Specific policies include the imposition of conditionality by foreign aid donors, as outlined in the introduction of this chapter, and most spectacularly, military actions undertaken by overseas powers in the name of rights.

Are these usages of rights "explosive" in the way that I have defined that term in this chapter? Their most prominent and seemingly sincere goal has been improvement in the plight of neglected, oppressed, or abused populations. Unsurprisingly, however, those who hold authority in target societies reject these rationales as cover for cultural imperialism by the world's most powerful countries. According to these local elites, the real goals are to transform indigenous cultures into dependent imitations of Western ones. More surprisingly, even the "victims" in these societies are divided about the wisdom of using women's and LGBT rights in such ways. By victims I do not mean those who might be too fearful or parochial to voice their true views openly, whether for or against. More tellingly, as we shall see, even many among the educated urban populations, who might seem most receptive to imported liberal rights, view their insertion from the outside as counterproductive and even dangerous.

The African cases that opened this chapter are an important example. As noted previously, these can be seen as cases of mutual dynamiting, situations where opposing forces make rights claims that would result in major change to (if not elimination of) their targets. When African states direct harsh criminal penalties against LGBT populations, they ground these actions in their ostensible right to maintain indigenous cultures and with the open goal of punishing same-sex "amorous relationships," as well as the scarcely concealed aim of eradicating homosexuality in their societies. For their part, Western countries demand that African governments accept LGBT rights. They threaten sanctions and cut development aid unless the African states change their laws, and ultimately their cultures, to accept LGBT people.

It is probably not the overt goal of such intervenors to change traditional cultures writ large. And it may be possible to bring about narrowly targeted change, involving only LGBT rights or even same-sex marriage, while leaving broader cultural practices intact. This is what has occurred in the West recently. Although LGBT rights and same-sex marriage represent real and major change, they have not destroyed broader aspects of society and culture. However, from the standpoint of social conservatives, even in Western countries and certainly in African ones, this is not so apparent. For them, LGBT rights and same-sex marriage not only are products of an already decadent culture but, more worryingly, contribute to further decline. For some, the only option is retreat from a modern Dark Age.[27] For others, the answer is to fight back at home, despite the odds, and to support those in other cultures who have not yet lost the battle, as some among the American Christian Right have done in Africa.

Whatever one thinks of the foregoing views, the conflict over LGBT rights in Africa and worldwide illustrates key aspects of how rights may be used as dynamite. The African countries that have strengthened laws against homosexuality framed these in the language of cultural or majority rights.[28] In promulgating these widely supported laws, the states' goals are explosive, even if only a few politicians or activists openly declare "death to gays." More often, political leaders and leaders of traditionalist civil society organizations avoid such statements but are not shy about stating other goals that will have profound effects on their LGBT targets. Consider the views of Theresa Okafor, the Nigerian leader of the Foundation for African Cultural Heritage and a regular attendee at international conferences on "traditional families." She has agreed that Uganda's law punishing gays and lesbians with a life sentence was "too harsh" and has said that "we love the [homosexual] person but condemn the deed." Yet at the same time, she has demanded that gays and lesbians be "rehabilitated," the goal again being to eliminate homosexuality entirely, albeit nonviolently. The Nigerian law's harsh penalties against LGBT organizations illustrate this further. It is also notable that at the international level, African states, along with other religiously conservative states in the Muslim and Orthodox worlds, have strongly opposed the term "sexual orientation and gender identity" (SOGI). By doing so, they hope to snuff out the very existence of the concept in international law and presumably in their own domestic laws and societies. As Iran's president stated in 2007, "we don't have homosexuals like in [the United States]."[29]

PROMOTING LGBT RIGHTS

With the rise of the LGBT movement and recent acceptance of LGBT rights by many countries in western Europe and the Americas, activists now demand that these states work to protect LGBT populations elsewhere. Increasingly, this encompasses not only calls to end violence and persecution, but also campaigns to bring LGBT rights to the world. The effort at the United Nations has addressed the most basic step: acceptance of the SOGI concept itself. For over a decade, Western nations and allies in NGOs and UN bureaucracies have sought to promote and even discuss SOGI. Like those involved in varied rights struggles before them, these activists seek to portray their rights as universal—or, as one UN report states (in necessarily guarded form about LGBT identities themselves), as having "global resonance." Given the UN's usual method of consensus decision-making, this effort has stalled, primarily because of opposition by socially conservative governments. In other international organizations, however, Western states have been able to act unilaterally. As Rachel Bergenfield and Alice Miller show, from 2011 to 2014, twelve of the world's largest multilateral development donors publicly voiced support for LGBT rights, including in recipient countries, and seven of these integrated LGBT rights or the SOGI concept into their core policies or missions.[30]

In addition, Western states have threatened to make aid to African countries conditional on their eliminating objectionable laws. In some cases, Western states have cut aid in response to harsh anti-LGBT laws. As Prime Minister David Cameron stated in answer to a question about whether the United Kingdom should take a "hard line" on discrimination in Commonwealth nations: "This is something we raise continually and . . . we're also saying that British aid should have more strings attached in terms of . . . do you persecute people for their sexuality? . . . We want to see countries that receive our aid adhering to proper human rights, and that includes how people treat gay and lesbian people. . . . We are saying it is one of the things that will determine our aid policy." Similarly, U.S. Secretary of State John Kerry condemned the Ugandan law, stating: "What is happening in Uganda is atrocious and it presents all of us with an enormous challenge because LGBT rights are human rights and the signing of this anti-homosexuality law is flat out morally wrong."[31] Within months, the United States and other countries cut about $140 million in aid to the country.

DESTROYING AFRICAN CULTURES?

These threats and actions were no doubt motivated by Western states' concerns over beleaguered LGBT communities in African states. Yet things looked different from the perspective of most Nigerians, Ugandans, and citizens of other African countries. LGBT rights, pushed by the world's most powerful states, seemed to menace their countries and cultures. It was not only political leaders who stated this, but also ordinary citizens, among whom belief in homosexuality's immorality was rampant, according to polls. In the international context, the Nigerian state and its citizens viewed themselves as relatively weak, if defiant. As Senate president Mark stated: "If there is any country that wants to stop giving us aid because we want to pass the bill on same-sex that country can go ahead." Nigeria would proceed on its own majority-approved pathway toward criminalizing same-sex marriage and LGBT activism. It would willingly pay the costs of maintaining its homegrown laws and local cultures against what it saw as an assault by Western powers dressed up in rights garb.[32]

But surely Western nations condemning the anti-gay law did not have such far-reaching and oppressive goals in mind? Rather, Western leaders acted for altruistic and defensive purposes: to protect Nigeria's endangered LGBT community. No foreign leaders demanded an end to the nation's culture, anyone's death, or, as some pundits fretted, the continent's recolonization. At most, Westerners were asking Nigeria to reject the marriage prohibition law and reform a small facet of the country's diverse cultures. But from the standpoint of the Nigerians and other Africans facing similar threats, something more ominous was afoot, albeit covertly (as is often the case in international uses of rights as dynamite). African leaders repeatedly denounced conditionality as gutting their nation's sovereign right to make its own laws and follow its own cultural practices. As Ghana's president, John Evans Atta Mills, stated in vowing never to legalize homosexuality: "No one can deny Prime Minister Cameron his right to make policies, take initiatives or make statements that reflect his societal norms and ideals but he does not have the right to direct other sovereign nations as to what they should do especially where their societal norms and ideals are different from those which exist in Prime Minister's society."[33]

In addition, while acknowledging Ghana's receipt of foreign aid, Mills vowed: "We will not accept any aid with strings attached." That, he said, would "worsen our plight as a nation or destroy the very society that we want to use the money to improve." In Uganda, reactions to international criticism similarly focused on majority, sovereign, and cultural rights. As a government-associated media outlet stated during the international controversy over the Anti-Homosexuality bill, if the foreign threats were credited, "Ugandans (read Africans) [would] have no right to discuss and no right to sovereignty. Uganda [would have] no mandate to make choices for its people and no role in shaping its destiny. . . . It would have surrendered [its] right to human rights."[34]

Such statements appear to reflect public attitudes in many African countries. From this perspective, any weakening of laws against homosexuality, particularly in the name of LGBT rights, would undermine the most basic tenets of the continent's traditional societies, with the kind of dire consequences supposedly visible already in Western countries. Western leaders did not openly or perhaps even consciously intend such broad effects. Many Nigerians and citizens of other African countries, however, saw LGBT rights and the practices thereby legalized as threatening to undermine if not destroy their traditional societies—and as intended to do so. At the Senate hearing on the bill, Michael Ekpenyong, secretary general of the Catholic Secretariat of Nigeria, said, "If we accept that two consenting adults can marry, we will soon . . . have to . . . argue whether mother and son, father and daughter are not free to marry." Senate President David Mark spurned "the importation of a foreign culture," stating, "My faith as Christian abhors it. It is incomprehensible to contemplate same sex marriage. I cannot understand it. I cannot be a party to it." In other contexts, African activists such as Theresa Okafor predicted an array of dire consequences. Same-sex marriage was "another ploy to depopulate Africa," an "assault on the family" in which "children are the ones who suffer." If marriage was "deconstructed and fragmented" in this way, it would lead to major societal problems, including divorce, drug abuse, suicide, single-parent pregnancies, and threats to free speech.[35] Put in this chapter's terms, African majorities transformed themselves into potential victims relative to the powerful countries promoting LGBT rights on behalf of a still weaker community.

These views of activists and politicians jibed with popular sentiments. Consider the results of a random national telephone poll of over one thousand Nigerians taken by a Gallup-affiliated survey organization in 2013, shortly after the House of Representatives unanimously passed the bill. The survey, indicating high levels of public awareness about the bill (69 percent), found that 99 percent of Nigerians supported it, 69 percent strongly. On more general issues, 15 percent agreed and 85 percent strongly agreed with the "claim that homosexuality is not part of the culture of Nigerians." Furthermore, 83 percent of Nigerians did not believe that the bill infringed on the rights of LGBT people, with only 4 percent believing that it did. Poll results such as these are obviously susceptible to biases. They are doubtless skewed because of their timing so shortly after the House vote. Nonetheless, they suggest strong public support for the Nigerian government's stance on the law. Similar popular views are common across sub-Saharan Africa, the only notable exception being South Africa, as a 2013 Pew Research Center poll found.[36]

AFRICAN LGBT GROUPS REACT

Given these elite and popular views, there seems little doubt that many in Africa view Western criticisms and conditionality as threatening—as cultural dynamite in the guise of LGBT rights. As further indication of the likely sincerity of these views, consider the reactions of African LGBT groups.

One might think that such organizations would be the most supportive of aid conditionality because their members would have the most to gain from transnational support. LGBT communities were certainly identified as "victims" by the international NGOs, foreign states, and development agencies that promoted these policies and called for immediate adoption of LGBT rights. From an academic standpoint, one might even assume that local activists helped spark the policies through the so-called boomerang pattern—appealing for help to sympathetic foreign activists and governments. None of these assumptions are valid in this case, however, because, as in other international uses of rights as dynamite, many of the "victims" opposed the conditionality policy.

Within weeks of Prime Minister Cameron's statement and in the wake of the Ugandan controversy, dozens of the continent's most important LGBT NGOs and activists issued a statement of "concern about the use of aid conditionality as an incentive for increasing the protection of the rights of LGBTI people."[37] The signatories described themselves as working slowly and cautiously "to entrench LGBTI issues into broader civil society issues, to shift the same-sex sexuality discourse from the morality debate to a human rights debate, and to build relationships with governments for greater protection of LGBTI people." But they expressed skepticism about Western motives, which the African NGOs refused to accept had anything to do with "protect[ing] the rights of LGBTI people." Pointedly, they stressed the "commonly held notion" that "countries like the U.K. will only act when 'their interests' have been threatened." By this, the statement was presumably referring to the possibility that LGBT lobbies in Western countries such as the United Kingdom and the United States influenced their own governments to act, whether through direct lobbying or indirect effects such as politicians' desires to appear sensitive to supporters' concerns. Worse still—and in line with this chapter's conjecture that those using rights as dynamite privilege their own needs over those of the victims they claim to help—Western governments took their actions without "recogniz[ing] the importance of consulting the affected" in African countries. Notably as well for this chapter's perspective, the African NGOs highlighted what they saw as the real basis for the use of LGBT rights against African states: the "disproportionate power dynamics between donor countries and recipients."

Explaining their staunch opposition to the West's use of LGBT rights on their behalf, the African NGOs pointed to the harmful repercussions they would face. First, LGBT people would be hurt by any aid cuts because they were among the most vulnerable of populations whose "access to health and other services are already limited." Second, such threats "create the real risk of a serious backlash." The measures could "exacerbate the environment of intolerance in which [African] political leadership scapegoat LGBTI people . . . to retain and reinforce national state sovereignty." Along the same lines, doing so would feed the "notion that homosexuality is unAfrican and a western-sponsored 'idea.'" Third, the NGOs argued that sanctioning states for violations of LGBT rights would divide LGBT communities from broader civil society groups. Singling out LGBT violations in a context of widespread violations of many other rights would "emphasize the idea that LGBTI rights are special rights and hierarchically more important than other rights." Again, this would undermine the important indigenous tactic of "entrench[ing] LGBTI issues into broader civil society issues." In a similar vein, consider the reactions of a Ugandan LGBT leader after the United States cut $140 million in development aid in 2014: "I'm not an advocate for aid cuts. Neither am I an advocate for bullying. There are so many horrible laws in this country, but to single out, to radically react to the [Anti-Homosexuality Act] is not only patronizing but also further enhances LGBTI persons' vulnerability to both non-state and state-sanctioned homophobia."[38] From this chapter's perspective, all of this describes predictable injuries resulting from outsiders' explosive uses of LGBT rights in African contexts dominated by traditional views.

International Dynamite: Women's Rights and the Afghanistan War

As a final example of rights being used as dynamite, consider the 2001 U.S. invasion of Afghanistan and associated efforts to bring women's rights to the country. The invasion began as a response to 9/11, initially justified as a means of removing a government that had harbored persons responsible for the attacks. However, rationales for the invasion soon began to balloon. Within weeks, the strongest nation in the world started emphasizing the goal of bringing women's rights to one of the world's poorest and weakest countries. It is no doubt true that women's rights served in part as camouflage—to divert attention from the war's huge cost in blood and treasure, as others have noted.[39] More important, however, women's rights were used as a tool to serve three more fundamental purposes. First, it was hoped that they would improve the plight of Afghan women. Officials, contractors, and NGOs explicitly and no doubt in most cases sincerely stressed women's real victimization by the Taliban government. Second, policymakers and activists also, if less openly, envisioned the broader dismantling of traditional Afghan society, with the imposition of women's rights as a catalyst. Women's forceful incorporation into police, government, education, and other institutions would, in this more submerged view, save Afghanistan from itself. Third, women's rights in Afghanistan would improve security for the Western societies that promoted these rights from afar. As this chapter's concept of rights as dynamite would expect, in making this expansive and questionable claim, the powerful foreign purveyors of women's rights transformed themselves into victims. Promoting an idea that has come to be known as the "Hillary Doctrine," they argued that only by bringing women's rights and concomitant liberal ideals to Afghanistan (and presumably the rest of the world) could liberal societies ensure their own national security. To do anything less would subject the world to continuing threats, as exemplified by the 9/11 tragedy.

Within weeks of the war's start in October 2001, women's rights and women's rights organizations were enlisted into the Afghan war, with millions of dollars of development and reconstruction aid to support them. Their deployment on the ground followed years in which the Taliban government had committed significant human rights violations, including abuses against women. At best, one could argue that during its government, from 1996 to 2001, the Taliban had brought a measure of peace and stability to a country that had been torn by decades of war and the severe human rights violations attendant thereto. Weeks after the United States began fighting in Afghanistan, First Lady Laura Bush delivered a national radio address in which she stated that the "brutal oppression of women is a central goal" of al-Qaeda and the Taliban. These groups had imposed "poverty, poor health, and illiteracy" on the country's women, presenting a vision of what they "would like to impose on the rest of us." In Bush's view, therefore, "the fight against terrorism is also a fight for the rights and dignity of women." Similar ideas spanned the political spectrum. In an opinion article in *Time* magazine welcoming the invasion of Afghanistan, Senator Hillary Clinton rejected the view that the United States was engaging in "cultural imperialism, destined to arouse the animosity of Muslims throughout the region." Part of the reason the United States was not doing so and indeed was justified in promoting women's rights, according to Clinton, was simply the right of conquerors: "we, as liberators, have an interest in what follows the Taliban in Afghanistan." Beyond that blunt statement of power, Clinton provided further justification by universalizing U.S. actions. Spreading women's rights was "the right thing to do," and consistent with the "universal values which we have a responsibility to promote throughout the world, and especially in a place like Afghanistan."[40] Left unspoken but implied in this argument, as in other international uses of rights as dynamite, was the necessary concomitant of pushing universal values on the country—the destruction of traditional Afghan cultures primarily through explosive outside intervention rather than gradual indigenous processes.

In addition, for Clinton and other policymakers, promoting women's rights was the "smart" thing to do for U.S. national security. It would help prevent a powerful America from being the future victim of terrorism. To make this point, Clinton posited an "immoral link between the way women were treated by the oppressive Taliban in Afghanistan and the hateful actions of the al-Qaeda terrorists." In this view, mistreatment of women was "an early warning sign of the kind of terrorism that culminated in the attacks of September 11." Conversely, imposing a new regime marked by the "proper treatment of women . . . can be a harbinger of a more peaceful, prosperous and democratic future." A new Afghanistan could "become a symbol for people elsewhere," and America could promote "values that will act like antibodies against the virus of evil that exists in too many hearts around the planet." Notably, Clinton provided no empirical evidence of the "immoral link" between violation of women's rights in Afghanistan, terrorism worldwide, and threats to U.S. national security. However, as secretary of state several years later, while the Afghanistan war festered and the United States "surged" troop levels and assistance for development and rights, she stressed this viewpoint more strongly. "Women's equality is not just a moral issue, it's not just a humanitarian issue, it is not just a fairness issue; it is a security issue. It is a prosperity issue and it is a peace issue . . . in the vital interest of the United States. . . . Give women equal rights, and entire nations are more stable and secure. Deny women equal rights, and the instability of nations is almost certain. The subjugation of women is, therefore, a threat to the common security of our world and to the national security of our country."[41]

Applying the concepts discussed earlier in this chapter, it is important to note that Clinton not only justified the explosive uses of women's rights on the accurate claim that Afghanistan's women had been marginalized and victimized under the Taliban, but also justified America's long-lasting and expensive interventions made partly in the name of women's rights by portraying the United States itself as a victim or potential victim—with women's rights a useful means of reducing the threat. Even if it seems farfetched to believe that the admittedly terrible conditions of women in an impoverished and backward country thousands of miles away could affect the national security of the world's most powerful liberal state, Clinton's subjugation claim made the link. More than that, it offered a new weapon for securing American national security: women's rights abroad.

THE HILLARY DOCTRINE

Although Clinton's 2010 statement provided little in the way of causal mechanisms—or definitions of such vague terms as "subjugation"—policy and academic followers have reiterated her points. Most expansively, former U.S. ambassador to the United Nations Samantha Power has claimed that "it is now objectively the case that our national interests are increasingly affected" by "how people are treated within states." As a result, she asserts, it is "precisely our self-interest that requires us to get better at improving human security in the service of national security." From academe, Valerie Hudson and Patricia Leidl's 2015 book *The Hillary Doctrine* supports a "very aggressive interpretation" of these views. They hold that "if the security of women and the security of states are linked, then the use of force by the international community to protect and liberate women from severe oppression might eventually have a salutary effect on national and international security."[42]

None of these exponents of the "immoral link" between oppression of women and U.S. national security provide a clear model of the causal mechanisms involved, although Hudson and Leidl devote many pages to discussion of a possible association between them.[43] Whatever those mechanisms, ending women's oppression in traditional societies necessarily entails explosive change in the target society and its dominant culture—and, in most cases, in the ruling political structure. However, as expected where rights are used as dynamite across national borders, few foreign activists publicly admit the profundity and comprehensiveness of what they seek, preferring to focus on a positive future to be achieved "eventually" rather than the immediate destruction required to arrive there. In a few cases, however, the veil drops and the explosive aims are revealed. For instance, in a 2013 interview for Hudson and Leidl's book, former Bush administration ambassador to Iraq Ryan Crocker put it bluntly, decrying the Obama administration's peace efforts in Afghanistan at the time: "The forces of darkness are just waiting and . . . they are not just the Taliban, it's the thrust of Afghan society. . . . It is a fundamentally chauvinistic, traditionalist society. And that applies to those who hate the Taliban as well as those who are them." In this view, the rights project is revealed at its most expansive and aggressive: it is Afghan culture, not simply the Taliban government, that must be replaced, with the enforcement of women's rights helping to dismantle it. As Crocker exhorted: "If I hear anymore about ending wars—well, you don't end wars by disengaging. You end wars by prevailing!"[44]

In another striking example, Amnesty International urged NATO to continue fighting in Afghanistan in May 2012. This was eleven years after the invasion of Afghanistan and shortly after President Obama announced plans to withdraw most American forces from the country. At the time, the NATO Summit was being held in Chicago. To counter the withdrawal plan, Amnesty plastered advertisements around the city depicting burqa-clad women and calling on NATO to "keep the progress going!" for "human rights for women and girls in Afghanistan."[45] Such absolutist rhetoric matched that of former first lady Laura Bush, who that same month decried "negotiat[ing] away women's rights" and treating Afghan women "as a bargaining chip." Other proponents of the Hillary Doctrine, such as U.S. representatives Martha Roby and Niki Tsongas, argued that because policies imposed during the U.S. occupation "elevated women's place in Afghan society," the United States could withdraw its forces only "in a responsible way that secures these gains."[46] To do otherwise would be to risk "losing everything," not only women's rights but also their personal security. Having once improved the rights of some Afghan women through years of military intervention and democracy promotion, the progress must be kept going.

For how long? According to Crocker, approvingly quoted by Hudson and Leidl, "if we can buy them another decade, this [progress for women] probably is sustainable on its own momentum. . . . It's up to us. It could go either way, and it's really up to us." As expected with any external effort to topple an existing culture using rights and military force as the means, prospects are uncertain—progress for women is "up to us" and only "probably" sustainable ten years on—even according to true believers. Still, Hudson and Leidl condemned the Obama administration's "unfortunate . . . undermin[ing of] the full implementation of the Hillary Doctrine in Afghanistan," calling it a "betrayal of the women of Afghanistan." They went further, offering a detailed blueprint of what should have been done "if the United States were serious" about implementing the doctrine and supporting Afghan women, in essence adopting Crocker's call for complete dismantling of the "thrust of Afghan society." As one example of the breadth of these goals, consider Hudson and Leidl's own call for externally promoted enlargement of Afghanistan's clan-based society: "It is time to think of woman as an Afghan clan of their own, [with] a right to representation in all councils of the nation."[47]

AFGHAN WOMEN'S RESPONSES

Important Afghan voices opposed these external, rights-based fixes for their society. Of particular relevance to the concepts discussed in this chapter, many of the ostensible "victims," Afghanistan's women, condemned the unintended and harmful effects on women and women's rights. Others raised doubts about the staying power of changes in women's roles forcefully imposed by powerful outsiders in the name of rights.[48]

Before examining that opposition and skepticism, one must acknowledge that some women in Afghanistan's most advanced cities responded favorably to the advent of women's rights. In areas cleared of Taliban control, women's NGOs formed and received foreign funding. New opportunities for education and employment sprang up, particularly in cities. In the American-installed government, the political process was opened to female voting and participation at all levels. There is some evidence that certain programs may have changed at least certain women's attitudes toward their own empowerment.[49] Moreover, leaders of some Afghan women's organizations have welcomed the linkage between war and rights, demanding the former's continuation so that the latter's far-reaching goals may be fully achieved. As Afifa Azim, coordinator of the Afghan Women's Network, has stated, "We all want stability and peace, but not at the price of women's rights. We're told that women's rights are a development issue, not a security issue. But women's rights are part of what the fighting is all about." Similarly, Mary Akrami, director of the Afghan Women Skills Development Centre, argues that "Afghan women have the most to gain from peace and the most to lose from any form of reconciliation [peace process] compromising women's human rights. There cannot be national security without women's security, there can be no peace when women's lives are fraught with violence."[50] As with some of the previously cited statements by American exporters of women's rights, these Afghan women appear to endorse rights' explosive effects, military accompaniment, and predictable harms to women themselves.

For other Afghan women, however, the effects of internationally imposed women's rights are too high for the country and especially its women.

To understand this view, it is first important to note that there was a small, but real, indigenous base for women's rights in the country before the U.S. invasion, including Afghan women's groups that had promoted rights even during the Taliban era. This should come as little surprise given that prior to the Taliban regime, some among Afghanistan's women were highly educated and participating in work and public life. This was true during the Soviet-allied government of the 1980s and in earlier decades as well, at least in certain urban areas. One of the best-known independent civil society groups promoting women's rights is the Revolutionary Association of the Women of Afghanistan (RAWA), founded in 1977. For decades, this group has advocated for women's rights despite strong opposition and in the face of war and violence.[51] Given RAWA's indigenous credentials and long-standing work in Afghanistan, its views of the use of women's rights in the U.S. invasion should be given weight.

For one thing, the women of RAWA and similar groups refuse to see themselves as victims, despite the belief among many in the West that the country's women are, as Afghan critic Spogmai Akseer puts it, "silent and passive victims of their culture, their men and their politics." As noted earlier, such paternalistic foreign views help justify external rights-promotion policies. In this view, local women are too oppressed to help themselves and only forceful foreign intervention can make a difference. Indeed, as former Loya Jirga member Malalai Joya charges, "foreign powers" have "propagated" the view that Afghan women are "merely passive victims" incapable of "standing up for our rights." The reality is far different, however. As Joya has written, in Afghanistan "democratic-minded people have been struggling for human and women's rights for decades. . . . They cannot be imposed by foreign troops." Similarly, RAWA denounces Western-imposed war and rights as interlinked—and as having horrific and indiscriminate consequences in Afghan society. In 2014, for instance, RAWA vehemently denounced the "U.S. and NATO occupiers" for "stag[ing]" the war under the "false and deceptive purposes" of the " 'war against terror', defending human rights, women's rights, and democracy." Furthermore, RAWA vows to continue "fighting against occupation and fundamentalism . . . to annihilate these two notorious enemies. . . . Freedom, democracy, and justice are attainable by the people and not superpowers and foreign countries."[52]

In this, RAWA's quest for an indigenous, Afghan form of women's rights grounded in independence, democracy, and secularism remains central. In its very name, as well as in numerous of its publications, the group acknowledges how revolutionary those goals are. Yet RAWA, like other supposed beneficiaries of foreign military interventions in the name of rights, rejects such outside help because it is counterproductive, a view evidenced by the fact that the group must still work underground in Afghanistan even years after the American intervention. Or as Malalai Joya stated in a 2013 interview: "When we don't have independence, talking about democracy, human rights, and women's rights is just a painful joke. . . . The U.S. is there for their own strategic, regional, and economic interests."[53]

Purveyors of the Hillary Doctrine have stated as much by claiming that the United States should pursue women's rights as much because of the plight of women as because they are needed to secure American national security. Many American officials also appear unwilling to admit the carnage caused by war in the name of rights. For instance, according to Joya, in a 2006 meeting the State Department's senior coordinator for international women's issues refused to listen to Joya's criticisms about the "suffering that the U.S. occupation had wrought in my country." As the Pakistani analyst Rafia Zakariah has written, many ordinary Afghans view American-sponsored women's rights as "female rebellion," imperiling "not just family or tribal honor . . . but also national honor, whose reclamation from the Americans requires even greater control over women. . . . Imperial interventions . . . cannot produce the ground-level moral shifts that must occur within Afghanistan to make its women safe."[54]

In sum, the Afghan case is a key example of rights as dynamite. The United States and its powerful allies used women's rights, along with conventional military power, not only to help women but also, as sometimes openly admitted, to upend traditional Afghan society as a whole. This entailed the identification of victims, especially the country's women. They were indeed oppressed by the Taliban, but they were not consulted about the explosive imposition of "universal" women's rights on their behalf. In addition, the association of women's rights with war was justified by identifying another potential victim of women's suppression: populations in powerful Western countries, based on the novel Hillary Doctrine. Although some Afghan women supported these moves, others opposed them. For groups such as RAWA, the horrendous costs of years of war, even if justified by the plight of women, was indefensible and perverse. As essential as RAWA believed women's rights to be, the group favored indigenously based change to achieve them, rather than dynamite thrown across their borders by outsiders.

Conclusion

There is nothing unique about the cases discussed in this chapter. In many conflicts, rights are similarly used to undermine or even destroy a foe's core institutions and way of life. The key ingredients are substantial power asymmetries that permit such explosive actions, sustained and forceful action by the dominant, and the extension of rights against weaker groups. In domestic settings, majority, sovereign, and states' rights are most commonly used in these ways against vulnerable domestic minorities. France's veil ban and Nigeria's anti-gay laws exemplify these usages. But it is not only such group rights that are used explosively. In contemporary international contexts, individual rights are also used in this way.

Whatever the context, there are recurrent features to the use of rights as dynamite. The powerful portray themselves as under threat from the weak—as victims or potential victims. Outsiders may find this depiction implausible, but it is necessary, particularly in domestic contexts, to justify the forceful measures taken against weak and minority communities. In addition, the powerful find other "victims" on whose behalf they claim to act—groups such as France's veil wearers, Afghanistan's women, or Nigeria's LGBT population. These groups may suffer genuine oppression, but they often reject outsiders' use of rights as dynamite. They also reject their designation as "victims," not only because of their own brave actions at home, but also because they are seldom consulted by outsiders about the wisdom of imposing "universal" rights, with their maximal goals and minimal time frames. Rather, the powerful act alone—or with pliable clients fronting for them—and use rights rhetoric that camouflages their ulterior purposes. In addition, those portrayed as victims of oppression and as beneficiaries of rights fear the explosive consequences of related force and violence. Particularly in international deployments of rights, the supposed beneficiaries may be the first casualties of rights advanced on their behalf.

PART III

Thwarting Third Parties

7

Rights as Blockades

SUPPRESSING SUBORDINATES

Since 2002, Britain's Labour Party has required all-women short lists of candidates for Parliament and other political institutions. Instituted as a matter of women's rights, the rule has significantly boosted female numbers in elective offices. In 2018, however, controversy erupted when the party began allowing transgender candidates—those born biologically male—to self-identify as female for the all-women short lists. Protesting the decision, three hundred members resigned from the party, and ten of them, including a former member of Labour's constitutional committee, issued this statement: "Self-identity, 'I am what I say I am,' reeks of male authority and male supremacy. In contrast, women . . . are rarely listened to, as this very issue demonstrates." As one of the women told the BBC, "Why should we be the ones to give up our space?" Or as others wrote on a GoFundMe page, "Trans representation must not happen at the expense of female candidates and we are furious that we are having to fight another battle for women's representation, just 100 years after the suffragette victories."[1]

Although signatories to the statement claimed to support transgender rights and some even urged a separate Labour Party quota for trans people, they used women's rights as a barrier to protect "our space." Trans women would be blocked from the all-women quotas, with women's rights as the means. Only people born biologically female, they argued, should be allowed to enjoy women's rights and quotas, whatever the gender with which a person later identified.[2] This controversy, in which one group uses rights to block another from enjoying its rights, may seem novel and contemporary. Certainly, the trans movement is recent. But even if little studied, the blockade tactic is a far older and recurrent way in which rights movements interact with third parties.

This chapter first conceptualizes key aspects of the blockade tactic. I then examine a common variant in which a movement that has previously attracted a weak group as a third-party supporter later narrows or *hones* the movement by excluding the group. Next, I look at the use of these tactics in an important historical case, the quest for voting rights in nineteenth-century America. Finally, I analyze the contemporary conflict between women's rights and transgender rights.

Blockade Tactics

Studies of interactions between rights movements and third parties have focused on activists' appeals to elites. Such groups already enjoy the right, hold significant resources, and may therefore vault a movement to victory if they lend support. However, movements may also seek aid from subordinate third parties—those deprived of the same or similar rights but distinguished from the original movement's constituents by other characteristics. Even though such marginal groups may not hold significant material resources, they may be large in number or avid for activism. For their part, subaltern groups may join the movement spontaneously, believing that its success will conduce to their own benefit. If the movement triumphs, they assume, their members will receive the same rights demanded by the original movement.

DEFINITION AND PURPOSES

But there is another way in which movements may treat other subordinate groups. Far from reaching out, movements may use rights as blockades against the weak to advance their own interests alone. Britain's feminist Labourites did just that in rejecting trans candidates for the all-women short lists. Scrambling to hold on to their own rights and quotas, they refused to share them even with another subordinate group that claimed to be women too. In other cases of blockading, a movement may forge an alliance with power-holders against another subordinate group. Such alliances are formed even when both the movement and the other needy group seek the same right. Movements that engage in this tactic offer a deal to their powerful foes: grant us, and us alone, rights to help keep the other subordinate down. If the power-holder fears or reviles the third party more than the rights movement, it may accept the movement's offer.

Most rights movements are not above using their rights claims against other weak groups to advance their own interests, at least under certain circumstances. True, idealistic adherents may refuse to go along and urge a wide tent. In the Labour Party case, only three hundred out of about fifty thousand members resigned. But the controversy received major coverage in the press and is part of a bigger conflict between wings of the women's rights and transgender rights movements. For strategically minded leaders of rights movements, achieving their own group's cherished goals is paramount, even if doing so redounds to the detriment of other outcast groups.

INTERSECTIONALITY OR DIVISIONALITY?

When are rights used as blockades? Movements are most likely to resort to such tactics in societies where several distinct groups lack the same or similar rights. The groups may be separated on any number of grounds: ethnicity, class, religion, or sex, for instance. Often they are also ranked in a hierarchy of status. When rights movements form, the substantive good provided by the right is therefore scarce, creating the potential for competition among deprived groups for the right and its underlying benefit.

Despite this potentially competitive context, discrete communities may sometimes join together to form a single movement, seeking the right for all. Broad-based civil rights or nationalist movements exemplify this possibility. "Intersectionality"—banding together against powerful oppressors—has become a watchword among marginal groups (or at least among the academics who study them). However, a politics of "divisionality" is equally possible, as the blockade tactic suggests. Movements most frequently form around preexisting institutions and identities that are strongest within one of a coalition's communities.[3] The rise of separate movements (or movement organizations) rooted in each of the member communities may be the result, even if all lack the same or similar rights. In such cases, each movement faces a choice about how to address similarly disenfranchised parties: ignore, include, or blockade them.

Because movements look ceaselessly for ways to advance their causes, the first of these possibilities is rare. Which of the two remaining options a movement chooses will hinge most importantly on its leaders' view of how likely it is to succeed in the fight for rights against its main adversary.[4] If leaders believe that the movement can achieve its rights relatively easily, they are more likely to tolerate other marginalized groups joining with the movement and may even encourage them to do so. The result is then likely to be a cross-community movement. By contrast, if leaders believe that the movement's chances of success are smaller, they will be warier of allying with other subordinate groups, even when they come bearing gifts of support. On the one hand, subordinate allies may provide material assistance to the movement, perhaps because they are large in number, even if not in resources. Some such allies may help psychologically, by showing constituents that they are not alone. On the other hand, support from other subordinate groups always carries risks. Among movement constituents, association with another subordinate group may undermine morale, particularly if that group is despised, not only by the common foe, but even by the movement's own members. In addition, accepting help from a reviled minority might harden the attitudes of a movement's enemies, making it even more difficult for the movement to gain its rights. Under such circumstances, the movement may reject the other subordinate group's offer of support, especially if that group is small in number or lacking in resources.

When deciding whether to align with or blockade against another marginalized group, a movement uses a calculus not directly based on social, economic, or ideological distance between it and the other subordinate, nor on the warmth of their historical relationships. Such factors play a role, but in the end movement leaders are hard-nosed. They will overlook major differences with other excluded groups when forming an alliance—and will amplify minor differences when proposing a blockade.[5] What matters most is how each alternative affects the movement's quest for its rights. When allying, groups of varied classes, beliefs, or ethnicities come together, collectively seeking one right, sometimes dissolving their differences into a single overarching, if tenuous, identity. Anticolonial movements in countries such as Nigeria played down deep-rooted ethnic and religious differences among their constituents when seeking self-determination for the country. Contrariwise, as we shall see in the empirical section of this chapter, movement leaders may rebuff or blockade a willing subordinate group if its aid appears counterproductive. To justify its rejection of the other group, the movement may then stress or exaggerate differences from the group. Doing so can make the movement more appealing to a power-holder with whom the movement seeks to form an alliance. If the tactic is successful, the movement gains its rights from the power-holder and in the process checks a mutually abhorred subordinate's own quest for rights.

BLOCKADE BUILDERS AND SUBORDINATE GROUPS

Which movements are most likely to use a blockade tactic? One might assume that the tactic is most common among movements whose members share certain identities with their oppressors, such as ethnicity, culture, or religion. Alternatively, one might suppose that a history of antipathy pitting members of the rights movement against the other excluded group will lead activists to raise barriers against that group. These factors undoubtedly play a role, but they are secondary, serving as post hoc rationales for decisions motivated by the movement's quest to achieve its desired rights and their substantive ends. Such strategic motivations are shared by all movements, meaning that there is no a priori way of identifying those that will use the blockade tactic. Any movement may exclude other subordinate groups if it believes that this move is necessary to achieve its own rights.

Similarly, one cannot identify a priori the types of subordinate groups that will bear the brunt of blockading. One might suppose that these groups are found at the very bottom of the social hierarchy, and that they face disdain, discrimination, and repression from all other groups. Such factors undoubtedly increase vulnerability to being blockaded, but more important is the political calculus outlined here.

OVERT OR COVERT BLOCKADES?

In the contemporary world, where norms of equality and democracy are pervasive, movements seldom openly acknowledge blockading another needy group. Rather, movements portray their actions as necessary for the achievement of their own rights, downplaying any related handicaps imposed on others. Less extreme forms of blockading, such as simply refusing to aid a subordinate group in its parallel quest for rights, are more frequently used in the open. Even then, however, contemporary movements are unlikely to flaunt such tactics, preferring instead to project an image of fellow-feeling. In earlier eras when equality norms were less prevalent, movements seeking rights had fewer compunctions. They would more openly urge power-holders to grant "our" rights alone—or use a grant of such rights to weaken or block a mutual enemy's claims. As a result, it is probably easier to find overt instances of rights blockading in the past than the present.

PERMEABLE AND IMPERMEABLE BARRIERS

Which rights are most likely to be used as blockades? As with any effort to prevent another group from advancing, the most effective barriers are the highest or least pregnable—rights that the inferior will have little possibility of jumping or breaching. Rights based on permanent or inherent characteristics work best for this purpose. Rights to which the inferior group or even a portion of the inferior group might gain access, by contrast, form weaker barriers. To put this in specific terms, broad-based civil rights, such as the right to expression or association, make poor barriers because all can access them. Rights based on property holdings are more promising because in many societies, particularly in the past, the difficulty of accumulating wealth raised a formidable hurdle. The rights of groups defined by ethnicity, national origin, or sex function even better as full blockades because these characteristics are not easily changed, even if the boundaries between certain groups may be unclear.

Notably, movements using blockades sometimes prefer erecting lower, rather than higher, walls against another subordinate group. Movement leaders may believe that once members of the out-group obtain a certain characteristic, they will be similar enough to movement members to be acceptable or to be trusted with the right. Historically, this has sometimes been the case with voting rights, which were long keyed to property ownership, a status difficult but not impossible for the propertyless to gain. As another example, consider women's rights, a major aim of which is improving and eventually attaining equality between the sexes in key political, economic, and social arenas. One way of reaching this goal has been the creation of impermeable barriers to men in certain spheres. For instance, in the United States, federal Title IX policies helped create equal but separate spheres for activities such as college sports. In the United Kingdom, all-women short lists did something similar for Labour Party candidates for political offices. With the rise of the trans movement, however, some in the women's movement have recently embraced the lowering of what was once seen as an insurmountable biological barrier, by accepting trans women as women. Others in the women's movement, such as the ex-Labourites discussed in this chapter's introduction, seek to maintain and enforce women's rights as a barrier—by excluding trans women from women's spaces and from recognition as women at all.

To specify one assumption of the foregoing discussion: leaders have some degree of choice in deciding how they will characterize and identify a movement. Of course, there are limits to this malleability—most importantly, the attitudes and identity of the movement's core constituency. Still, in certain circumstances, leaders of an ethnic movement may reframe it as multiethnic or as a broad national or civil rights movement. On the other hand, leaders may prefer to portray the movement more narrowly, or they may face strong incentives to do so because rival leaders engage in ethnic outbidding, denouncing them as sellouts for seeking to work with others.[6] With this assumption in mind, one can hypothesize that the right chosen as a blockade depends chiefly on the goals of the movement that is considering the tactic. If movement leaders believe that they are most likely to achieve their goals through permanent exclusion of the other subordinate group, they will use a right related to an immutable characteristic that they possess and the other group does not. On the other hand, if leaders believe that only short-term exclusion is required to reach their goals, they are less likely to choose such a characteristic and more likely to choose an alterable one.

BLOCKADING TO SUCCESS

When is a rights movement's offer of a blockade strategy against a fellow subordinate group likely to be accepted by the powerful foe that currently represses both groups? Initially, it must be stressed that a movement's offer to blockade another excluded group represents a boon to the power-holder. Indeed, following divide-and-rule tactics, the latter may well have played a role in inflaming enmity between the groups, perhaps by favoring one of the groups, even if not giving it full rights. Following this logic, a power-holder is most likely to accept a movement offering a blockade strategy if it believes that such an alliance is needed to preserve its own position or otherwise advance its agenda. If, on the other hand, it can preserve this status alone, it will be more likely to refuse the offer. In making this assessment, the power-holder gives significant weight to the social distance between itself and the movement, especially to preexisting prejudices against the movement's members, because the power-holder, unlike the movement, has greater room for choice. It has the power and therefore the luxury to indulge its prejudices against the weaker group, rebuffing its advances. Moreover, it may believe that allying with one subordinate, even against another, is beneath its dignity or creates too great an association with a group it still shuns. In the end, those in positions of power look to their own interests, both material and status, in deciding whether the blockade offered by a subordinate group is worth accepting.

HONING

A common variant of the blockade tactic occurs when a movement that formerly included a subordinate group as an ally later sheds it as a means of advancing or prioritizing its own rights at the expense of this third party. I call this variant "honing," because it involves the narrowing of a movement, followed in some cases by the movement's raising a blockade against its erstwhile ally.

How does honing work? To begin, it is important to recapitulate that, early in their development, movements often proclaim their rights to be human, universal, apolitical, and absolute, hoping to attract all who feel deprived. Eager to secure their own rights, as apparently promised by a movement's high-flown rhetoric, other subordinate groups may join the movement spontaneously. However, just because a movement once offered abstract rights to all does not mean it will share them when victory appears to hang in the balance. Rather, its leaders may apply their new rights more narrowly than earlier rhetoric suggested, abruptly claiming to cover only their own group. Honing embodies this phenomenon. It restricts rights, as actually implemented, to the movement's core constituency, leaving one-time subaltern allies to fend for themselves.

In the most extreme forms, honing involves a complete turnabout. A movement that had formerly welcomed another subordinate group now uses its newfound rights to repress it, in conjunction with its former foe. In honing's lesser forms, one movement is subordinated within another, more powerful one, either explicitly or tacitly. Calls for "unity" around a particular right may lead to neglect of other rights. The dominant movement may downplay the role of other groups, even if their constituency is also needy. As a small-scale example, consider controversies among participants in the Women's March on Washington (first called the Million Women March) held after Donald Trump's 2017 presidential inauguration. The march was organized by women who had been part of an ideologically diverse opposition to Trump during the campaign. Top organizers most feared that hard-won rights such as abortion would be lost under the new president, leading them to exclude a small but vocal number of anti-Trump women who opposed abortion. In addition, the march generated controversy among black activists who had formed part of the loose-knit anti-Trump coalition. They charged that the focus on women blotted out concern for the rights of minorities. Although organizers quickly moved to change that impression, the perception that the march for women's rights neglected minority rights created deep rifts in the newly formed coalition.[7]

Why hone? As conflict reaches its denouement, the movement's core group may see advantages to sacrificing one of its allies for the success of the struggle. Honing can reassure the movement's foe that its aims are more moderate than previously believed: even the movement now recognizes who or what remains beyond the pale. By removing an inconvenient ally from impending rights protection, the movement makes it more likely that members of the powerful opponent will accept it. For example, in the 1990s, as LGBT rights moved from the fringe toward the center of politics in the United States, certain longtime supporters became liabilities. In particular, the core of the movement publicly ejected groups that promoted pedophilia, hoping thereby to make itself more acceptable to mainstream America.[8]

From the standpoint of the movement, there is another reason to hone newly won rights narrowly: doing so burnishes its constituents' novel and hard-won status. Constituents may bask in the notion that they have attained righteous glory because they truly deserve it. By contrast, rights may lose their symbolic value if shared too broadly with hangers-on to the movement. Pleasant feelings of distinctive worthiness dissolve if "our" rights are granted to hands too alien, too grubby, or too many. In addition, in the wrong hands, rights can be turned against their original bearers, undermining the movement's interests. In early American history, as Rogers M. Smith has argued, many of those who had just won their rights quickly moved to restrict their reach, despite the expansive words of the newly instituted national and state constitutions. Although imbued with liberal ideas for themselves, powerful political leaders used civic republicanism and Anglo-Saxon ethnocentrism to argue that only white male property-holders had sufficient civic virtue, cultural understanding, and moral purity to be trusted with full citizenship rights.[9]

For new rights-holders at any historical moment, the demands of "inferiors" have been a constant worry. The latter may use the lately successful movement as a model to build another one out of their own organizations, grievances, and rights claims. But copycat movements with the temerity to loft their own rights banners too soon can be problematic for new rights-holders. Insecure about their novel status because of their own recent oppression, they remain vigilant that their efforts to overturn the old order do not go too far. They protect their own interests and self-conception against the churlish claims of the hoi polloi. Failing to do so can threaten the new rights-holder psychologically and materially.

Honing's how-tos. Honing of rights occurs in a number of ways. As the fight for rights reaches its climax, leaders of the core group within the movement may come to believe that seeking to achieve rights for all will mean failure for all, whereas seeking them only for its own group offers better chances of success. In such cases, movements that had previously welcomed all comers may suddenly begin emphasizing differences within the movement or urging certain allies to "wait your turn." That admonition might seem a minor matter of timing, but many times such a move can have lasting effects. Opportune moments for major political change, the product of long-term struggle and pressure, are rare. If one group alone gains its rights, the moment may pass for others. Of course, it is never possible for leaders to know with certainty how much they can gain at a particular time and for how many groups within the broad movement. The issue is always a matter of debate among activists, who must make decisions in real time (as well as among scholars later). In the heat of conflict, therefore, movement leaders may take what they think they can attain for their core constituency alone, leaving onetime allies behind.

A less obvious but equally potent approach to honing is to claim that one segment of a more narrowly based movement is not, after all, part of it. If classification as a group member is necessary for access to certain rights, then reclassifying a segment as something other than the preferred group will effectively hone the right. In ethnically plural societies such as Malaysia, Nigeria, and Fiji, for instance, "indigenous" groups receive rights that "migrants" do not, even when the latter are fellow citizens or have lived in a territory for generations. These may include rights to hold political office, to own land, or even to remain within a region. In Nigeria, citizens who lack a government-issued certificate of indigeneity from their state may lose their rights to schooling, jobs, or land—a major deprivation in a poor country with limited opportunities. On the other hand, depriving such groups benefits the indigenes, who then have greater access to scarce goods. As one final example, the Indian government has developed an elaborate system of "reservations" for public university seats, government jobs, and political offices for members of "backward classes." Originally, these preferences were intended for Untouchables and tribal peoples, designated as scheduled castes (SCs) and scheduled tribes (STs). These groups had faced generations of poverty, ostracism, and victimization under the Hindu caste system. For much of its post-independence history, however, India's economy, with limited opportunities for education and employment, grew slowly, leading to resentments and violence by groups excluded from such benefits. To gain them, these groups began calling themselves "other backward classes" (OBCs) and eventually won special rights for themselves as well. Conflict over which castes, subcastes, or even individuals are classified as OBCs or SC/STs remains important in Indian politics today.[10] In sum, in all three of these countries, certain citizens of a single polity face honing of their rights that deprives them of valuable opportunities.

Honed away. What of the individuals and groups that face such exclusion? Much like a "mark" in a confidence game, as described by the sociologist Erving Goffman in a classic article, excluded subordinate groups are understandably frustrated and angered by the reversal involved in honing. Why should they be omitted from the rights they helped achieve through their joining and suffering with the movement? Having been offered a vision of universal, absolute, and apolitical rights, why should they accept further subordination, least of all by false friends? In response, as Goffman hypothesizes, the winning movement may need to "cool out the mark" by offering it something real, even if not the rights it thought it would receive. Even then, the honed group may use its dashed expectations and fresh humiliations to form a new rights movement—against the erstwhile allies that so recently betrayed it. As Goffman writes: "A social stratum that has lost its status may decide to create its own social system [or its] own splinter group."[11]

Overseas supporters may be shocked by a movement's honing as well. Viewing the movement from afar, these international allies form an idealized vision of its expansiveness and probity, based on historical ignorance or naive acceptance of the movement's earlier inspiring rhetoric. Outsiders, however, do not feel the sting of exclusion. Thus, they are often divided over whether they should push their long-standing ally to be more inclusive or accept its rationalizations for honing. Consider Aung San Suu Kyi, leader of the Burmese democracy movement. After decades of internationally supported prodemocracy activism, her movement succeeded in reducing the power of the army, and for her courageous efforts, she won the Nobel Peace Prize. However, soon after a new and more democratic government took office, with Suu Kyu as chief councilor, it turned indifferent or worse to attacks on the Muslim Rohingya minority in western regions of the country.

Thousands of Rohingya were massacred by Buddhist extremists, government forces, and paramilitaries, and tens of thousands more were forced to flee. Yet Suu Kyi remained quiet as claims were made that the Rohingya were not citizens of the country, or did not even exist as an ethnic group, to justify their exclusion by violence from the people's newly won rights. Many in the transnational Burmese solidarity movement, previously little aware of the Rohingya or of the frequency of honing in rights movements, were shocked at the actions and inactions of a longtime darling of the human rights movement. In response, some overseas supporters deferred to the apparent political needs of the new government. Others pushed Suu Kyi to either end the honing and take a stand for the Rohingya or give up her medal. South Africa's Archbishop Desmond Tutu expressed both attitudes in an open letter to his "dearly beloved younger sister" and fellow Nobel laureate. He hailed her as once "symbolizing righteousness" and called on her to "allay our concerns about the violence" against the Rohingya. With renewed reports of horrific crimes against these people, he wrote, "it is incongruous for a symbol of righteousness to lead such a country. . . . If the political price of your ascension to the highest office in Myanmar is your silence, the price is surely too steep." He urged her to "speak out for justice, human rights, and the unity of your people," even as others called for her to be stripped of her medal.[12]

Before leaving this discussion of honing, it is important to note that many subordinate groups have the insight, the experience, and sometimes the leverage to recognize and parry the threat of honing, thus avoiding the fate of a Goffmanian "mark." They know from long, hard experience that movement activists who suddenly mouth universalist language in an ongoing conflict may not follow through later on. Alert to the peril, they demand guarantees against honing, or at minimum some lesser but still significant right. As one example of such preemptive action, consider India's Untouchables in the years leading up to independence, when the Indian National Congress was led by upper-caste Hindus. After being radically excluded from Indian society for generations, Untouchables demanded separate electorates for themselves, which would have allowed them to choose their own parliamentary representatives independent of other Indians. For Congress leaders, this posed a major threat to the independence movement and, in Mahatma Gandhi's eyes, to the unity of Hindu society itself. To counter this threat, Gandhi fasted near to death against the proposal in 1932. Under enormous pressure, Untouchable leader B. R. Ambedkar backed down and accepted a lesser but still important concession in the Poona Pact: reserved seats for Untouchables in the national parliament, a precursor of reservations in many other aspects of society. This key moment in the Indian independence struggle, when the rights of various subordinate groups were pitted against one another, shows the lengths to which those chastened by exclusion will go to guard against honing. In the event, the reservations system has not eliminated abuses against Untouchables, and it has led to struggle with the OBCs for rights and reservations, but it has probably helped avert more extreme marginalization.[13]

Voting Rights in Nineteenth-Century America

The history of voting rights movements in the nineteenth-century United States presents a number of important blockading and honing cases.[14] The social context made such tactics likely: it was a highly unequal society in which a number of disfranchised groups struggled against power-holders— and each other—to gain voting rights. This section of the chapter focuses on three subordinate groups: those without significant property (non-freeholders), African Americans, and women.

In 1790, historians estimate, only about 30 to 35 percent of the adult white population had the right to vote. They were primarily male landowners; women and non-freeholders were generally excluded. The exclusion of African Americans and Indians reduced the percentage of adults eligible for voting still further, although the population of these groups is less clear.[15] (Voting rights were a matter of state law at the time.) In this context, movements for the vote among non-freeholders, blacks, and women developed in the early decades of the nineteenth century. However, rather than rising together for the common goal of universal adult suffrage, these groups responded to their shared deprivation in a piecemeal and even antagonistic manner. Although the abstract concept of voting rights was occasionally voiced in universalistic language, and although the practical idea of universal suffrage was sometimes pursued, the dominant trend, particularly at the most critical moments, was for each group to pursue its own particularistic goal—securing the vote for its group alone. Indeed, as they struggled against the entrenched political elite of white male property owners, these groups used their own claims to block those of the other subordinate groups. Political necessity, reinforced by prejudice, drove them to do so. At times, elites used divide-and-rule tactics to exacerbate preexisting tensions between the groups. This historical case helps tease out the key factors involved in honing and blockade tactics. It highlights in particular this chapter's core hypothesis that a movement's shifting perceptions about its own prospects and its foe's vulnerabilities affect the way it uses these tactics.

ENDING PROPERTY TESTS, RAISING RACIAL BARRIERS

In the first decades of American independence, voting in the United States was largely confined to white men of significant property. This was in keeping with the views of Founding Fathers such as James Madison, who, as Alexander Keyssar summarizes, saw property qualifications as a "bulwark against the landless proletariat of an industrial future." From about 1790 to 1840, those excluded from the vote on this basis repeatedly petitioned state legislatures for an end to or reduction in property qualifications. For the most part, however, these loose-knit, state-based movements sought only white manhood suffrage. Women of all races were excluded from the voting rights movements, and especially in the South the movements promoted white male voting rights as a blockade against black men.

Before examining this example of one disfranchised group using its own rights claims to block the claims of other disfranchised groups, it is useful to understand the arguments that this narrow movement faced from its main foe: propertied men holding the vote. Two points dominated the views of men such as Madison. First, they believed that men without property lacked the autonomy and judgment necessary to exercise voting rights. Their ballots would be bought by employers, landowners, oligarchs, or demagogues, corrupting the political process. Second, and contradictorily, defenders of property qualifications, such as New York chief justice Ambrose Spencer, held that the propertyless might be *too* autonomous and would therefore "vote taxes with much less caution and care [than the propertied because] they do not expect themselves to pay any part." Spencer claimed that only property-holders had a sense of the common good, respect for limited government, and "that attachment to the preservation of all rights incident of real estate." The only way to preserve society and property was therefore to block the propertyless from the franchise. In this, Spencer was much like his Whig predecessors in England. As the historian Michael Kammen puts it, when "mainstream Whigs spoke of defending the liberties of the people, they invariably meant protecting the privileges of men of substance. . . . The measure of an individual's right to participate in the political process . . . was his possession of real estate (and not just movable goods)."[16]

This barrier was not impermeable, however, even if penetrating it was not easy at the time. If a man—in most states, a white man—gained sufficient property, the vote would be his. Notably, however, the property barrier's permeability only reinforced the blockade against the remaining property-less. The expectation was that when a poor man obtained enough property to vote, he would be transformed. He would attain enough sense and stake in society that, in Spencer's words, he would "exercise this important privilege in a manner compatible with the interests of society itself."[17] The relative openness of the property qualification also had an element of "cooling out" the propertyless, or at least industrious members of the group. With enough work and saving, they could secure not only property but also the vote. By gradually and judiciously increasing the ranks of the franchised, this real but permeable barrier would be strengthened against the remaining propertyless and other disfranchised groups.

For the most part, however, this cooling-out effort was not enough to keep the propertyless from seeking an unqualified vote immediately. With rapid urbanization in the early nineteenth century, the numbers of the propertyless swelled. Unwilling to wait for their own possible enrichment to receive the franchise, many mobilized for the vote in loose-knit, state-based, and narrow movements that blockaded other disfranchised groups. In 1829, for example, the non-freeholders of Richmond, Virginia, decried the "odious distinction between members of the same community" that "ignominiously [drove] them from the polls, in time of peace," but "summoned them, in war, to the battlefield." Importantly, however, these white male non-freeholders, like others nationwide, honed their movement narrowly and only for themselves. Carefully couching the vote as a "social" rather than "natural" right, they stressed that their demand excluded, "for obvious reasons, by almost universal consent, women and children, aliens and slaves."[18]

As this quotation should make clear, an expansive voting rights movement was not unthinkable at the time. In some states, black freedmen of property did have voting rights, and in at least one state, New Jersey, so did women (until 1807). Despite these exceptions, and despite the greater mass of supporters that a movement for universal suffrage might have generated, most state-based movements against property qualifications framed their demands in limited terms that usually covered only white males. As Keyssar notes, most white men who fought against property qualifications "feared the universalist implications of natural rights claims" and opposed voting by other excluded groups. This stance was rooted in part in deep-seated beliefs that those groups, especially women and African Americans, did not have the capacity for voting, although the fact that certain states had allowed both groups to vote without incident demonstrated the baselessness of this claim. In addition, this was a decision grounded in the logic of using rights as blockades. Non-freeholders believed that opening their movement would hurt its chances of success given the "almost universal consent" against including women and blacks. By limiting the breadth of their arguments, they hoped that propertied power-holders would accept them. In some cases, they actively promoted their rights to property owners as a barrier against those of the other disfranchised groups. Particularly in the South, white male suffrage was presented as a means of creating "white solidarity" and strengthening state militias against the possibility of slave revolts.[19]

In the North, there was a similar dynamic. Demands for an end to property qualifications often excluded black freedmen or proposed different standards for them than for white men. In the face of such blockading, abolitionists would at times oppose an end to property qualifications for voting. In 1842, for instance, the most powerful abolitionist organization, the American Anti-Slavery Society (AASS), unsuccessfully fought a law abolishing Rhode Island's property qualifications for white men. In abolitionists' view, this law, and others like it nationwide, would unite all white men and obstruct black progress, creating what they later called an "aristocracy of race." As one scholar has observed of arguments simultaneously made in this period against property qualifications and for enfranchisement of white males only, rights arguments are "not always the language of greater empowerment and inclusion [but] can be the language of exclusion as well."[20]

ABOLITION, BLACK SUFFRAGE, AND WOMAN SUFFRAGE

By the mid-nineteenth century, white male suffrage had triumphed in part because of the movement's strategic use of the blockade argument. According to C. Vann Woodward, "the advance of universal white manhood suffrage in the Jacksonian period [was] accompanied by Negro disfranchisement."[21] Only in a few states could black men vote on the same basis as whites, and in others, such as New York, property qualifications were maintained for blacks, even as they fell for white men. An effect and intent of those pressing for the expansion of voting rights to the unpropertied was to hurt the cause of abolition and block that of black suffrage. Meanwhile, women remained almost completely disfranchised, although they did not face the hostility and violence directed at blacks.

In this period, distinct movements for black suffrage and woman suffrage began to develop, at first primarily within the abolition movement. However, for the AASS, which had been active since 1833, enfranchisement of blacks, and even more so of women, was a secondary issue, notwithstanding the group's opposition to the 1842 Rhode Island law noted earlier. Particularly for white abolitionists, ending slavery, not post-slavery rights, was paramount. By contrast, free black activists in the North, who personally faced discrimination and disfranchisement, began to think more broadly about the issues. In the 1830s, these freedmen began to meet on their own in "colored conventions."[22] These formed the basis for a broader negro rights movement seeking goals beyond ending slavery—most importantly, voting rights. In this decade as well, women such as Susan B. Anthony and Elizabeth Cady Stanton became important within the abolition movement, and some began promoting women's rights, especially the franchise.

Until the end of the Civil War, however, the nascent movements for black rights and women's rights were dwarfed by abolitionism in terms of both membership and resources. As Faye Dudden writes, the two new movements were "positioned as supplicants for crumbs from the table of white abolition."[23] In this difficult context, tensions with abolitionist leaders ran high, with some abolitionists urging that the movement remain narrowly focused on ending slavery. For instance, in 1840 the AASS split in part over the "woman question." Making a strategic calculation emblematic of the honing tactic, conservative opponents of including woman suffrage in the abolitionist movement, such as AASS cofounder Elizur Wright, argued that in the difficult political climate abolition faced, it "is downright nonsense to suppose that the anti-slavery cause can be carried forward with forty incongruous things tacked on to it. You can't drive a three-tined fork through a hay mow, [but] you can drive in the handle."[24] In this view, women might be encouraged to participate in the movement, but only in the background, where their activism would not alienate potential allies, and only in support of abolition, not simultaneously for their "incongruous" vote. However, at this time (although not later, as we shall see), leading abolitionists such as William Garrison and Wendell Phillips believed that promoting woman suffrage as a secondary goal and employing women in the movement would not hurt abolition. Indeed, they saw talented women such as Stanton and Anthony as assets to the abolitionist cause. On the other hand, opponents who thought inclusion of women and women's rights "nonsense" left the AASS to continue a narrower fight for abolition alone.[25]

Despite this fracturing, the AASS remained the most powerful abolition-ist organization, and the much weaker woman and black suffrage move-ments worked for the most part within it until the end of the Civil War. In part because of their precarious situation, neither movement permanently embraced a joint strategy to achieve universal voting rights, nor did the AASS itself. Relations among the three movements were sometimes cordial and cooperative; Frederick Douglass in particular maintained good relations with all of them.[26] Just as commonly, however, the movements for woman and black suffrage worked apart and even antagonistically. Particularly as resources and political opportunities contracted in the 1850s and 1860s, the two movements honed their rights claims narrowly. They also used their own claims sometimes in efforts to block those of the other, even though they shared the common goal of enfranchisement, had substantial overlap-ping constituencies embodied in the persons of black women, and operated largely within the umbrella of the abolition movement until the 1860s.

Although a complete analysis of relations among the three movements is beyond the scope of this book, a brief account helps illustrate this chap-ter's analytic points about the blockade and honing tactics. In 1840, as we have seen, the AASS accepted the push for women's rights and the critical support of women for the antislavery cause. Similarly, the nascent move-ment for black enfranchisement at first worked together with the early women's suffrage movement. The 1848 black convention in Cleveland de-clared, "We believe fully in the equality of the sexes," and proclaimed "three cheers for women's rights."[27] That same year, at the Seneca Falls Conven-tion, Frederick Douglass worked with Elizabeth Cady Stanton to win ap-proval of a demand for female suffrage.

Prospects for slave emancipation dimmed, however, with passage of the Fugitive Slave Law in 1850 and the Supreme Court's *Dred Scott* decision in 1857. In these harsher conditions, as Dudden concludes, black conventions, if not yet the AASS, came to see "women's rights as an unaffordable luxury, a separate cause that had no place on their agenda."[28] Thereafter, black con-ventions for the most part promoted voting rights only for black men, not for women. When the prospects for black male enfranchisement seemed dimmest, this honing tactic reached its height.

For their part, leading women's rights advocates engaged in blockade tactics against black men in the pre–Civil War era, owing in part to the rac-ism, common in the day, that infected many women despite their member-ship in the abolition movement. In addition, at critical moments leaders of the women's movement purposefully torpedoed the idea of black enfranchisement to advance their overriding goal of woman suffrage. Stanton was the best-known practitioner of this opportunistic and instrumental approach, but many others, such as Anthony, did so as well. Despite a personal friendship with Frederick Douglass, Stanton often maligned black men when she demanded votes for women. In an 1854 address to the New York State legislature, for instance, she sought to promote woman suffrage at the expense of black men: "We [women] are moral, virtuous, intelligent, and in all respects quite equal to the white man, yet by your laws we are classed with idiots, lunatics, and negroes."[29] In 1860, she again addressed the legislature, arguing that both women and black men were unjustly deprived of their rights and that granting them both the franchise would not harm the rights of white men. However, she also suggested that women were more deserving of the ballot because the "prejudice against sex is more deeply rooted and more unreasonably maintained than that against color."[30] She railed against the fact that educated women were deprived of the vote whereas uneducated men, whether ex-slaves or new immigrants, could vote.

In the crucible of the Civil War, the black and woman suffrage movements for the most part worked together under the aegis of the abolition movement in support of the Northern war effort. For instance, Stanton and Anthony joined other abolitionists in vigorously pressuring a reluctant President Abraham Lincoln to emancipate the slaves. He finally did this in the 1863 Emancipation Proclamation, which was followed in 1865 by the Thirteenth Amendment abolishing slavery. Believing strongly in abolition, they also took this position because they hoped that women would benefit in the postwar era, when the rights of free persons, both men and women, would need to be redefined.[31]

HONING WOMEN'S RIGHTS IN THE "NEGRO'S HOUR"

As the war ended, however, the prospects for black suffrage suddenly appeared uncertain. Congress and a newly installed president, Tennessean Andrew Johnson, were anxious to reintegrate the South as soon as possible and on favorable terms. The AASS, which since 1840 had accepted women's rights and benefited greatly from the energy of female abolitionists, concluded that now all its efforts must go to securing black suffrage. In May 1865, AASS leader Wendell Phillips told the Society: "As Abraham Lincoln said, 'One war at a time,' so I say one question at a time. This hour belongs to the negro."[32] Pursuit of women's suffrage, he said, should be postponed until votes for blacks had been attained. Activists, he argued, should support universal male suffrage and not risk losing it by demanding suffrage for all. Putting this in the terms I have used in this book, even key abolitionist allies, such as Phillips, who had long supported women's rights, opted to hone the movement sharply as victory on their core issues began to look doubtful. Despite the decades when the two movements had worked together almost as one, the top abolitionist leaders sacrificed women's rights, arguing that demanding them would slow progress for blacks. Before discussing this change of position in detail, it is worth noting that a small minority of abolitionists, including some black activists, objected to it. They, along with women such as Stanton and Anthony, argued against separating the two issues. In other words, the honing of the movement was a debatable political choice at this time—but one that the movement's leaders, such as Phillips and Douglass, ultimately embraced.[33]

Phillips sometimes wavered from his own prescription, raising the possibility of a "women's hour" whenever it appeared that prospects for black suffrage had increased. Initially, he may also have believed that the "negro's hour" would be short and successful, allowing an early turn to woman suffrage. But the postwar years were far less hospitable to black suffrage than many had predicted, and passage of the Fourteenth and Fifteenth Amendments was long and difficult. In the end, however, both amendments reflected, if imperfectly, the "negro's hour" idea, although power-holders in Congress in turn narrowed the two amendments far more than leading abolitionists would have preferred. The Fourteenth Amendment granted citizenship to slaves and established a representational penalty for states that failed to permit "male" suffrage. Most abolitionists opposed the amendment, however, because it glaringly omitted the right of ex-slaves to vote. The Fourteenth Amendment was anathema to women's suffrage leaders even more because, for the first time, it introduced the word "male" to the Constitution. The Fifteenth Amendment was also problematic. It declared that the right to vote should not be abridged by reason of race, color, or previous servitude—omitting sex. It also opened the door to abridgments of manhood suffrage through literacy tests, poll taxes, and violence.

BLOCKADING BLACK VOTING WITH WOMAN SUFFRAGE

Unsurprisingly, these constitutional developments and the AASS's honing incensed many woman suffrage leaders, who had worked so hard for so long in the organization. In response, Stanton and Anthony formed the American Equal Rights Association (AERA) in mid-1866. On paper, the AERA favored simultaneous black and woman suffrage.[34] However, AERA leaders used blockade tactics and harshly racist language against black enfranchisement. For one thing, they openly maintained that if women were granted the franchise, they would neutralize the effect of suffrage for black (and immigrant) men. Running for Congress in New York in 1866, Stanton warned: "In view of the fact that the Freedmen of the South and the millions of foreigners now crowding our Western shores, most of whom represent neither property, education, or civilization, are all in the progress of events to be enfranchised, the best interests of the nation demand that we outweigh this incoming pauperism, ignorance, and degradation with the wealth, education, and refinement of the women of the republic."[35]

Stanton, Anthony, and other movement leaders would repeat this "outweighing" argument often in coming years.[36] Similarly, in an 1867 pamphlet entitled "What Can the South Do: How the Southern States Can Make Themselves Master of the Situation," the well-known abolitionist and women's rights proponent Henry B. Blackwell urged Southern legislators to accept the Fifteenth Amendment, but offered them an easy way of subverting its effects. By granting woman suffrage, "your four millions of Southern white women will counterbalance your four millions of negro men and women, and thus the political supremacy of your white race will remain unchanged." Even better, according to Blackwell, granting woman suffrage could lead to the permanent exclusion of blacks: "The negro question would be forever removed from the political arena," and "the black race would gravitate by the law of nature towards the tropics." Over the ensuing decades, racist overtures to white supremacy, grounded in the idea that female enfranchisement would undercut black voting power, became suffragists' "single most important argument used in the South."[37]

To return to Stanton and the AERA, when pressed about whether she was willing to have the black man enfranchised before women, she publicly said, "No; I would not trust him with all my rights; degraded, oppressed himself, he would be more despotic with the governing power than even our Saxon rulers are." In 1867, when Kansas voted on separate referenda for woman suffrage and black suffrage, Stanton, Anthony, and fellow activists traveled to the state, where they argued for women's rights by invoking stereotyped fears of black men. In the desperate closing weeks of the campaign, they openly embraced notorious white racists such as George Francis Train, who offered them money to support the AERA and its journal, *The Revolution*. In the 1868 national elections, Stanton endorsed the virulently racist vice presidential candidate Frank Blair after he hinted of support for woman suffrage. In 1869, she and Anthony opposed the Fifteenth Amendment. But rather than arguing against it for the omissions to its text that would rapidly permit the rise of Jim Crow, they predicted that it would create an "aristocracy of sex" that would prevent woman suffrage for decades. Invoking again the specter of black rapists, they claimed that the amendment would "culminate in fearful outrages on womanhood especially in the southern states," because black men were "more hostile to women than any class of men in the country."[38]

As Dudden concludes, Stanton and Anthony compromised with racists and abandoned their egalitarian commitments because they sensed that a historical window of opportunity for women's rights was closing. Certain other leaders of the women's movement at that time did not dangle women's suffrage before white racists as a barrier against black empowerment, or at least not in such openly racist terms. But the movement's core leaders were willing to do so, despite their abolitionist roots, their occasional tactical alliances with the black suffrage cause, and their personal friendships with black men such as Douglass—all in the interest of the female franchise. Erstwhile allies such as Phillips condemned the Stanton wing of the women's movement as "essentially selfish." With greater understanding of the factors that could lead any movement to embrace a blockade strategy against a fellow subordinate group, Douglass remarked that "it is natural and habitual" to seek one's own rights by denying those of others.[39]

"BULWARK OF WHITE SUPREMACY"

In later decades, Stanton and Anthony staunchly adhered to these tactics. Placing a positive spin on them, they claimed that by "standing alone we learned our [women's] power." As Lori Ginzberg has written, Stanton had been "arguing for years that it was women's lack of self-respect that caused them to defer their demands." In the Reconstruction era, "white women's self-respect . . . could be heightened by comparison with people of 'lesser' races,'" bolstering women's own mobilization.[40]

More negatively, however, Stanton and others repeatedly promoted woman suffrage as a way of blocking the political power of voters they portrayed as ignorant, whether immigrant or black. This tactic was particularly evident in the South. During the late nineteenth century, suffragists argued to racist male politicians that woman suffrage would help preserve white supremacy because white women statistically outnumbered black men and women. As one example, the Equal Suffrage Association of North Carolina printed a broadside emphasizing that, "if white domination is threatened in the South, it is, therefore, doubly expedient to enfranchise the women quickly in order that it be preserved." Some political leaders, such as Mississippi senator John Sharp Williams, agreed, opining in 1876 that "woman suffrage might be made a bulwark of white supremacy in the State."[41]

For a variety of reasons, including their paternalistic attitudes toward women, Southern (and Northern) legislatures rejected suffrage in the late nineteenth century, with only a few lightly populated Western states granting it. Although Southern legislatures considered using woman suffrage as a bulwark against the black male vote, they ultimately settled on suppressing it through Jim Crow laws and violence, practices condoned by much of the rest of the country. Kammen well captures the subversion of one set of rights by another in the Reconstruction era: "States' rights lived whereas civil rights were dying."[42] On the other hand, most Southern legislators did not reject the blockade tactic in principle but simply believed that woman suffrage was too permeable a barrier to preserve white power. Even if black women's votes would be offset by white women's, white supremacy might be weakened. Passage of the Fifteenth Amendment had impelled Southern racists to develop procedures such as literacy tests, poll taxes, and outright violence to prevent black voting, and Southern legislators feared that such Jim Crow measures would be less effective against newly enfranchised black women than men. As the *Richmond Evening Journal* argued in 1915, "the literacy test would not work in choking off the colored woman vote" because black women were "decreasing their percentage of illiteracy very fast." Nor would the poll tax deter them because most "would be willing to go hungry, if necessary to pay it."[43] In other words, guardians of white supremacy saw nothing intrinsically wrong with using women's rights to blockade blacks. They rejected the tactic only because the barrier of women's rights was too porous and the pressure from black women too great to achieve their most important goal of keeping blacks down.

STATES' RIGHTS SUFFRAGISM

With that critique in mind, Southern suffragists clamored to make women's voting rights an impermeable barrier to black votes. Many insisted on a states' rights approach to suffragism, eschewing a national constitutional amendment and instead working for state-by-state grants of the vote, which in the South were sure to exclude black women. With Southerners' growing importance to the national movement in the late 1800s, the preeminent

National American Woman Suffrage Association (NAWSA) officially endorsed states' rights in its 1903 convention in New Orleans. It thereby allowed each state association to determine its membership and the "terms upon which the extension of suffrage to women shall be requested of the respective State Legislatures." Few objected at the time, although William Lloyd Garrison Jr., son of the famous abolitionist, remonstrated that "to purchase woman suffrage at the expense of the negro's rights is to pay a shameful price." The resolution led to the exclusion of black women, the free expression of racist views in NAWSA, and the open promotion of woman suffrage using the blockade tactic against blacks. Nor were such resolutions confined to the South. Across the country, as Kraditor writes, NAWSA's "two principal arguments involving the Negro [were] that white women ought not to be the political inferiors of Negro men and that woman suffrage would insure or at least not threaten white supremacy in the South."[44]

In the late 1910s, some Southern suffragists went so far as to work against NAWSA's renewed efforts to amend the U.S. Constitution to grant all women the right to vote. For activists such as Louisiana's Kate Gordon, who had earlier served in high positions within NAWSA, a federal amendment would place black women "on the same par with white women, and . . . while white men would be willing to club negro men away from the polls they would not use the club upon black women." To overcome this shortcoming, Gordon and other Southerners favored state-by-state legislation. This would maintain the principle of states' rights and allow Southern states to open voting only for white women. Importantly, even the NAWSA leadership, which repudiated the state-by-state approach by 1916, did so while continuing to embrace the "statistical argument." As Kraditor concludes, NAWSA maintained that woman suffrage "would render Southern Negro votes meaningless" and "den[ied] that the [federal] amendment would endanger states' rights or white supremacy." Or, as Walter F. White lamented in 1919, if NAWSA "could get the Suffrage Amendment through without enfranchising colored women, they would do it in a moment." In turn, according to W.E.B. Du Bois, "the reactionary attitude of most white women toward our problems" led many black men to oppose woman suffrage.[45]

Despite the latter's opposition to women's rights, and in part because of NAWSA's embrace of the blockade tactic against blacks, the Nineteenth Amendment granting women the vote came in 1920. For decades afterwards, white Southern women, both suffragists and antisuffragists, exercised their newfound rights to support white supremacy. Whereas white supremacist men specialized in violent suppression of the black vote, their wives, daughters, and mothers exercised their power in the voting booth. As Elna Green notes, after ratification of the Nineteenth Amendment, even "female antisuffragists registered and voted in order to outvote their black neighbors."[46] Viewed from the perspective of this chapter, once the Nineteenth Amendment had been adopted, even those white women who had earlier opposed the vote used it to fend off what they perceived as the greater threat of making voting rights effective for African Americans.

To conclude this discussion, it should be clear that the tactics discussed in this section do not represent merely the unfortunate effects of societal racism or sexism at the time. Both sets of attitudes were widespread in the nineteenth century and shaped the political environment in which the abolition, black rights, and women's rights movements operated. Nevertheless, using women's rights as a blockade against black empowerment was also a considered strategic move with predictable, negative consequences for African Americans. In this, it was akin to the abolition movement's earlier honing of women's rights in the "negro's hour" and the non-freeholder's even earlier exclusion of blacks and women from the movement for white male enfranchisement. In each case, a movement's quest for its rights in an inhospitable political climate led it either to jettison other subordinate movements or to portray a grant of its own rights as a means of putting down other subordinate groups.

Women's Rights versus Transgender Rights

The voting rights cases just examined are historical. One might think that in the contemporary world the context is so different, with egalitarianism so prominent, that rights claimants would not use blockades against others—or at least would not do so openly. However, subordinate groups continue to do so today when they perceive themselves to be in competition with one another for the same rights and their related benefits. A case in point is the one that opened this chapter—the British Labour Party controversy, which is part of a broader conflict between parts of the women's rights and transgender rights movements. Many women, of course, support transgender rights. But others, such as those who resigned from the Labour Party, do not—at least not if "trans representation must . . . happen at the expense of female candidates and of women's rights."[47]

To understand this contemporary example of rights blockading, it is helpful to focus on a self-described group of "radical feminists" (sometimes called "gender-critical feminists") that has been vocal about the "threat" of transgender rights and willing to use women's rights against them. It is hard to know the exact number of radical feminists, but they have had significant influence in this debate in the United States, Britain, and other countries. The radical feminists believe that transgender rights are a profound threat to women. They see trans rights as a form of rights dynamite unleashed by a male-dominated transgender movement whose aim is the destruction of the feminist movement, women's rights, and womanhood itself.[48] Against what they perceive as an existential menace, radical feminists such as Germaine Greer, Mary Daly, and Sheila Jeffreys mount their own blockade tactics. In the nineteenth-century voting rights case discussed previously, groups that perceived themselves as different from one another competed for the same right (even though, alternatively, all of them could have seen themselves as part of the same group—the disfranchised). In the contemporary transgender case, something similar occurs between radical feminists and trans women, with the former using women's rights to block anyone not born female from enjoying those rights.[49]

This fight over who is a woman and who may enjoy women's rights might seem an unlikely one, but transgender rights are a major area of rights conflict today. In countries around the world, transgender people face harsh persecution and violence. In many liberal democracies, however, the rights to change one's gender identity and to have that identity recognized by the state have become more liberal in recent years, even if discrimination persists. In 2012, Argentina passed the world's most sweeping law, permitting persons over the age of eighteen to choose their gender identity and gain official recognition of this without judicial or medical approval. A growing number of countries have passed similar laws since then.[50] More relevant to this chapter, heated debates over "bathroom bills" have erupted in many countries, with the broader question relating to the basis on which transgender people should have access to public facilities long open to women alone. In 2016, the U.S. Justice and Education Departments generated much controversy by issuing guidance requiring all educational institutions receiving federal funds to "treat a student's gender identity as the student's sex for purposes of Title IX."[51] Of course, in these and other countries, social conservatives have loudly objected to transgender rights, using as their primary argument the rights of "traditional" families to maintain their values and lifestyles. Radical feminists oppose the traditional values agenda but use women's rights to blockade what they see as the transgender movement's incursions.

RADICAL FEMINISM AND THE TRANSGENDER THREAT

For the radical feminist wing of the women's movement, contemporary Western society is a patriarchy, a "sex caste system" with men exercising domination over women. As suggested earlier in this chapter, if activists live in such a society, or even if they simply believe that they do, they are more likely to use blockade tactics against other subordinate groups. Most radical feminists would agree that the women's movement has made progress toward greater equality, with the rights of women representing a signal achievement in reducing, if by no means ending, patriarchy. Particularly important in this regard are the hard-won rights of women to settings where they may enjoy privacy and separation from men. The fight for women's toilets in nineteenth-century Europe and America, and similar struggles in the developing world today, are basic but important examples.[52] In the United States, the original Title IX was a landmark achievement in this regard, prompting creation of women-only spaces, events, and competitions. In some cases, such as women's shelters or prisons, such spaces provide places of refuge or safety from men. From a political standpoint, women-only spaces afford room for women to speak, plan, and organize independently of men. All of this, according to radical feminists, is a necessity as women seek rights in "male-supremacist" societies and work ultimately for an end to patriarchy itself.[53]

Given the pervasive societal discrimination they face, why would radical feminists not want support in their quest for equality from trans women, another subordinate group seeking a similar set of rights? Although some radical feminists agree that trans women are an oppressed group (victimized by men), they reject an alliance with them as self-defeating. Because the radical feminists view trans women not as women but as biological men, including them as women would be a blow to feminist morale and to the very concept of womanhood. To ally with them would be to surrender the cause of *women's* rights. Given the enormity of the risk that these radical feminists perceive from the transgender movement, it is unsurprising that in this contemporary context they use blockade tactics openly. Indeed, as we shall see, radical feminists explicitly promote women's rights as an absolute bar to trans women's enjoyment of those rights.

In the view of these feminists, the transgender movement and the rights it espouses are grounded in a pernicious conflation of two distinct concepts, sex and gender identity. For the radicals, the former is an unchangeable biological given, an objectively determinable fact. Except in the rarest of cases, people are born genetically male or female. They then enter societies in which females face relentless discrimination, with subordinate roles and oppressive stereotypes imposed on them. In this view, medical, pharmaceutical, or psychological interventions cannot alter the physical and social realities of sex.

By contrast, according to one of the basic documents of the transgender movement, the International Bill of Gender Rights, "gender identity" is subjective and changeable. Gender identity is "all human beings['] . . . ever-unfolding idea of who they are [, which] is not determined by chromosomal sex, genitalia, assigned birth sex, or initial gender role . . . [and which they] have the right to define, and to redefine as their lives unfold."[54] From this perspective, gender identity transcends biological sex. Identity, rather than biology, constitutes an apolitical fact, and gender rights must transcend the rights of women. To promote these ideas, the transgender movement has used mobilizing tactics common to other rights movements. First, it has humanized trans rights, with the International Bill stating that it expresses "fundamental human and civil rights," not "special rights applicable to a particular interest group, i.e. transgendered people." Second, it holds that all ten articles of the International Bill are "universal rights" expressing "universal truths." Among these rights are rights to "define gender identity," to "control and change one's own body," and to "enter into marital contracts." Finally, the International Bill proclaims these rights absolute: "no individual shall be denied access to a space or denied participation in an activity by virtue of a self-defined gender identity." Although the International Bill of Gender Rights has no legal force, as the document itself admits, it has provided a model and basis on which activists in a number of countries have recently promoted transgender rights—with some success, as noted earlier.

But according to radical feminists, the transgender movement's root concept, gender identity, is misconceived and incoherent. It originates in today's patriarchy, which is marked by gender roles that subordinate women. Gender identity is therefore "founded upon stereotypes" that help bolster the hierarchy. In this context, donning a new gender identity is little more than a sexual amusement, eccentricity, or abnormality (autogynephilia, a man's arousal by the thought of himself as a woman) for those in the dominant sex caste. Worse still, according to radical feminists, when men demand women's rights on the basis of this novel and transitory identity, it infringes on the space and rights of the subordinate female caste.[55]

For radical feminists such as Sheila Jeffreys, the transgender movement is "hostile to the rights of all women" and poses three main threats. First, males who have never experienced biological womanhood, let alone the social stereotypes and discrimination women face, can take full advantage of women's rights as transgender females. As Jeffreys and others claim, "men's rights to personate women are promoted above the rights of women." Men identifying as women may compete equally with biological women despite their physiological differences. They may enter private spaces that women have worked hard to create for their own safety, privacy, and well-being. They carry with them male privilege and continue to exercise power over women based on their biological and social background. As Ruth Barrett complains: "Fighting women for the right to share their spaces, organizations and meetings . . . pressur[es] an already oppressed class to relinquish rights, freedoms and structures they have fought to create and [it] is plainly unfair and destructive." From a more political standpoint, "entryism" by male transgenders undermines women's autonomy to organize, develop strategies, and fight for their rights "without," in Jeffreys's words, "members of the ruling group present." As Patricia McFadden concludes, allowing trans women into "women's spaces . . . would be a major political blunder for the future of the Women's Movement."[56]

Second, according to these radical feminists, the transgender movement undercuts decades of toil to end harmful stereotypes about feminine looks, fashion, and mannerisms. According to Jeffreys, these pillars of male domination have long been "enforced through cultural expectations, legal systems, street harassment, the influence of the sex industry, and workplace and school requirements." These stereotypes have harmed women in countless ways. Feminists such as Janice Raymond write that they also harm trans people because "sex-role stereotyping" is a "primary cause" of transitions, with all of their costly and mutilating interventions by psychiatrists and surgeons. But leaders of the transgender movement, whom Jeffreys describes as "often very conservative and hypermasculine" men, celebrate and flaunt these feminine stereotypes—"skirts, high heels and a love of unpaid domestic labour"—not least in their own dress and actions. As the International Bill of Gender Rights proclaims, all people have the "right to free expression of their self-defined gender identity"—the right to wear clothing and engage in behaviors believed to be associated with the chosen gender.[57] But if, as these feminists argue, gender represents the stereotyped and discriminatory manifestation of patriarchy, this "right" makes it all the harder for women to achieve their own rights. More bluntly, if trans rights succeed, women's rights fail, undermining women's advances and reinforcing women's subordination.

Third, radical feminists such as Barrett denounce the transgender movement for what they see as its most explosive goal: "gyn-ocide." At the individual level, this occurs when transgender activists physically attack or silence women they condemn as TERFs—trans-exclusionary radical feminists. There have been a number of high-profile examples of this in recent years. At the societal level, "reducing 'woman' to an identity erases women's biological reality." In Jeffreys's terms, it blots out "all the experiences that those with female biology have of being reared in a caste system based on sex." As Raymond argued decades ago, "the creation of man-made 'she-males'" makes "the biological woman obsolete." If anyone can be legally recognized as a "woman" based merely on their subjectively felt gender identity, biological women, they argue, are extinguished as a category, along with all the rights they have won for themselves over centuries. More politically, as Jeffreys warns, "without women feminism cannot exist, since feminism is a political movement for the liberation of a specific category of oppressed persons."[58] As noted previously, using the terminology of this book, these feminists clearly believe that transgender rights are a form of dynamite intended to destroy the women's movement, women's rights, and womanhood itself.

WOMEN'S RIGHTS AS AN IMPERMEABLE BLOCKADE

Radical feminists have responded to these threats by honing women's rights to apply only to people born biologically female and by blockading trans women with women's rights. At the most elementary level, these tactics use language to mark a sharp boundary between the sexes. In the 1970s, feminist critics used the terms "male-to-constructed-females" or "she-males" to fight what they then called the "transsexual empire." In today's era of gender identity theory, these critics speak of "male-bodied persons identifying as women" or "male-bodied transgenders."[59] Whatever the label, the intent is exclusion from womanhood, albeit a rejection that these feminists see as wholly justified by biology and upbringing.

As the theory presented in this chapter would predict, trans women respond harshly to this rhetorical effort to omit them from the very category of woman. They denounce this honing tactic and the radical feminists themselves as "transphobic" or "transexclusionary." Judith Butler, a prominent gender theorist and proponent of trans rights, condemns this honing as illegitimate radical "feminist policing of trans lives and trans choices." Other trans activists seek to exclude or marginalize the radical feminists who ostracize them. For instance, in the British Labour Party debate over the scope of all-women shortlists, the party's first trans women's officer greeted the news about the "300 transmisogynist women" resigning from the party with an exultant tweet: "Today is a good day."[60]

Beyond honing trans women out of the category of woman, feminist critics seek to blockade the transgender movement. Given the dire threat that these radical feminists have long perceived from the transgender movement, it is not surprising that the rights blockade they erect would be insurmountable: women's rights, in radical feminist eyes, are available only to those born women. More concretely, radical feminists oppose trans women's access to women's bathrooms, changing rooms, prisons, and more—all based on the rights of women. In this view, trans women should enjoy none of the rights women have *qua* women, even if other rights as citizens should remain open to them. Nor in this view should efforts at "gender equality" be pursued; they are pointless and incoherent because gender itself is a hierarchy.[61] Equality between the sexes, not gender equality, should be the primary goal. By contrast, according to radical feminists, recent laws that recognize a right to gender identity represent an erosion of women's rights and equality because they place legal recognition and state power behind a concept grounded in patriarchy. Worse still, these laws represent "female erasure" (the title of a recent book collecting radical feminist views).

Most fundamentally, radical feminists reject the claim that those born with a male anatomy can ever be female, no matter the psychological, chemical, or surgical means used, on the grounds that they are not biological women and have not experienced concomitant societal subordination. As Raymond argues, the interventions wrought by medicine or psychology are "superficial, stereotypical, and artifactual changes that reinforce socially constructed roles and identities." Or in Mary Daly's terms: "The surgeons and hormone therapists of the transsexual kingdom . . . can be said to produce feminine persons. They cannot produce women." Men, she maintains, can never be women, or women men. In this, these groups find common cause with conservatives, whom they ordinarily view as foes, in efforts to blockade trans rights. For instance, in the House of Lords debate over Britain's Gender Recognition Act of 2004, which allowed transgender people to change their legal gender, Sheila Jeffreys admitted that "those I agree with most are the radical right," who argued that if the "savage mutilation of transgenderism . . . was taking place in other cultures," the British would denounce it as a "harmful cultural practice."[62]

THE TRANS MOVEMENT COUNTERS

How do trans activists and their defenders respond to the honing and block-ading against them? As we have seen, trans activists abhor it, they denounce radical feminist leaders as a "strident" and "inflammatory" fringe within a more welcoming feminist movement, and they engage in the countering tactics common in clashes over rights.[63] First, trans activists deny that their movement threatens those they call cis women. Rather, they claim to be allies, envisaging that acceptance of fluid gender identities will "liberate and empower humankind."[64] Moreover, they claim to share similar formative experiences with cis women, most importantly the discrimination and vio-lence inherent to a world in which cisgender identities dominate. Politically, they seek to spread these views widely, even by entering women-only con-claves uninvited, despite the tense standoffs with radical feminists that sometimes follow. On an individual level, trans women have sought to help cis women victimized by men, for instance, by working at rape crisis centers as counselors—unsurprisingly provoking controversy and lawsuits.[65]

Second, as we have seen, trans activists raise a rival set of rights, which they claim to be universal, apolitical, human, and absolute. The Interna-tional Bill of Gender Rights sets out the broadest vision of a world in which these rights are fully recognized. More recently, an international network of organizations has worked to promote trans rights in legislatures and de-fend them in courts.

Third, following reversal strategies, trans activists publicize their fre-quent victimization. According to the National Center for Transgender Equality (NCTE), a leading American organization founded in 2003, trans people in the United States, especially trans women, "face extraordinary levels of physical and sexual violence, whether on the streets, at school or work, at home, or at the hands of government officials." Internationally, they "face extreme discrimination and violence," and their "very identities . . . [are] criminalized" in many countries. Along with physical attacks, many activists view themselves as under rhetorical threat from those they label TERFs. Consider again Judith Butler's critique of radical feminists' "painful, unnecessary, and destructive . . . prescriptivism, which . . . aspire[s] to a kind of feminist tyranny." So opposed are trans activists to such alleged "tyranny" that they have sought to impose something similar on those who question their views, as recent controversy over an academic philosophy article comparing transgenderism to transracialism shows.[66]

Conclusion

When different subordinate groups seek the same or similar rights against a common enemy, joint action is possible. Broad civil rights or self-determination movements may form. However, there is a temptation for one group to seek precedence over another. In hierarchical contexts, this temptation can easily become a reality. Some movement leaders may bemoan this fact or seek to avoid making hard choices. They may urge a focus on individual rather than group rights, praise the virtues of universalism, or claim that there is no need to prioritize rights. But when resources are scarce and opportunities fleeting, jettisoning another group to save one's own is common. Put another way, far from the ideal of "intersectionality," in which groups that are multiply disadvantaged work together to help the weakest among them make gains, this chapter reveals a politics of "divisionality": identifying first with one's own group—that is, the group with which one feels the strongest ties. If choices need to be made about who receives a right—as is common given the reality of limited resources and powerful opposition—one's primary loyalty, however reluctant, is to one's own group. This choice is not inevitable, and as I discussed in conceptualizing the blockade tactic earlier in this chapter, coalitions of the weak do form under certain circumstances, but divisions among them are also common.

As a more general conclusion, it is not always the case that insurgent groups fighting powerful interests will look to expand their movement. This view about the utility of enlarging the scope of conflict is associated with the writings of E. E. Schattschneider. There is little doubt that Schattschneider's ideas have merit. Gaining a larger number of supporters and resources for a minority cause can improve one's chances of achieving one's ends. However, blockading and honing are powerful and recurrent impulses in rights campaigns. Allying with one's supposed foe against one's presumed "natural" ally is common in the quest for one's own rights. The inevitable differences among subordinate groups—cultural, religious, status, and more—are easily seized upon as the basis for blockade tactics.

Is there a way for oppressed groups to avoid blockade tactics and the divisions they entail? Clearly, they hurt the overall quest for rights and are a gift to power-holders who oppose all grants of new rights to others. And of course, we do have historical examples of unity winning out over division. Blockade tactics are not inevitable. However, as noted previously, when movements face difficult prospects of success, they are more likely to resort to blockade tactics. If those circumstances can be ameliorated, the tactic becomes less likely and a coalition among diverse subordinate groups may develop. However, coalitions of all kinds are potentially unstable, and foes will seek to weaken them, as shown in the next chapter on the use of rights as wedges or crowbars.

8

Rights as Wedges

BREAKING COALITIONS

In the summer of 2011, a young gay American uploaded a video to YouTube. Peering earnestly into the camera, Marc related his heartfelt efforts to support the Palestinian solidarity movement. Enthralled by the movement's rhetoric of national liberation, he had contacted organizers of the Gaza flotilla, urging them to include an LGBT solidarity group. But Marc was in for a shock. As he gravely informed his audience, flotilla organizers rejected his proposal. Puzzled, Marc did some quick internet research on the Palestinian movement. To his shock and distress, he found that LGBT people faced repression in Palestine and nearby Muslim countries. Filled with indignation, Marc took to YouTube to warn other activists against supporting the Palestinian movement. Doing so would mean undermining LGBT rights and supporting terrorist groups such as Hamas.[1] On the other hand, Marc's research revealed that Israel was the Middle Eastern country most supportive of such rights.

But there were problems with the video, with the research—and with Marc himself. He didn't exist. He was an Israeli actor, and the video, far from being the *cri de coeur* of a disappointed idealist deeply offended by homophobia, was a professional public relations job. Its goal seemed to be embarrassing the flotilla movement and weakening the Palestinian cause as much as caring for threatened LGBT populations in the Middle East. At its core, the video aimed to use LGBT rights to loosen international solidarity with Palestinians. As Marc intoned to LGBT and straight audiences alike, supporting the flotillas would mean getting "in bed with Hamas."

It is hard to know how effective the video was. Within days of Marc's debut, the *New York Times* and other outlets revealed the video as a fabrication. But much remained unknown. Media speculation swirled around who might have produced it: pro-Israel activists—or the Israeli government itself?[2] Whatever the details, this use of LGBT rights as a wedge to pry supporters from the pro-Palestinian coalition was far from unusual. For Palestinian activists, the video amounted to "pinkwashing"—the use of LGBT rights to tarnish the Palestinian cause and chip away at international support. The broader tactic is not unique to the Israel-Palestine conflict: other rights have long been employed to damage rival coalitions.

This chapter explores the ways in which these tactics work, highlighting several questions: Why are rights so frequently used this way? Who are the foes? Which rights are fashioned into wedges? And how does wedging work? I begin with these conceptual matters and then turn to key examples both historical and contemporary. In the early Cold War, I examine the Soviet Union's ballyhooing of America's poor civil rights record to weaken the "free world" coalition that the United States anchored. Next, I analyze a number of contemporary cases involving LGBT rights, including the use of LGBT rights as wedges in the Israel-Palestine conflict, human rights as crowbars against anti-gay coalitions, and religious freedom as pries against pro-gay alliances.

Wedge Tactics

Most studies of wedge politics focus on the United States, especially presidential campaigns. Well-known examples include campaign appeals by Republicans Richard Nixon and Ronald Reagan to traditionally Democratic Southern voters using racially tinged rhetoric. More recently, George W. Bush used moral issues such as abortion and LGBT rights to appeal to Catholic voters in 2000 and 2004. In these campaigns, as Sunshine Hillygus and Todd Shields show, the wedge tactic aimed both to win voters from the opposing candidate and, if that failed, at least to dampen voters' enthusiasm for their initial favorite. Other scholars, such as Roger Cobb and Marc Howard Ross, have placed wedge issues into a broader context, looking at how political adversaries use such strategies to gain advantage by redefining the political agenda. E. E. Schattschneider focuses on the strategic displacement of conflicts: when one side is losing or stalemated, it seeks to shift the terms of debate to attract additional supporters and, more pointedly, subtract some of the foe's allies. As Schattschneider writes, "each new cleavage produces a new allocation of power." International relations scholars such as Timothy Crawford, have examined the use of wedges as counterbalancing tactics among states. Facing a powerful international coalition, states seek to peel off certain members by offering selective bribes or making particularized threats.[3] But few scholars have moved beyond these areas to examine broader uses of wedge tactics. Nor have scholars noted how frequently rights are used as the pry by political movements in non-electoral campaigns around the world.

DEFINITION AND PURPOSES

Wedging occurs when a political contestant raises a rights claim either to weaken an opposing coalition, alliance, or network or to thwart its growth preemptively.[4] The context for such usages is not primarily a fight over the right itself but over a different and deeper issue dividing the rival sides. In the anecdote that introduced this chapter, the Israel-Palestine conflict is the core issue. However, LGBT rights are a useful tool for backers of Israel aiming to weaken the international support network for the Palestinians. This network spans conservative Muslim groups in the Middle East and left-leaning audiences in other regions. In such a grouping, the various allies obviously agree over the central issue but may disagree over others, including rights that are tangential to the main dispute. In addition, their reasons for participating in the network vary, ranging from a principled agreement with its goals to a purely strategic alignment. The intensity of their commitment to the cause varies as well. When a political tactician inserts a wedge, he seeks to exploit and widen these latent cracks in the opposing coalition to gain an advantage in the larger conflict. Put another way, rather than making a frontal assault on the foe or the core issues, the tactic represents a flank move against the foe's support coalition, using a rights claim to loosen vulnerable members.

If successful, the wedge tactic will reduce the coalition's strength, scope, and effectiveness. At minimum, leaders of the coalition must spend scarce time and resources defending its rights record, upholding its good name, or even changing its practices. The aspersions cast on the coalition member maligned by the tactic—abuser! savage!—impugn the entire coalition's bona fides. More concretely, by highlighting the right—or more precisely, its violation—the tactic aims to scare off potential supporters or, if a coalition has already formed, to demobilize and detach key components. Faced with news of violations by one coalition member, particularly if the finger is pointed at the core member, others may reduce their commitment and effort, making it possible that the coalition will wither or collapse. Or, to avoid public association with a disgraced coalition, allies may insist that their aid be kept covert. Secrecy causes another disadvantage to the targeted coalition, however, by foreclosing the demonstration effect achieved when overt aid by one prominent ally attracts further support by signaling to other potential supporters the legitimacy and merit of the cause.

For the tactician using a rights wedge, an even better outcome is the departure of a member from the targeted coalition. The loss of an adherent not only weakens the coalition directly but also exposes its vulnerabilities, exacerbating the effects just discussed. Worse still, members of a targeted coalition who suddenly become aware of their ally's rights violations may join forces with the group that inserted the wedge. This does not happen often, because usually the estranged partner disagrees with the wedge-wielder even more than with its former friends. When it does happen, however, the triumphant tactician heralds the fresh recruit for seeing the light, whereas the rejected rump damns it for joining the dark side.

VICTIMS AND COLLATERAL BENEFICIARIES

In seeking to break an opposing coalition with a rights-based wedge strategy, the tactician not only advances his own cause directly but also may help the group on whose behalf he ostensibly raises the rights violation. In this chapter's opening anecdote, those who created "Marc" sought to split supporters of LGBT rights from the Palestinian solidarity movement, weakening the latter and strengthening themselves directly. Doing so might also have helped LGBT Palestinians, by shining light on abuses of their rights. Such "collateral beneficiaries" of the wedge tactic sometimes suffer real violations. And sometimes those inserting the wedge may really care about the abused group. Whether or not that is so, the tactician hopes that the collateral beneficiary will either affirm the validity of the wrongs it suffers or mobilize against its oppressor. Either way, the tactician's goal of weakening the foe in the main fight is helped if the collateral beneficiary joins in swinging the rights crowbar.

The beneficiary's positive reaction is not assured, however, as we shall see in later discussion of the Palestinian case. Collateral beneficiaries may reject a "helping hand" because it could give their oppressor an excuse for deeper repression. Or, despite their current problems, they may expect worse from or identify less with those who inserted the wedge. Spurning offers of aid, "victims" may even come to the defense of their oppressor in its larger struggle—with the hope that taking this position will advance their goals in the long run.

To draw out several points about the use of rights as wedges: Tacticians do not see the rights they flourish as fundamental to their main goals. Nor is sympathy for the victim of rights violations their primary motivation. Rather, they aim to hurt the enemy by weakening or destroying the coalition supporting it. This again raises the question whether the tactician actually believes in the right she asserts. There is no doubt that those at the receiving end of the blow will cry hypocrisy and manipulation. From an objective standpoint, however, such claims will be difficult to judge, and any determination will in any case be ignored or rejected by the tactician. At most, we can say that those publicly raising a rights issue must believe in it to some minimal degree. Otherwise, they would open themselves to the same line of disparagement. But this does not negate the possibility that the right is being used strategically, even cynically—or, alternatively, the possibility that its user sincerely believes in the right, at least as long as it does not contradict its primary goals.

CONSUMMATE CROWBARS

Rights are not the only issues that can serve as wedges or crowbars. Any issue can be used this way, depending on the context of a particular conflict. However, rights are peculiarly amenable for several reasons. First, their individualistic nature makes them well suited for sowing division. As Mary Ann Glendon argues, "rights talk" makes it "difficult for persons and groups with conflicting interests and views to build coalitions and achieve compromise."[5] Glendon makes this point with sorrow for the future of American democracy. But for political tacticians everywhere, this is welcome news! By their very nature, rights can serve a key goal of any campaign—fracturing the opposition. Fashioning rights into wedges is therefore commonplace. Of course, to do so effectively is not necessarily easy, as we shall see. The requirement that, at minimum, the tactician have considerable knowledge of the enemy highlights the central importance of strategic intelligence to any political campaign.

Second, rights wear the garb of morality and the face of legitimacy. Talk of rights is so pervasive and the aura surrounding them so positive that coalition partners are at least likely to give rights arguments a hearing. This is true whether the tactician acts overtly or covertly. In short, crowbars coated with a sheen of righteousness are more likely to gain credence and are therefore more likely to fracture a rival coalition.

Finally, the absolutist pretensions of rights lend them heft as wedges. With any wedge, the tactician hopes to temporarily supplant the main conflict with a different one. If successful, certain members of the rival coalition may rethink and even drop their support. In this, the all-or-nothing aspect of rights encourages the rise of the new issue over the old, at least for susceptible members of the support coalition. Nonrights issues are less effective in this regard because they lend themselves to compromise and accommodation. Talk of rights, by contrast, aims to place the abuser beyond the pale. Even if the violations initially appear tangential or secondary to the main conflict, they can catch a coalition partner's eye, forcing it to confront the ugly, if previously veiled, features of the bedfellow it has chosen.

WEDGE USERS AND TARGETS

Wedge tactics may be used by any political actor confronting a foe backed by a support coalition. Which coalitions are most likely to be targeted? As a general matter, the more diverse the coalition, the more likely it is to face wedging. A coalition of convenience, one formed for purely strategic reasons, is particularly vulnerable. Similarly if the core political actor within a network attracts an ideologically disparate group of supporters, its members may disagree with the actor (and one another) on a host of other issues, making it susceptible to rights-based wedge tactics. By contrast, an ideologically coherent coalition or one based on a principled commitment to the core member's goals is a less tempting target for wedging.

In some cases, coalition diversity correlates with size, or, more precisely, with the number of discrete members. Of course, broad coalitions can come in many sizes, but larger coalitions tend to be more diverse than smaller ones. More importantly, coalitions whose members span different beliefs, cultures, and nations are likely to include divergent perspectives on issues other than the one that brings them together. Transnational networks, such as collections of NGOs that advocate for a global policy goal or work in solidarity with a national liberation movement overseas, are examples. Typically in such cases, a lead group builds international support widely, hoping to improve its ability to achieve a policy or pressure a government. If leaders become aware of ideological or other cracks within the coalition, they will seek to ignore them or paper them over. Supporters, intent on achieving the coalition's primary goals, may bracket internal differences on "side issues" or willfully avoid inquiry about controversial matters. Opponents, however, will not be reticent. Acting strategically, they ferret out, expose, and inflame even latent cracks.

Against which coalition member will a rights wedge be directed? As noted previously, damaging the reputation of the core member will have the greatest effect on the coalition as a whole, although more peripheral members may also be targeted by a wedge tactic. Either way, the goal is to weaken the commitment or stop the support of powerful members of the coalition. In this context, a member's power can be measured first by the magnitude of the resources it supplies to the coalition. Of equal or greater import, however, is the extent to which the member's participation attracts the support of others. Such "gatekeeper" members facilitate the growth of additional support because of their connections, status, or credibility. Whatever the source of their influence, gatekeepers serve as models or attractants for others and therefore are tempting targets for wedging. If they can be dislodged, other coalition members may leave too.[6]

THE RIGHT WEDGE

Which rights are best converted into wedges? Any right can be used in this way, but a trivial or utopian right is usually too insubstantial to fashion into a worthwhile wedge. More basic rights, such as those pertaining to core matters of identity and equity, are more serviceable. Among these, the tactician will choose his weapon by scrutinizing the target coalition, looking for a right accepted by a powerful partner but rejected or, better yet, violated by the core member. Allegations that the latter has violated a widely accepted and well-established right make formidable wedges. By the same token, however, the core member is less likely to violate such rights.

For that reason, less-established or accepted rights can also make good crowbars. "New" human rights—those omitted from the Universal Declaration of Human Rights or other major human rights instruments—are good examples.[7] Their relative novelty makes it likelier that members of a diverse coalition will differ over them. Both within and among nations, new rights have proliferated in recent decades, despite purists' grumbles about rights "inflation." The purists are correct: many new rights are infeasible and ignored—such stuff as dreams (not crowbars) are made on. Some new rights, however, relate to pressing and vexed issues that political movements have fashioned into ringing claims, proposed norms, and hard law, even if these rights remain controversial. Sturdier stuff, such rights make good wedges. An example of a new right never contemplated in the UDHR is LGBT rights, which are today honored in some parts of the world and reviled in others.

OVERT OR COVERT WEDGES?

Precisely because new rights are controversial, members of the wedge user's own coalition may also be divided on them. This raises yet another question: how are wedges employed—openly or secretly? As a general matter, covert action and plausible deniability provide an advantage. Working in secrecy makes it more difficult for the coalition to raise its defenses, discredit the charge, and dismiss the wedge as merely a stratagem. Particularly powerful are covert wedges that only the targeted member, not the coalition leader, will notice before damage is done.

Wedge users will especially prefer secrecy when the right is controversial among their own allies. If raising the right might lead to internal contention, the tactician will prefer covert action. Rather than inserting the wedge himself, he may feed information to a proxy, preferably a seemingly neutral third party such as a journalist, activist, or academic, who then raises questions about rights violations by a coalition member. If wielded adroitly, the wedge will not bear the tactician's fingerprints, even if circumstantial evidence or *cui bono* inference point to his wile. In such cases, the target coalition will appear to fissure "naturally." Meanwhile, the tactician may sit back and enjoy his handiwork, secretly savoring his enemy's pain.

On the other hand, if the tactician's own side solidly supports a right, brandishing it against a vulnerable member of the opposing coalition may be the preferred option. In addition to weakening the target, driving the wedge in openly may burnish the tactician's own reputation for righteousness among his supporters.

WINNING AT WEDGING

When are wedge tactics most likely to weaken or break a target coalition? As the foregoing discussion suggests, a number of factors come into play, most relating to the key players involved. One is the identity of the coalition itself: the stranger the ideological bedfellows it includes, the more likely it is that a wedge can pry away a member. The reaction of collateral beneficiaries makes a difference. If LGBT Palestinians had affirmed the wedge driven in by "Marc" by emphasizing their own oppression at the hands of the Palestinian Authority, wobbly members of the international Palestinian solidarity coalition would have been more likely to remove themselves. Beyond these points, the critical factor in the success of a wedge tactic is the character of the wedge itself. The more the rights issue used as a wedge reveals a contradiction among members' fundamental values and commitments— especially between those of the core member and its supporters—the more likely it is that the wedge will crumble the coalition.

Of course, the core member's reactions to a well-placed wedge matter as well. Although it may initially ignore or deny the violations revealed, in some cases it may acknowledge the charges, however grudgingly, and reduce its own abuses. From the standpoint of the wedge driver, such acknowledgment is the worst-case scenario, because it may appease coalition members that might otherwise exit. But if the tactician has chosen his wedge wisely, the foe will have little ability to reform itself. If the rights violations are central to the core member's cultural system or political structure, reform will be difficult. If the targeted group cannot correct these violations without sacrificing its identity or interests, it may have to accept the loss of coalition partners uncomfortable with the unbridgeable divides revealed by the wedge. For its part, the targeted member will be unable to avoid the inconsistency between its own values and the practices of its partner. A well-placed wedge will force each group to choose: my ally or myself?

Civil Rights as a Wedge in the Cold War

Consider first an important historical example: the use of rights as wedges by the United States and the Soviet Union in the early years of the Cold War.[8] Each side used the other's violations to embarrass its foe, catch it in hypocrisies, and, most importantly, loosen its global support coalition. Soviet exploitation of the U.S. civil rights record to wedge apart America's "free world" coalition was particularly prominent. At times, non-aligned authoritarian regimes such as Argentina's Peronist dictatorship used similar strategies against the United States.

America's Cold War coalition spanned NATO members, other established democracies, and, it was hoped, the non-Communist countries of Asia, Africa, and Latin America. As noted, such broad-based coalitions make good targets for wedge tactics. In addition, most members or potential members, especially those from the developing world, were particularly susceptible because they did not have strong preexisting ties to the United States. Unsurprisingly, the Soviets chose civil rights as their wedge because these rights were controversial within the free world coalition—or, more exactly, they were controversial within the core member of the coalition, the United States. Particularly between the 1940s and 1960s, serious state-sanctioned or condoned rights violations against African Americans, especially in the American South, provided an obvious opportunity for Soviet leaders to pry away certain members of the coalition or dissuade the non-aligned from joining it. The abuses in America echoed the colonialist treatment of local populations in many newly independent states. Such states were therefore vulnerable to being wedged from the U.S.'s support coalition. As Uganda's prime minister Milton Obote wrote in an open letter to President Kennedy shortly after police violence against the civil rights movement in Birmingham, Alabama: "Nothing is more paradoxical than that these events should take place in the United States and at a time when that country is anxious to project its image before the world screen as the archetype of democracy and the champion of freedom." Released during a May 1963 meeting of African heads of state, Obote's letter warned the president that "the eyes and ears of the world are concentrated on events in Alabama." In the Cold War context, the Soviet Union made sure that the world's eyes and ears stayed concentrated on the U.S. South more broadly. However cynically deployed, this Soviet tactic meshed with the American civil rights movement's simultaneous use of international institutions and global public opinion to pressure for racial equality, as discussed later in this section.

Nor did the Soviets envelop their wedge tactic in secrecy. To deepen latent cracks among America's allies, Soviet media repeatedly published articles describing segregation, poll taxes, repression, and lynching in the South. Counterposing America's claims about rights against its reality of abuse, the Soviet Union underscored the hypocrisy of the "leader of the free world," raising questions among certain allies about its real intentions. As one article in the Soviet journal *Trud* reported: "The absence of economic rights [in the United States] is accompanied by the absence of social rights . . . of negroes."[9] Making this overt wedging more dangerous to the U.S.-led coalition, the Soviets could use reporting by the American press itself. The Communist media simply republished American press reports on government or Ku Klux Klan treatment of African Americans in the South. Indeed, for the Soviets, keeping a lower profile and allowing American sources to do the work probably made the tactic more effective. Media in non-aligned countries also took the initiative in reporting on segregation, discrimination, and violence.

U.S. policymakers at the time clearly recognized the dangers of the wedge tactic. President Harry Truman's Committee on Civil Rights, for instance, claimed that totalitarian countries used "our civil rights record [as] a convenient weapon with which to attack us," and the commission sought ways to "deprive them of that weapon" to maintain the "good opinion of the peoples of the world." The U.S. government's amicus curiae brief in *Brown v. Board of Education* highlighted harms to U.S. foreign policy, concluding that "racial discrimination furnishes grist for the Communist propaganda mills." Foreign policy officials, such as Dean Rusk, promoted the Civil Rights Act in part to counter Soviet propaganda. They also pressured state officials, particularly in the South, to ease discrimination and uphold civil rights for all. In Maryland, African diplomats driving between the UN and Washington, DC, were refused service by racist business owners as late as the 1960s. When lobbying the Maryland legislature to pass a bill against discrimination in public accommodations, one State Department official demanded: "Give us the weapons to conduct this war of human dignity" against the Soviet Union. Passage of the Maryland bill would "eliminate a source of embarrassment that greatly damages our relations with not only the neutral nations of the world, but many nations which are stoutly with us in the fight for freedom." As the American ambassador to India, Chester Bowles, stated in 1952, "How can the colored peoples of Asia be sure we are sincere in our interest in them if we do not respect the equality of our colored people at home?"[10] Of course, this was precisely the question that the Soviet Union wished to raise in the mind of potential American allies, particularly in the developing world, by highlighting Jim Crow policies and egregious acts of violence against African Americans.

Although the Soviets used civil rights to advance their own interests, there were collateral beneficiaries: African Americans. However, for the most part, the black community reacted independently of the Soviets' rhetorical wedge. To do otherwise in the Cold War context would have discredited the homegrown civil rights movement. Nevertheless, the movement came under suspicion from powerful government officials for supposed Communist sympathies.[11] Carol Anderson argues that fear of being delegitimized as Soviet stooges contributed to civil rights leaders' rejection of Soviet-endorsed international economic and social rights that might have improved African Americans' status as much as the civil rights they sought.[12]

At the same time, however, the National Association for the Advance-ment of Colored People (NAACP) and the Civil Rights Congress entered the UN and other global arenas to pressure the U.S. government. They hoped that by internationalizing America's civil rights problems, U.S. offi-cials would come under greater pressure to address them, if only to avoid losing out in the Cold War competition with the Soviets. In one of the most striking instances of this tactic, the NAACP issued *An Appeal to the World*, which denounced the United States for "profess[ing] democracy with one hand and deny[ing] it to millions on the other." The *Appeal* avoided mention of Communism, dwelling instead on American racial injustices. Like other political actors striving to advance their own cause, however, the Soviet Union pounced on the *Appeal* to bolster its claims about American civil rights violations. As Anderson summarizes, "The Kremlin, with *An Appeal to the World* strapped in its holster, went gunning for the United States."[13] There is little doubt that this searing victims' account strengthened Soviet efforts to fracture the free world coalition, even if the NAACP's aim was to compel the United States to improve domestic race relations.

Understanding this threat, the U.S. government fought back, following the menu of reactions typical when a core member's support coalition faces wedging. As noted earlier, certain officials appreciated that America's civil rights record was problematic and urged improvements. In key incidents, such as the *Brown* case, the national government publicly acknowledged America's racial problems. But its power to resolve them quickly was limited given political realities in the South and the strictures of America's federal system. In the short term, foreign policy officials therefore took other mea-sures to blunt the effects of the civil rights wedge. For one thing, the United States retaliated by raising rival rights as crowbars of their own. Officials pointed to various Soviet violations, not only of civil and political rights but also, and probably more effectively, of the economic rights that the Soviets claimed to champion. Repeatedly, American diplomats, such as Jonathan Daniels, pointed to the hypocrisy of Soviet charges against the United States, arguing that the Soviet Union had "achieved equality by uniformly suppressing human rights."[14]

The United States also engaged in denial to weaken the rights wedge. Government officials subtly downplayed the significance of civil rights prob-lems, placing them instead in a larger story of progress toward civil rights and racial equality. As an internal 1954 publication of the U.S. Information Agency (USIA) urged its staff: "It is unwise to focus attention on bad condi-tions unless this helps maintain credibility, or shows the U.S. is attacking its social problems. . . . *A lynching should be reported without comment*, but the following week there should be a general report of U.S. progress in race relations."[15]

In addition, American officials used covert means to keep civil rights problems from weakening their coalition. Particularly important were actions against expatriate African Americans who spoke to the foreign press about institutionalized racism, discrimination, and violence. Such testimony of victims and witnesses lent visibility, credibility, and therefore heft to the Soviets' wedge tactic, whether or not the witnesses intended this effect. From the U.S. government perspective, the problem was how to offset or silence these voices, whether they had strengthened the foreign wedge deliberately or inadvertently. An obvious and much-used means was to sponsor overseas visits by African Americans who portrayed a rosier picture. Less savory means were also used in secret. Consider the U.S. government reaction to the African American entertainer Josephine Baker in the 1950s, as documented by Mary Dudziak. Baker, who had renounced her American citizenship over her home country's racial injustices, frequently decried segregation, discrimination, and violence. Her statements found a ready audience in countries such as Peronist Argentina, where U.S. officials, such as Ben Brown, claimed in secret cables that she was "permitting herself to become the tool of foreign interests which are notoriously unfriendly to the United States and which are only interested in the causes which she sponsors in so far as they can be made to embarrass the United States." To blunt Baker's impact, officials sought to "avoid any appearance of having sent someone to 'offset' J. Baker," because doing so would "put ourselves on the defensive" and could serve to "weaken our arguments." Instead, American officials in Argentina and elsewhere secretly persuaded (or bribed) local officials and theater owners to cancel her appearances, harass her, or require her to sign damaging or limiting statements regarding her activities.[16]

In sum, Soviet uses of civil rights as wedges were doubtless cynical and were denounced as such at the time. Yet the tactic, along with the underlying violations it publicized, threatened to weaken or even break America's "free world" coalition. By deftly playing the foreign policy angle, the civil rights movement inadvertently added pressure, even though most civil rights leaders pointedly rejected Soviet support of their cause. In response, U.S. officials took a variety of countermeasures, working to blunt, deflect, or parry the wedge and raise their own rights claims against the Communist bloc. Although it was only one of many Cold War tactics used by the United States and the Soviet Union against each other's support coalition, the rights crowbar played an important role in the overall struggle.

LGBT Rights as a Wedge in the Israel-Palestine Conflict

For a contemporary example of how rights are used as wedges, consider the recent use by Israel and supportive NGOs in various countries of LGBT rights against the Palestinian solidarity network. Palestine's allies are broadly united by their desire for Palestinian liberation and a free Palestinian state. But support for Palestine also spans an array of states and NGOs, many of whom have conflicting interests on other matters. The YouTube video starring the Israeli actor "Marc" is but one example of efforts to crack this coalition. A broader examination of this case casts much light on the use of rights as wedges.

As background, it should be noted that secular Israelis and the Israeli state are relatively open to LGBT rights. Although Orthodox Jews in Israel view homosexuality as problematic and have opposed the expansion of LGBT rights, gays and lesbians enjoy far greater rights there than elsewhere in the Middle East. In this context, LGBT rights have increasingly become a wedge used by both domestic and foreign supporters of Israel to break apart the pro-Palestinian coalition. This is not to say that Israel and its defenders are insincere about LGBT rights. There is little doubt that they believe in such rights, as Israeli law and society affirm (even if there are rare cases of violence against LGBT people). But in the context of the Israel-Palestine conflict, the use of LGBT rights has an additional, aggressive purpose: to substitute new conflict lines for old ones, weakening the Palestinian solidarity network. As core members of the Palestinian network describe the tactic, it seeks to "promote LGBT issues over the universal human rights of all Palestinians."[17] The goal is to drive away LGBT supporters of Palestine and, more importantly, a larger number of straight activists around the world who strongly back those rights.

As noted earlier, wedge tactics are often conducted covertly. The tactician using them hides his identity, motivations, and strategic considerations, thereby hoping to make the wedge more effective. Marc's YouTube video is a good example. One illuminating exception to such secrecy involves the nongovernmental group Stand With Us (SWU), a stalwart American supporter of Israel that has sought to embarrass and undermine the Palestinian solidarity movement in the United States.[18] SWU describes itself as "an international, non-profit Israel education organization . . . dedicated to educating people of all ages about Israel and to combating the extremism and anti-Semitism that often distorts the issues." As part of its efforts, SWU has repeatedly criticized the Palestinian Authority and the Palestinian solidarity network in the United States, highlighting violations of LGBT rights in Palestine. SWU advertisements on the internet, for instance, highlight the Palestinian Authority's arrest and torture of gays and lesbians, or they ask: "Why does Israel look like paradise to gay Palestinians?" These ads aim to delegitimate the Palestinians and create doubts among supporters. In 2011, when Marc's video first appeared on YouTube, SWU quickly posted a link on its own YouTube channel, although the organization removed it after the hoax was revealed.[19]

In a more sustained effort at wedging in 2010, SWU targeted an important American component of the Palestinian solidarity movement: the U.S. Palestinian Community Network (USPCN). USPCN's goals include "self-determination and equality for the Palestinian people; the right of all Palestinian refugees to return to their original homes, lands, properties and villages (a natural right supported by international law and UN Resolution 194); [and] ending Zionist occupation and colonization of Palestine."[20] From the standpoint of this chapter, USPCN is a ripe target for wedge tactics because the network's membership, although united by support for Palestinian rights, is large and diverse in its views of other rights issues. One major institutional member of USPCN is the U.S. Social Forum, the American wing of the World Social Forum (WSF). The U.S. Social Forum, like the WSF, is itself a network composed of numerous organizations and activists. Both forums began with a vague "anti-neoliberal" agenda related to concerns about the threat of economic globalization, which erupted in the mid-1990s.[21] Initially, they attracted support from labor and environmental activists who had earlier coalesced around opposition to the North American Free Trade Agreement (NAFTA), the World Trade Organization (WTO), and other international trade institutions. By the late 1990s, support for the WSF and the U.S. Social Forum had mushroomed to include a variety of left-leaning organizations promoting issues as diverse as environmentalism, women's rights, Dalit (Untouchable) rights—and LGBT rights. The U.S. Social Forum therefore represented an important gatekeeper within the USPCN, not only because of its own large membership, but also because, by certifying causes such as Palestinian statehood, the U.S. Social Forum influenced other like-minded groups and individuals. Reciprocally, the Palestinian network lends its support to the U.S. Social Forum by being part of its "national planning committee." As such, ties between the two networks are mutually beneficial, and the U.S. Social Forum represents an important part of the international Palestinian solidarity network.

From the standpoint of defenders of Israel such as SWU, however, the U.S. Social Forum's prominence in the broad-based Palestine solidarity network has made it a tempting target for detachment or demobilization through wedge tactics. As noted previously, gatekeeper members of a coalition are the most likely targets for wedging. And the fact that the U.S. Social Forum's left-leaning members had generally come to support LGBT rights by the late 2000s provided all the more reason to seek to dislodge it. All that was needed was an opportunity. That came in June 2010, when the U.S. Social Forum held its multiday annual meeting in Detroit, Michigan. Michigan is one of the few states in the U.S. with sizable concentrations of Muslims, making it likely that the USPCN hoped to make a mark in this seemingly friendly setting. Months beforehand, the U.S. Social Forum issued a public call for proposals, looking for people to present workshops to the thousands of activists expected to attend. Sensing an opening, SWU alertly inserted its wedge, a proposal innocently entitled "LGBTQI Liberation in the Middle East." On its surface, SWU's proposal sounded unobjectionable to those supportive of LGBT rights: "The purpose of this workshop is to expose the underground LBGTQI Liberation movements that currently exist across the Middle East. . . . Some stories are harrowing and gut wrenching, while others are triumphant, but all are inspirational. The end goal is to engage the participants in supporting the cause of LGBTQI Liberation, and to connect them with outlets through which they can offer their support. We plan on having information available on how to connect with the offices of different Middle Eastern LGBTQI non-profits, and will offer material produced by StandWithUs."[22]

As noted previously, there is usually a kernel of truth behind a rights crowbar, and there are often collateral beneficiaries. In this case, those beneficiaries would seemingly be the "Middle Eastern LGBTQI non-profits" mentioned in the proposal, as well as their individual members. It may even be that members of SWU sincerely hoped to help these groups. But there were other, more strategic reasons for SWU's application to the high-profile U.S. Social Forum conference. As its leaders Roz Rothstein and Roberta Seid stated months later, in words that reveal its wedge tactic, SWU's goal was to "force [left-wing members of the coalition] to take a hard look at themselves and ask why they aren't doing more for the tragic suffering of gays in the Middle East, even in Palestinian communities."[23] As we shall see,

SWU hoped that some U.S. Social Forum members might "do . . . more" for gay and lesbian Palestinians by doing less for Palestinian liberation. Of course, SWU did not disclose these purposes at the time. To the U.S. Social Forum, words such as "liberation," "struggle," and "LGBTQI" proved mesmerizing. Unaware of SWU's identity and seeing a proposal that seemed to fit so well with the U.S. Social Forum's embrace of LGBT rights, conference organizers promptly accepted the proposal and placed the workshop on the agenda.

All seemed well until weeks before the conference. Then Palestinian groups that had previously clashed with SWU discovered its plans and publicly rebuked the U.S. Social Forum for allowing SWU on the agenda. Among others deprecating the U.S. Social Forum were four "victim" groups that SWU ostensibly hoped to help. These collateral beneficiaries rejected the wedge inserted by SWU, ostensibly on their behalf. Identifying themselves as "queer Arab organizations," these groups denounced SWU's "pinkwash[ing] Israel's crimes in the region." In particular, they condemned SWU for using LGBT Palestinians for its own pro-Israel agenda. According to the Arab groups, SWU "deceptively uses the language of LGBT and women's rights to obscure the fact that institutionalized discrimination is enshrined within the state of Israel." In their view, SWU did not raise LGBT rights to help gay and lesbian Palestinians but wanted to make the Palestinian cause look "unworthy" as a whole.

In addition, the Arab groups defended against the absolutist edge of SWU's rights crowbar. They accepted the damaging charge that LGBT people face mistreatment and even persecution in Palestine, although they phrased the point vaguely: "homophobia . . . exists within Palestinian society." Indeed, the facts show this to be the case, and there would be little point in denying it, although the USPCN's response to SWU largely ignored the plight of LGBT Palestinians. What SWU's rights tactic forced the Palestinian groups to fight against therefore was the suggestion that these rights violations—and Israel's superior if hardly spotless record on LGBT rights—should mean rejection of the Palestinian cause *tout court*. Against that view, the LGBT Palestinians proclaimed that they would not "compartmentalize our beliefs, lives, and identities so that solidarity with the queer struggle would preclude solidarity with others." Finally, the Palestinian LGBT groups proclaimed their refusal to be "instrumentalized by anyone, be it our own oppressive governments or the Zionist lobby hijacking our struggle to legitimize the state of Israel and its policies, thus providing even more fodder for our own governments to use against us."[24]

Although the collateral beneficiaries' resounding rejection of SWU's wedge dampened its effects, the U.S. Social Forum was nonetheless thrown into disarray, just as SWU had hoped. The forum faced a dilemma: maintain SWU's presentation and alienate its Palestinian allies, perhaps even risking their leaving the U.S. Social Forum, or eject SWU and potentially offend its own increasingly LGBT-friendly supporters. After long and contentious debate, it opted for the latter.[25] But this decision came not only with internal disruption to the two left-wing networks, but also with bad publicity in local and national media. To this, SWU bitingly contributed, not least in an online press release titled "The Stench of Hypocrisy." It proclaimed that the U.S. Social Forum was indifferent toward LGBT rights, intolerant of free speech, and neglectful of Palestinian homophobia.

In many ways, SWU had achieved its strategic goals. As the group's leaders acknowledged, SWU had hoped that the focus on LGBT oppression in Palestine and the Muslim Mideast would produce "cognitive dissonance" among international solidarity activists. It would force them to "reassess their belief system and their self-image" and to recognize that "there are good things about Israel, and that it shares many of their values." The goal was to pry apart the Palestinian coalition or at least loosen the resolve of key allies—and even turn some of them into friends of Israel. Those in solidarity with Palestine would have to ask whether "the allies they have chosen share [their] progressive values [and] tolerance." In this way, LGBT rights were the wedge that could weaken the coalition and open it to broader questioning: "If any real facts about Israel slipped through, it would have been difficult for the USSF to motivate attendees to support these hate-filled anti-Israel campaigns."[26]

In the end, SWU's use of LGBT rights was relatively successful. Like most wedges, the tactic did not break its target coalition, probably in part because the Arab queer organizations refused to legitimate the tactic. But the disruption caused during the lead up to the U.S. Social Forum conference was significant. The tactic also may have caused longer-term damage by raising doubts among some left-wing audiences about the Palestinian cause. At minimum, controversy over SWU's expulsion magnified media coverage of its pro-Israel views, particularly in outlets sympathetic to LGBT rights. In these contexts, SWU could continue to batter the U.S. Social Forum for "shameless and destructive hypocrisy [that] effectively silenced the voices of this persecuted minority." As SWU proclaimed, the U.S. Social Forum, "allegedly committed to mobilizing against persecution and oppression, ended up supporting the world's worst persecutors and oppressors by ignoring the pain and suffering these governments inflict on gays and others. Their anti-Israel obsession trumped all their other human rights values."

Wedge Politics in Conflicts over LGBT Rights

HUMAN RIGHTS AS WEDGE

In the foregoing case, supporters of Israel used a secondary issue, LGBT rights, as a wedge in the primary conflict over Israel-Palestine. In many parts of the contemporary world, of course, controversies over LGBT rights are themselves the main issue. In these cases, the antagonists use other rights as crowbars. First, consider how proponents of LGBT rights, including both broad-based human rights groups and single-issue LGBT groups, have used other rights as wedges against their foe, a loose-knit network that opposes LGBT rights. From the perspective of this chapter, this network is again a prime target for wedging. It spans Catholic, evangelical, and Orthodox conservatives from the United States and Europe, including the Holy See, the World Congress of Families, and the Russian Orthodox Church. As we saw in chapter 6, it also includes religious activists and governments from socially conservative parts of Africa, as well as the Caribbean and Islamic worlds. In some ways, this is a classic coalition of convenience, uniting strange bedfellows around a small set of issues. On the one hand, members of this "traditional values" coalition agree in their opposition to LGBT rights. For decades, this transnational, transreligious network has worked together both within states and in international institutions such as the United Nations to block LGBT rights initiatives, with considerable success.[27] On the other hand, members of the network have deep theological and cultural differences. On the issue of LGBT rights, they differ on how sharply and with what tactics they should attack such rights and homosexuals themselves.

Against this powerful and diverse traditionalist network, proponents of LGBT rights have frequently used rights crowbars, along with affirmative tactics to advance their own cause. The prominent human rights group Human Rights Watch has issued reports criticizing "an alliance of fundamentalisms." This alliance, HRW notes, includes both states where gays and lesbians are jailed or killed and more moderate opponents of LGBT rights, including American evangelicals and the Holy See, which oppose such harsh penalties. Sensing an opportunity to insert a wedge and weaken the traditional values coalition, HRW has sought to widen this fracture line and pry away powerful Western members. For instance, HRW sought to shame more moderate foes into weakening their commitment by highlighting the extreme measures of other members, such as Uganda's Anti-Homosexuality bill. More broadly, it has driven home the claim that attacks on LGBT rights "attack the logic and essence of human rights themselves."[28] From this chapter's perspective, HRW's tactic is textbook wedge politics: sow doubts among moderate LGBT rights opponents about their highly repressive overseas allies, supplant the LGBT conflict at least temporarily with a wider array of human rights issues, and thereby reduce the cohesion and power of the anti–LGBT rights coalition.

RELIGIOUS RIGHTS AS WEDGE

Lest one think that only supporters of LGBT populations use rights as wedges in this multi-arena contest, consider how those who opposed same-sex marriage fought against it in the United States. This is part of a larger trend in recent decades in which the Christian Right has embraced rights politics.[29] In this case, groups such as the National Organization for Marriage (NOM) used a different right, religious freedom, as a wedge against a broad coalition of same-sex marriage proponents, both before and after the U.S. Supreme Court's 2015 *Obergefell v. Hodges* decision legalizing same-sex marriage. Unsurprisingly, NOM has sought to keep its destructive purposes hidden. However, internal organizational documents became public in 2012 as part of a campaign finance investigation by the state of Maine. The documents reveal the NOM leadership's strategic thinking in this case and open a window to understanding wedge tactics more broadly.

In the main conflict over same-sex marriage, NOM's opponents were LGBT advocacy groups such as the Human Rights Campaign (HRC). After years of difficult activism, HRC had by 2009 assembled a diverse coalition of other rights groups and, more importantly, political party leaders, primarily from the Democratic Party. The expanding membership of the coalition made it a prime target for wedge tactics, and by 2009 the need for such tactics had become pressing. According to NOM, its religiously conservative constituents faced increasing threats to their beliefs and values from this coalition and the rights it promoted. Well-known examples include controversies over whether socially conservative cake makers and photographers had to provide marriage services to LGBT couples. In addition, NOM saw such threats in the harassment of public opponents of same-sex marriage. For NOM, a prominent victim was beauty queen Carrie Prejean, 2009 Miss

USA runner-up, who allegedly lost her shot at the title when she answered a competition question about her views on same-sex marriage from openly gay celebrity Perez Hilton.[30]

With these and other cases as backdrop, NOM's leaders proposed a wedge tactic to fight back by weakening the same-sex marriage coalition. In a confidential document entitled "Marriage: $20 Million Strategy for Victory," NOM called for "developing side issues to weaken pro–gay marriage leaders and parties and develop an activist base of social conservative and Christian voters." These side issues—examples of the kinds of rights that are ideal for use as wedges—would include "pornography, protection of children, and the need to oppose all efforts to weaken religious liberty at the federal level." Explicitly mentioned as a primary purpose would be to "drive a wedge between . . . key Democratic constituencies": LGBT Democrats and the top party leaders supporting them, on the one hand, and socially conservative Democrats, such as African Americans and Hispanics, on the other. The latter's conservatism is evidenced by a 2015 survey by the Public Religion Research Institute (PRRI) showing that 38 percent of black Protestants, 35 percent of Hispanic Protestants, and 28 percent of white evangelical Protestants supported same-sex marriage, whereas 62 percent of white mainline Protestants did so, along with larger majorities of Catholics and Jews.[31]

Seeking to break Democratic conservatives from the party, NOM used religious freedom as a wedge, highlighting alleged violations of the right resulting from same-sex marriage laws. Most publicly, it mounted a $1.5 million "religious liberty ad campaign," featuring two YouTube videos, one of them including Prejean. According to NOM, these "brought the message of religious liberty threats posed by same-sex marriage to millions more viewers" and highlighted the "intolerance shown by many same-sex marriage supporters."

In the once-secret documents, NOM was candid and specific about plans for its "Not a Civil Right Project," illuminating the dynamics of wedging more generally. The first goal was to collect and disseminate stories of people "harassed, threatened, or intimidated" because of their opposition to same-sex marriage. This "Document the Victims" project would "capture the oppression of people's rights, the disregard of their feelings and interests, on video, as it happens, in real time." Next, NOM would enlist members of the "victim" group to use their rights as a wedge: "Find, equip, energize, and connect African American spokespeople for marriage; develop a media campaign around their objections to gay marriage as a 'civil right'; . . . find

attractive young Black Democrats to challenge White gay marriage advocates electorally." Going further about how it envisioned the tactic might
undermine the same-sex marriage coalition, NOM voiced the secret hope
that this African American backlash would "provoke the gay marriage base
into responding by denouncing these spokesmen and women as bigots." The
controversy aroused might then reduce the appetite of the Democratic
Party for same-sex marriage: "No politician wants to take up and push an
issue that splits the base of the party. Fanning the hostility . . . is key to raising the costs of pushing gay marriage to its advocates and persuading the
movement's allies that advocates are unacceptably overreaching on this
issue."[32] As a final aspect of the campaign, NOM urged taking the wedge
tactic to the international level, stating that "we have learned how to make
the coercive pressures on religious people and institutions in the United
States an issue. We will use this knowledge . . . to problematize the oppression of Christians and other traditional faith communities" and thereby "halt
the movement toward gay marriage worldwide."[33]

As in most clashes of rights, some restriction on religious rights is made
possible in the expansion of LGBT rights and same-sex marriage. And NOM
clearly cared deeply about religious freedom issues. Witness this statement
by NOM: "Gay marriage is the tip of the spear, the weapon that will be and
is being used to marginalize and repress Christianity and the Church [so
that] faith communities that promote traditional families should be treated
in law and culture like racists."[34] In addition, as a fallback position, NOM
advocated for religious opt-out provisions in any same-sex marriage laws
that they failed to halt. Nonetheless, as NOM's secret motives and public
actions demonstrate, another key reason for raising the religious freedom
issue was tactical: in the pre-*Obergefell* era, a rights wedge might undermine
the same-sex marriage coalition, just as the other rights wedges discussed
in this chapter were meant to bruise and break the coalitions they targeted.

Conclusion

The cases discussed in this chapter are far from unusual. In all political conflicts, activists seek not only to advance their interests directly but also, and
as an equally important goal, to damage the entities that oppose them. In
most cases, such opponents include a diverse set of groups working in
league with one another. Political tacticians alert to the utility of negative
tactics will therefore deploy wedge strategies against opposing coalitions

frequently. As we have seen, because rights issues lend themselves so well to use as wedges, they are often central to this tactic.

To deploy such a wedge, the tactician surveys the opposition coalition and identifies a rights issue on which its members differ. Inflaming latent differences over the right or, even more effectively, exposing violations of the right by the coalition's core member can weaken or break the coalition, even if those violations have nothing to do with the raison d'être of the coalition. Whether the coalition is shattered, fractured, or impaired, those deploying the rights wedge to advance their cause will benefit, even if they do not truly care about the right itself.

9

Conclusion

This book has analyzed rights as aggressive weapons of political conflict, rather than viewing them primarily as defensive concepts. The book's premise is that rights themselves are not the fundamental goals over which groups fight. Rather, they fight over any number of underlying matters, with rights providing an important means of achieving these. If a rights claimant succeeds in institutionalizing a correlative duty as law and, most crucially, practice, that claimant will attain the substantive goal she has sought. Reciprocally, another entity has a new duty imposed upon it, either to act or refrain from acting in a way that permits the rights-holder to gain her due. Of course, that is seldom the end of the story because conflict then erupts over the interpretation, conditions, and scope of the right/duty to whatever goals the claimant has sought. In that new flare-up, rights arguments will again be a means to achieve those ends.

Beyond these starting points, the book has illustrated three broad ways in which political adversaries, whether based in states or nongovernmental entities, use rights offensively. First, they voice them as rallying cries: naturalizing, universalizing, absolutizing, and depoliticizing rights—and publicizing violations—to mobilize constituents and sympathizers. Second, those whose interests or values are threatened not only raise rights as shields but also counter with their own specialized parries: denial, reversal, rivalry, and repudiation. Finally, throughout these engagements, all sides deploy rights in aggressive ways: as camouflage, spears, or dynamite against their foes, and as wedges and blockades with regard to third parties.

This view of how political actors use rights and of what rights really are does not omit a moral component. As I discussed in chapter 1 and as I have indicated elsewhere in this book, the instrumental uses on which I focus hinge on rights' profound but restricted moral appeal. People must believe in a right for it to gain heft. The more people there are who believe in it and the more powerful those believers, the weightier the right becomes. These beliefs have a strong ethical component. Many believers trust simply in the virtue of their right. Others, more clear-sighted, gauge their interests first, then encase them in a moralistic cover. Either way, the ethical appeal of rights cannot be denied and is certainly played upon by political leaders, even if this aspect of rights is not intrinsic to the concept itself. Each of the cases examined in this book has demonstrated these points. In all of them, activists could use rights as weapons only because they had political movements or states behind them, lending strength to their claim. Their success hinged on the breadth of their movements, itself augmented in some cases by the appeal of the rights claim relative to competing ones. In the *Lautsi* case, when Italy's Union of Rational Atheists and Agnostics raised the claim of individual freedom of conscience in the country's courts, the claim ultimately failed. Although UAAR members deeply believed in this right, most other Italians were far from convinced that it applied in the circumstances of the case. Indeed, the Italian government responded to this challenge with a fervent appeal to the rights of national majorities to determine their own cultural practices. This appeal had deep resonance in Italy and across the religiously conservative countries of Europe, except among secularists.

Notwithstanding the important ethical component of rights, this book has emphasized the limits of such appeals. Rights exercise their attraction within preexisting moral communities, and those communities are often at odds with one another over a range of values, interests, and concerns. True, in any conflict, there will be third parties and sometimes authoritative decision-making institutions. The competition over their attention, loyalties, resources, and judgments is fraught—and fought using moralistic rights rhetoric. But the larger point is that among communities in conflict with one another, one group's rights will have little appeal to another. Indeed, one group's rights will be seen as another's violation.

Abraham Lincoln put this point eloquently, remarking in 1864 that "we behold the processes by which thousands are daily passing from under the yoke of bondage, hailed by some as the advance of liberty, and bewailed by others as the destruction of all liberty."[1] This phenomenon is prominent in all of the conflicts studied in this book. Powerful Western states may now declare (rightly in my view) that "LGBT rights are human rights," but leaders and citizens in other regions revile the claim. Nor do the lines of communities correspond simply with state borders. Several of the conflicts examined in this book were largely domestic. Yet zealous appeals to the morality of one community's rights often trigger resistance in another's, despite their all being citizens of the same state. Over long periods of time, one set of rights may win out over another and be established in national law, but there is nothing immanent in rights, or even human rights, that makes particular successes certain or permanent. All is a matter of ongoing political conflict, sometimes submerged but always present. Rights rhetoric plays a key, aggressive role in that conflict, with its weaponlike usages shaping and being shaped by equally critical material and human resources.

Analytic Implications

For scholars, viewing rights as weapons in addition to the more usual emphasis on them as ends of conflict has significant analytic implications. Most basically, scholars should take a clear-eyed view of the movements they study even if, in their private lives, they enthusiastically work as activists for one or another cause. If rights are tools manipulated to achieve substantive ends, analysts need to treat them as such. One simple way of doing this is to avoid confusing activists' underlying goals with the rights rhetoric within which they so frequently come wrapped. This view does not neglect rights, but it underlines the need to differentiate the aims that movements seek from the tools, including rights, that they use to achieve them. It recognizes that rights are empty and can be directed at any political goal. This is why many conflicts appear to be over clashing rights claims, even though the real issue is the substantive goals dividing the parties. Always, it is important to recognize that the use of rights language is a political move and part of an advocacy strategy. In the same-sex marriage dispute, for instance, the core issue is about marriages themselves, and secondarily the *right* to them. The right is a means that makes marriages possible legally, and claims to the right helped make them possible politically. In the U.S. case, these rights claims were used as rallying cries to mobilize support and as wedges to weaken Republican Party opposition. Importantly, however, LGBT leaders did not seek political power—or seek to erode the power of their opponents— merely for its own sake. Rather, LGBT groups sought same-sex marriage as an end. To gain it, they used rights claims as tools, and these in turn helped them gain sufficient political power to win (at least for now) on this issue.

Of course, given the ubiquity and political utility of the term "rights," political movements will inevitably continue to drape themselves in moralistic terms. They will proclaim their rights human, universal, apolitical, or absolute as a means of mobilizing and bootstrapping their way to realization of the underlying goals they seek. The scholarly literature on rhetorical framing by social movements has paved the way in this analysis, but more should be done to explore the reasons that activists choose particular rights rhetoric and its effect on receptive audiences.

This recommendation underlines another point: the importance of studying whole conflicts, rather than only one side (usually the one with which the scholar identifies). This book's empirical chapters sought to do that, examining how all sides to conflict (and third parties) strategically interact with one another. Taking that holistic perspective brought into focus not only the ways in which rights may mobilize receptive audiences, both constituents and potential allies, but also how they may harm foes and their allies. These aggressive usages deserve more attention from scholars, to match the many studies of rights as shields. As noted in chapter 3, when raised as shields, rights work to protect individuals and groups or to preserve or defend their interests and values. But defensive and offensive weapons are difficult to distinguish, particularly on rhetorical battlefields where all sides to conflict simultaneously guard and advance conflicting visions of society. Even if we could sort out purely protective rights actions, defenders use many of the same tactics as aggressors to mobilize their forces. In the many cases in which political actors pursue novel goals, offensive uses of new rights are at the fore. For analysts who seek to provide an objective view of conflicts—or even for those who prefer an activist stance sympathetic to one or another political actor—it is important to give equal billing to the conjoined aspects of rights, as both defensive and offensive weapons. Similarly, we need more studies of how rights are employed not only by individuals, minorities, and social movements, but also by corporations, majorities, and states in the many conflicts pitting one set of groups against the other. To neglect such powerful users of rights does a disservice to the movements we admire, by giving only a partial view of how they and their opponents behave.

Building on this book's foundation, scholars should do more to identify and analyze various usages of rights. I have developed some propositions about the rights tactics identified in this book, making it easier for scholars to test them in other cases, but I make no claim to comprehensiveness. It would be well worth exploring additional weaponlike usages of rights, including some that I have hinted at here. One example might be rights as provocations: one group asserting its rights not only to promote its own interests or beliefs but also to offend a rival. The intent of such an affront might be to demoralize the foe, extract concessions from him, or to draw him into actions that can be used as an excuse for further repression. In international disputes involving cross-border minorities, rights and violations are used frequently as *casus belli*. Russia, for instance, pays close attention to the treatment of Russian-speaking minorities remaining in various parts of the former Soviet Union. Violations of their rights, whether instigated by local majorities hoping to attract the support of their powerful international allies or by Russian speakers themselves, have served as the basis for diplomatic and military interventions.[2] Nor is such behavior confined only to cross-border minorities. Under the right circumstances, political actors of all kinds may seek to galvanize support from distant allies by engaging in similar provocations.

In addition to helping us better understand rights tactics, this book's perspective casts light on the historical rise of rights and the overwhelming current urge to "rightsify" claims. As noted previously, some scholars have decried this proliferation of rights. But the reason for this expansion seems clear and the trend unstoppable, at least as long as rights continue to hold appeal and serve as weapons of conflict. Movements need rhetorical instruments, whether or not they also use arms. Rights serve that purpose admirably. Movements of all political kinds and stripes therefore have every reason to proclaim their rights. In working toward its political goals, the more rhetorical weaponry a movement has, the more powerful its appeals and sallies can be. Similarly, the more skillful one's activists at using those tactics, the better one's chances of achieving one's goals. Scholars of international law who stand outside the fray may decry "rights inflation." But those in the scrum will have no ears for such criticisms. They will instead use every tool at their disposal to achieve their goals, whether by inventing a new right, mobilizing a constituency with righteous rallying cries, or deploying a right aggressively against foes or third parties.

As such, the "rights as weapons" perspective has important implications for how we view rights activists, both today and in the past. It stresses that they are active, strategic decision-makers who use rights in variable ways— and do not simply strive toward them as ends in themselves. Thus, from a practical standpoint, historical figures who have used rights with aggressive intents toward weaker groups cannot be dismissed as passive conveyors of their society's prejudices—mere reflectors of the prejudices of their times.

With regard to the nineteenth-century voting rights movements examined in this book, activists such as Elizabeth Cady Stanton cannot simply be said to have "caved in to the racism of the surrounding society" when she aggressively utilized women's rights to blockade newly enfranchised black men.[3] For one thing, even in their own times, similarly placed activists *refused* to use rights in these ways. Rather, these historical figures must be seen as strategists who accurately or inaccurately read their times and acted accordingly, raising rights as one of their weapons. Their decisions were deeply political, grounded in unbending commitment to their own group's goals. But they were also morally questionable, given that others at the time refused to take up these rights in such aggressive ways—or actively defended the weak with other rights.

The same, of course, goes for contemporary activists who use or abuse rights' firepower. As noted previously, in 2017 Myanmar used the rights of the nation to justify what the UN has called a "textbook example of ethnic cleansing" against the Rohingya minority. Nobel Peace Prize winner Aung San Suu Kyi's silence in the face of this move and attendant massacres has helped make the government's explosive use of rights possible. Suu Kyi's stance is perhaps wise strategically. She faces many political constraints at home, and her overriding goal is apparently a more democratic Myanmar—but only for those whom the state and its Buddhist majority consider citizens. This stance raises difficult questions about someone long seen as a champion of human rights, not just the rights of her own people.[4] From an academic standpoint, it suggests another area for future research: the effects of using rights weaponry on the movements and activists using them. Does this tactic lead to distortion or inequity in distributing the substantive goods that rights provide? To what extent, if any, does using rights aggressively contribute to the well-documented tendency among movements to serve the needs of their best-off constituents first, while neglecting, honing, or repressing weaker ones?[5]

Policy Implications

As all this suggests, and as I have been at pains to show throughout this book, rights are not somehow above or prior to politics. Activists of all ideologies may assert the transpolitical nature of their goals, and some may truly believe it. Others voice these views more for strategic reasons—to mobilize support and to strengthen their cause. In the end, however, the uses to which rights are put, rather than the sentiments with which they are voiced, matter most for their political effectiveness. As Hopgood has shown with respect to Amnesty International, the human rights NGO most closely associated with what has been portrayed as a purely moral stance, it quickly adopted a political approach in its activism. At its founding in 1961, it bravely stood up for the rights of prisoners of conscience in Eastern Bloc countries, in the West, and in the global South, striving thereby to "generate . . . a world conscience" on behalf of all individuals, whatever their politics.[6] But in doing so, it inevitably took a political stance. Even if its defense of the individual was seen as nonpolitical, a simple matter of right, Amnesty soon came under pressure to involve itself in an array of more obviously controversial matters such as abortion and LGBT rights. And within only a few years, it openly took sides in these and other "political" issues. It still does so today, even if it continues to promote itself as the guardian of a transcendent ideal.

Many have held that rights, or at least human rights, are innately liberating and inclusionary. Obvious shortcomings—slavery and disenfranchisement in historically "liberal" societies, or discrimination today—simply represent failures to achieve liberalism's ideal of extending rights to all. Others hold that if liberal societies fail to meet liberal ideals, it is because of the power of illiberal groups. In this view, the rise of contemporary civil and human rights is a progressive turn. Going forward, in the United Nations' words, we should continuously strive for a universal rights culture in which human rights are "indivisible and interdependent because all rights—political, civil, social, cultural and economic—are equal in importance and none can be fully enjoyed without the others."[7] The problem with these views, however, is that they fail to perceive that rights are means to substantive ends, and those ends come into competition with one another. Rights shape and tame conflicts. Things are no doubt better with rights available as tools of politics than if they were not—if only action, violent action, were available. But even as rights have helped lead to significant human progress, conflict does not disappear. Targets of campaigns fight back, sometimes in violent ways, but equally in ways that subscribe to the dominant approach, rights, using them as weapons as well. The idea that all rights could ever be indivisible, interdependent, and equal is clearly utopian.

Nor are rights, even human rights, the exclusive domain of the political left—or right. Rather, rights are malleable political tools, available to any group to pick up and use in a variety of ways. Denunciations of cynical misuses do not usually stand because of rights' ideological vacuity and status as a means rather than just an end of politics. Activist groups intuitively understand these points and use rights on their own behalf following these precepts. What they overlook is the depth of their foes' diametrically opposed views. Yet that divisive reality is important to a movement's ability to grasp the advantages and limitations of rights strategies. The most basic point is that activists must distinguish between their usages of rights for internal and external purposes. Although constituents and sympathizers may be galvanized by proclamations that certain rights are human, universal, apolitical, and absolute, opponents will be left cold. Against them, rights must be deployed—and will in turn be rebuffed—in the aggressive ways noted in chapters 4 to 8. Not all of the weapons analyzed in those chapters will be available to every actor in every conflict. Rather, as the hypotheses proposed in this book indicate, each is most appropriate to certain users, targets, rights, and methods. Of course, every political protagonist faces unique circumstances and opponents. Nonetheless, the concepts developed in this book may provide some indication of the best tactic to use at particular times and ways to employ it.

Because of my realism about rights, some activists and scholar-activists may view this book as hostile to rights. Yet much of it has been a theoretically informed account of how activists use rights to achieve their goals, usually in sharp conflict with others who react against such change. I disagree with some of the tactics used in particular cases and certainly some of the goals of those profiled in this book. But I do not think that there is something "wrong" about using rights in the ways examined here. Nor do I hold rights up for censure against some "implicit ideal," some better way of conducting politics.[8] I view rights' aggressive side as inherent to any tool of politics and do not fault rights for being means as well as ends. Although my focus has been on these understudied but important offensive usages, I fully acknowledge that rights have often been used as shields or as inspirations to spark great advances in human history. More generally, I do not hold that rights need saving from the uses to which activists of varied political persuasions put them.[9] As I have noted throughout, such usages are intrinsic to rights because rights are means of politics. Rights rhetoric, often deployed in aggressive ways, has been a critical part of some of the most significant advances in human history, particularly those that put limits on the arbitrary exercise of power, even if similar rhetoric has also been deployed for contrary purposes. Thus, there is no question of "saving" rights through purifying the tactics that activists adopt. Put another way, although this is a critical book, it is not critical of rights or rights activists as such. Rather, the book is critical in the sense that I scrape away the carapace of morality around rights to uncover what activists care most about and how they strive to achieve it. In doing this, I have come to admire the tactical genius of many activists, even if I may reject some of their goals.

Still, some might worry that in a small way this book has weakened the rights movement, or at least the liberal human rights movement and the rights it promotes. As a believer in many of the most important current rights and their underlying substance, I disagree with this view. It is true, of course, that I am skeptical of the view that rights, even human rights, have universal moral value or immanent political force. But as noted earlier, this does not mean that I believe there is something broken or wrong about rights—or about using them in the ways I have analyzed. The nonviolent politico-legal tactics that go along with rights politics are better than violence or war, although, as we have seen, the two may go hand in hand. Even if some of those usages might be seen as cynical or insincere, they can help achieve important political ends.

By taking a clear-eyed view of rights, I underline the need for activist groups to use politics to achieve their goals, rather than relying on any assumed appeal of norms or morality. Most activists intuitively recognize and follow this precept already, although as Ignatieff has warned, there is a danger of idolizing rights. For believers in rights to rely too much on the force of rhetoric and ideas alone is foolish, particularly with respect to influencing political outcomes in a conflictive environment. What is needed is better understanding of what rights are and what rights do. In some ways, this book offers a kind of guide book for these tasks, although its lessons must be fine-tuned for particular political circumstances. If the book has succeeded, political actors will find it valuable in developing more effective ways of using rights arguments to achieve their goals.

In this regard, I do not criticize human rights NGOs for their use of rights, even if I may disagree with some of the goals they pursue. Amnesty International and Human Rights Watch are not only champions of rights and, more importantly, the political goals that they encapsulate, but also masters of using rights in their pursuit. We have seen several examples in this book, including HRW's use of human rights as wedges against the traditional values coalition opposing gay rights or as spears against Italy's classroom crucifixes in the *Lautsi* case. In much of its work, the group supports vulnerable individuals and groups, mounting campaigns that employ many of the rallying cries discussed in chapter 2. Amnesty International's 2011 campaign to "keep the progress going" for women's rights in Afghanistan is another, if more ambiguous, example. It served both to camouflage a long and bloody war that many Afghan women opposed and, as some of the war's more candid advocates stated, as dynamite aimed at undermining the country's traditional cultures from without. In all of this, most observers will support one or another side politically and may have set views about what rights should provide. But as tools of politics, rights can be put to any number of defensive and offensive uses.

Some might question whether accepting and even highlighting the use of rights as weapons helps in the resolution of conflicts or makes conflicts more intractable. The absolutist quality of much rights rhetoric seems inimical to compromise. Conservative and communitarian critics have viewed "rights talk" with suspicion. Even in democracies, where judicial institutions may offer a means of ending particular disputes, such resolutions are limited and temporary. Activists raise new rights claims to challenge aspects of court decisions, on the streets, in election booths, or back in the courts. All the more so are rights claims difficult to resolve internationally, an arena in which "final" decision-makers are largely absent. To this extent, the critics may be right, but alternatives are difficult to find, particularly in diverse societies. One easy answer to the critics is that limiting the use of rights rhetoric is difficult and dangerous in a free society. Certainly, government controls risk being a cure worse than the disease. Self-control seems the only option, but groups that view the status quo as unjust or even inconvenient will be unlikely to exercise it.

Nor should they. Political conflict is healthy and inevitable in democratic settings and, particularly if conducted through peaceful means, at the international level as well. In societies that remain and probably will always remain unequal and unfair in the eyes of certain actors, rights offer critical tools for altering wrongs. Conversely, of course, rights offer the powerful invaluable means of maintaining and expanding their positions. At worst, even if we accept that rights have downsides in reducing social cohesion, they are necessary to liberal democratic systems. Rather than spurring conflict in themselves, rights are means of conducting it. As such, rights are preferable to warfare and bloodshed, even if they are as much offensive as defensive weapons.

ACKNOWLEDGMENTS

I incurred many debts during the time that I spent writing this book. For critical financial and academic support, I thank Duquesne University, particularly its Faculty Development Fund. Duquesne has been an excellent setting for my scholarship and teaching during this project, both in Pittsburgh and at our wonderful Rome campus. I thank my colleagues, especially in the Political Science Department, and Dean James Swindal. I also received support from a number of other institutions, which provided me with interesting new colleagues and workplaces. These included the Transatlantic Academy, where I owe particular thanks to Stephen Szabo; Ritsumeikan University, where I thank Kenki Adachi; and the Peace Research Institute Frankfurt (PRIF/HFSK), where I thank Claudia Baumgart-Ochse.

For help in honing the ideas and cases that I present in this book, I am grateful for speaking invitations from the Center for Research and Teaching in Economics (CIDE), the German Institute for Global and Area Studies, the International Politics Seminar at Columbia University, the Transatlantic Academy, the Political Science Speaker Series at George Washington University, the International Relations Group at Merton College at Oxford University, the Centre for International Relations Speakers Series at the School of Oriental and African Studies, the Peace Research Institute Frankfurt, the Normative Orders Cluster of Excellence at Goethe University, the Taft Research Center at the University of Cincinnati, the Batten School of Public Policy at the University of Virginia, the Colloquium in Ethics, Politics, and Society at Luiss University School of Government, the European University Institute, the Institute for Global and International Studies Research Seminar Series at George Washington University, and the Comparative Politics Workshop at the University of Pennsylvania.

In addition to the helpful comments I received at all these events and at regular professional meetings, a number of individuals took the time to write lengthy comments on my work at various stages. These include

Pasquale Annicchino, Phillip Ayoub, Jennifer Dixon, Neve Gordon, Will Kymlicka, Miguel Angel Simon, and Timothy William Waters. At Princeton University Press, Eric Crahan took an immediate interest in this project and has been a model of patience during the time it has taken me to complete it. In addition, I thank the activists and politicians who agreed to speak with me about my research and whom I have listed in the appendix.

Others who contributed insights, critiques, or encouragement include Peter Agree, Lori Allen, Karen Alter, Julia Amos, Michael Barnett, Jens Bartelson, Lewis Bateman, Nicholas Bouchet, Sarah Sunn Bush, Charli Carpenter, David Crow, Nicole Deitelhoff, Neil DeVotta, Eileen Dougherty, Amitai Etzioni, Martha Finnemore, Jörg Friedrichs, Michael Goodhart, Mark Haas, Fen Hampson, Ruth Hanau Santini, John Haslam, Jeff Haynes, Stephen Hopgood, Wade Jacoby, James Jasper, Anne Jenichen, Peter Katzenstein, James Lebovec, Lucian Leustean, Dan Lindley, Steven Livingston, Ian Lustick, Jarol Manheim, Willie Manteris, Raffaele Marchetti, John Markoff, David McBride, Michael McCann, Samuel Moyn, John Mueller, Harris Mylonas, Aryeh Neier, Nora Fisher Onar, Erin Pischke, Kateryna Pishchikova, Donatella della Porta, Eric Posner, Aseem Prakash, Tonya Putnam, Ted Reinert, Luc Reydams, James Ron, Marc Howard Ross, Richard J. Samuels, Rebecca Sanders, Anya Schiffrin, Frank Schwartz, Susan Sell, Kathryn Sikkink, Rudra Sil, Jackie Smith, Rogers Smith, Jack Snyder, Valerie Sperling, Kristina Stöckl, Andrew Strauss, Sarah Stroup, Mohammad Ayatollahi Tabaar, Sidney Tarrow, Trevor Thrall, Johannes Urpelainen, Rachel Wahl, Claude Welch, Steven I. Wilkinson, Carmen Wunderlich, Lisbeth Zimmermann, and Michael Zürn. Any errors that remain in the work—including my inadvertent omission of any who helped me in this project over the years—are of course my responsibility.

My thankfulness to my family is greatest. Although my children, Alex and Natalie, left the house for college, jobs, and graduate school during the years I took to finish this book, my continuing conversations and frequent visits with them kept me happy and fresh. I was particularly delighted that Natalie was there for the moment when this book first crystallized in my mind: while enjoying a family vacation with her and Joan in Barcelona, with Catalan nationalism and bullfighting bans very much in the air. Alex clued me in to the tenants' rights issues that make a cameo appearance in this book. I thank my mother Renate Bob for her interest in this project and her inspiring energy, enthusiasm, and love. As an intrepid octogenarian, she participated at an Oxford High Table where I presented an early version of this book.

Most importantly, I thank my wife Joan Miles, who shared the years of work with me and made research and writing sites, including Barcelona, Rome, Kyoto, Frankfurt, and Pittsburgh, even more pleasant than they would otherwise be. Joan kept me happy and on track. Without her great support and love, I could not have completed this book. I dedicate this book to her.

APPENDIX

Interviews

Much of the information on which chapters 4 and 5 are based comes from a limited number of one- to two-hour interviews I conducted in 2012. Most interviews involved a single person, although one was a joint interview with two subjects. I conducted all interviews in English or Spanish, with the aid of a translator. Although I entered each interview with a set of prewritten questions, I used a dialogic technique—and frequently uncovered new information and insights that I followed up in the exchange.

All interviewees signed a consent form approved by Duquesne University's Institutional Review Board. The form asked interviewees to provide separate consents to audiotaping and to a waiver of anonymity in publications resulting from my research. All interviewees consented to both requests and are identified below. All interviews were audio-recorded and are available at the Duquesne University Archive.

Leonardo Anselmi, Plataforma Prou (Enough Platform) leader, joint interview with Alejandra García, Barcelona, June 8, 2012

Raffaele Carcano, Union of Rational Atheists and Agnostics (UAAR) president, Rome, December 3, 2012

Williams Cardenas Rubio, International Bullfighting Association (AIT), president, Madrid, June 11, 2012

Alejandra García, Plataforma Prou leader, joint interview with Leonardo Anselmi, Barcelona, June 8, 2012

Marius Kolff, CAS International, director, Madrid, June 13, 2012

Pablo de Lora, Professor of Legal Philosophy, Universidad Autónoma de Madrid, and witness for the popular legislative initiative (PLI), Boston, May 22, 2012

Joaquim Nadal, Socialist Party of Catalonia (PSC), deputy, Barcelona, June 8, 2012

Luca Volontè, European People's Party (EPP), chairman at the Parliamentary Assembly of the Council of Europe, Rome, December 18, 2012

Alessandro Zara, EquaAnimal, director, Madrid, June 12, 2012

NOTES

Chapter 1. Introduction: The Uses of Rights in Political Conflict

1. United Nations, Office of the High Commissioner for Human Rights, "What Are Human Rights?," http://www.ohchr.org/EN/Issues/Pages/WhatareHumanRights.aspx; Ronald Dworkin, "Rights as Trumps," in *Theories of Rights*, ed. Jeremy Waldron (Oxford: Oxford University Press, 1984), 153–67.

2. "Hillary Clinton on Gay Rights Abroad: Secretary of State Delivers Historic LGBT Speech in Geneva," transcript with video, *Huffington Post*, December 6, 2011, https://www.huffington post.com/2011/12/06/hillary-clinton-gay-rights-speech-geneva_n_1132392.html; Ian Katz, "World Bank's Kim Halts Uganda Loan over Anti-Gay Law," *Bloomberg*, February 28, 2014, https://www .bloomberg.com/news/articles/2014-02-28/world-bank-s-kim-halts-uganda-loan-over-anti -gay-law.

3. John Locke, *Two Treatises of Government and a Letter Concerning Toleration* (New Haven, CT: Yale University Press, 2003), 155.

4. Mary Ann Glendon, *Rights Talk: The Impoverishment of Political Discourse* (New York: Free Press, 1991), 22; C. B. Macpherson, *The Political Theory of Possessive Individualism: Hobbes to Locke* (Oxford: Clarendon, 1962), 221.

5. John Boli and George M. Thomas, "World Culture in the World Polity: A Century of International Non-Governmental Organization," *American Sociological Review* 62, no. 2 (1997): 180–82.

6. United Nations, Office of the High Commissioner for Human Rights, "What Are Human Rights?," http://www.ohchr.org/EN/Issues/Pages/WhatareHumanRights.aspx.

7. Michael Ignatieff, *Human Rights as Politics and Idolatry* (Princeton, NJ: Princeton University Press, 2001), 68.

8. Jeffrey A. Winters, *Oligarchy* (Cambridge: Cambridge University Press, 2011), 22–23.

9. For exceptions, see Stuart A. Scheingold, *The Politics of Rights: Lawyers, Public Policy, and Political Change*, 2nd ed. (Ann Arbor: University of Michigan Press, 2004); Michael W. McCann, *Rights at Work: Pay Equity Reform and the Politics of Legal Mobilization* (Chicago: University of Chicago Press, 1994); Tom Buchanan, "'The Truth Will Set You Free': The Making of Amnesty International," *Journal of Contemporary History* 37, no. 4 (2002): 575–97. In international relations, the instrumental uses of law are a growing area of study. Ian Hurd, *How to Do Things with International Law* (Princeton, NJ: Princeton University Press, 2017). In the international security arena, scholars of "lawfare" have studied how nongovernmental groups use humanitarian and human rights laws in armed conflicts, and this book will show the multiple ways that states do as well. "About Lawfare: A Brief History of the Term and the Site," *Lawfare*, https://www .lawfareblog.com/about-lawfare-brief-history-term-and-site; Orde F. Kittrie, *Lawfare: Law as a Weapon of War* (Oxford: Oxford University Press, 2016).

10. Ignatieff, *Human Rights as Politics and Idolatry*, 56, 9.

11. Samuel Moyn, *The Last Utopia: Human Rights in History* (Cambridge, MA: Harvard University Press, 2010).

12. James Peck, *Ideal Illusions: How the U.S. Government Co-opted Human Rights* (New York: Henry Holt and Co., 2010); Stephen Hopgood, *The Endtimes of Human Rights* (Ithaca, NY: Cornell University Press, 2015); Costas Douzinas, *Human Rights and Empire: The Political Philosophy of Cosmopolitanism* (Abingdon: Routledge-Cavendish, 2007).

13. Ignatieff, *Human Rights as Politics and Idolatry*, 9–10.

14. Richard Thompson Ford, *Universal Rights Down to Earth* (New York: W. W. Norton, 2011), 53.

15. Philip Alston, "Conjuring up New Human Rights: A Proposal for Quality Control," *American Journal of International Law* 78, no. 3 (1984): 607; Glendon, *Rights Talk*; Amy Gutmann, "Introduction," in Ignatieff, *Human Rights as Politics and Idolatry*, x.

16. Nicola Perugini and Neve Gordon, *The Human Right to Dominate* (Oxford: Oxford University Press, 2015).

17. Sidney Tarrow, *War, States, and Contention: A Comparative Historical Study* (Ithaca, NY: Cornell University Press, 2015), 12. I am fully aware that the term "movement," as well as most of the other terms discussed in this paragraph, has been the subject of extensive definitional debate for many years. Rather than rehearsing that debate when the aims of this book are quite different, I use these shorthand definitions here.

18. Hohfeld developed a complex and influential typology of rights and other legal relations. The definition I use is based on what Hohfeld called a "claim-right," which he held all rights to be "in the strictest sense." See Wesley Hohfeld, *Fundamental Legal Conceptions* (New Haven, CT: Yale University Press, 1919), 36. Of course, philosophers and activists continue to debate definitions of rights, including Hohfeld's, but for my analytic purposes, his definition suffices.

19. Isaiah Berlin, "Two Concepts of Liberty," in *The Proper Study of Mankind: An Anthology of Essays*, ed. Henry Hardy (New York: Farrar, Straus and Giroux, 1997), 191–92.

20. Paul M. Sniderman et al., *The Clash of Rights: Liberty, Equality, and Legitimacy in Pluralist Democracy* (New Haven, CT: Yale University Press, 1996), 3; see also Henry Shue, *Basic Rights: Subsistence, Affluence, and U.S. Foreign Policy*, 2nd ed. (Princeton, NJ: Princeton University Press, 1996), 15–16. The historian Michael Kammen makes a similar but broader point: that the abstract concept of liberty only takes on meaning "in relation to some other quality," such as property, authority, or justice. Michael Kammen, *Spheres of Liberty: Changing Perceptions of Liberty in American Culture* (Madison: University of Wisconsin Press, 1986), 5.

21. Notably, Hohfeld wrote that the term "claim" is "a synonym for the term 'right,'" expressing its "best" and "proper meaning." *Fundamental Legal Conceptions*, 38; see also Sniderman, *Clash of Rights*, 78.

22. Micheline R. Ishay, *The History of Human Rights: From Ancient Times to the Globalization Era* (Berkeley: University of California Press, 2004), 3. In downplaying the moral dimension of rights to focus on the strategic, I do not question the legitimacy of philosophical debate about these issues. Philosophers, however, often follow political trends in defining rights, and in the end, their ideas must be turned into politically palatable terms to be useful to the movements that might put them into practice.

23. John Dewey, "Force and Coercion," *International Journal of Ethics* 26, no. 3 (1916): 359–60, 367, 366. For critical discussion of the related "instrumental" view of law, see Brian Z. Tamanaha, *Law as a Means to an End: Threat to the Rule of Law* (Cambridge: Cambridge University Press, 2006).

24. The priority of the first set of rights, so-called negative rights, is often claimed to stem from their being achievable if governments and others simply refrain from action and expense, whereas positive rights cannot be attained without action and expense—and potentially coer-

cion. Maurice Cranston, "Are There Any Human Rights?" *Daedalus* 112, no. 4 (1983): 1–17; Aaron Rhodes, *The Debasement of Human Rights: How Politics Sabotage the Ideal of Freedom* (New York: Encounter Books, 2018). From a more strategic standpoint, others point to the relative ease of identifying violations, violators, and remedies in the case of negative rights, and the relative difficulty of doing so with respect to positive rights. Kenneth Roth, "Defending Economic, Social, and Cultural Rights: Practical Issues Faced by an International Human Rights Organization," *Human Rights Quarterly* 26, no. 1 (2004): 63–73. For discussion, critique, and an alternative view, see Shue, *Basic Rights*.

25. Scheingold, *Politics of Rights*, xxxii; Perugini and Gordon, *Human Right to Dominate*, 16–17; John Emerich Edward Dalberg-Acton, *Essays on Freedom and Power*, ed. Gertrude Himmelfarb (Boston: Beacon Press, 1948), 14.

26. Perugini and Gordon, *Human Right to Dominate*, 10–12. Some would claim that such perversions should not be considered "rights" at all. If one adopts a morally based definition, that is a valid point. But such definitions and their implementation in specific circumstances always remain controversial. By contrast, the definition of rights used in this book encompasses all manner of rights, allowing for broader analysis.

27. Louis Henkin, *The Age of Rights* (New York: Columbia University Press, 1990); James Ron, Shannon Golden, David Crow, and Archana Pandya, *Taking Root: Human Rights and Public Opinion in the Global South* (Oxford: Oxford University Press, 2017); Lynn Hunt, *Inventing Human Rights: A History* (New York: W. W. Norton, 2007); Jack Donnelly, *Universal Human Rights in Theory and Practice*, 3rd ed. (Ithaca, NY: Cornell University Press, 2003); Seyla Benhabib, "Claiming Rights across Borders: International Human Rights and Democratic Sovereignty," *American Political Science Review* 103, no. 4 (2009): 691–704; Ishay, *History of Human Rights*; Margaret E. Keck and Kathryn Sikkink, *Activists beyond Borders: Advocacy Networks in International Politics* (Ithaca, NY: Cornell University Press, 1998); Moyn, *Last Utopia*.

28. E. H. Carr, *The Twenty Years' Crisis: An Introduction to the Study of International Relations* (Basingstoke: Palgrave, 2001), 65.

29. Daniel T. Rodgers, *Contested Truths: Keywords in American Politics since Independence* (New York: Basic Books, 1987), 10.

30. Joseph Margulies, *What Changed When Everything Changed: 9/11 and the Making of National Identity* (New Haven, CT: Yale University Press, 2013), x; Kammen, *Spheres of Liberty*.

31. Sidney Tarrow, *The Language of Contention: Revolutions in Words, 1688–2012* (Cambridge: Cambridge University Press, 2013), 3; David A. Snow and Robert D. Benford, "Master Frames and Cycles of Protest," in *Frontiers in Social Movement Theory*, ed. Aldon D. Morris and Carol McClurg Mueller (New Haven, CT: Yale University Press, 1992), 133–55; Sidney G. Tarrow, *Power in Movement: Social Movements and Contentious Politics*, 3rd ed. (Cambridge: Cambridge University Press, 2011), 146.

32. See, for example, John J. Mearsheimer, *Liddell Hart and the Weight of History* (Ithaca, NY: Cornell University Press, 1988), 36, 61n; Colin S. Gray, *Weapons Don't Make War: Policy, Strategy, and Military Technology* (Lawrence: University Press of Kansas, 1993).

33. Robert Jervis, *Perception and Misperception in International Politics* (Princeton, NJ: Princeton University Press, 1976).

34. Paul J. Nelson and Ellen Dorsey, "At the *Nexus* of Human Rights and Development: New Methods and Strategies of Global NGOs," *World Development* 31, no. 12 (2003): 2013–26; Craig M. Kauffman and Pamela L. Martin, "Can Rights of Nature Make Development More Sustainable? Why Some Ecuadorian Lawsuits Succeed and Others Fail," *World Development* 92 (2017): 130–42.

35. Tarrow, *Language of Contention*, 17.

36. Samuel Moyn, *Not Enough: Human Rights in an Unequal World* (Cambridge, MA: Harvard University Press, 2018).

37. Julian E. Barnes and Scott Shane, "Cables Detail CIA Waterboarding at Secret Prison Run by Gina Haspel," *New York Times*, August 10, 2018, https://www.nytimes.com/2018/08/10/us/politics/waterboarding-gina-haspel-cia-prison.html; Rebecca Sanders, *Plausible Legality: Legal Culture and Political Imperative in the Global War on Terror* (Oxford: Oxford University Press), 29.

38. Harry Eckstein, "Case Study and Theory in Political Science," in *Handbook of Political Science*, vol. 7, *Strategies of Inquiry*, ed. Fred I. Greenstein and Nelson W. Polsby (Boston: Addison-Wesley, 1975).

39. Scheingold, *Politics of Rights*, 7.

Chapter 2. Rights as Rallying Cries: Mobilizing Support

1. John Gaventa, *Power and Powerlessness: Quiescence and Rebellion in an Appalachian Valley* (Urbana: University of Illinois Press, 1980).

2. Doug McAdam, *Political Process and the Development of Black Insurgency, 1930–1970*, 2nd ed. (Chicago: University of Chicago Press, 1999), 35; Phillip M. Ayoub, *When States Come Out: Europe's Sexual Minorities and the Politics of Visibility* (Cambridge: Cambridge University Press, 2016).

3. James C. Scott, *Weapons of the Weak: Everyday Forms of Peasant Resistance* (New Haven, CT: Yale University Press, 1985); Samuel Johnson, "Taxation No Tyranny; An Answer to the Resolutions and Address of the American Congress" (London: T. Cadell, 1775), 67–68, https://archive.org/stream/cihm_20501#page/n71/mode/2up; McAdam, *Political Process*; Tarrow, *Power in Movement*.

4. Keck and Sikkink, *Activists Beyond Borders*; Clifford Bob, *The Marketing of Rebellion: Insurgents, Media, and International Support* (Cambridge: Cambridge University Press, 2005); James Ron, Howard Ramos, and Kathleen Rodgers, "Transnational Information Politics: NGO Human Rights Reporting, 1986–2000," *International Studies Quarterly* 49, no. 3 (2005): 557–88.

5. Ara Wilson, "Lesbian Visibility and Sexual Rights at Beijing," *Signs* 22, no. 1 (1996): 214–18. The term "LGBT" may soon be superseded by broader formulations such as LBGT+ or a twelve-letter acronym covering the eleven groups, LGBTQQIP2SAA. Joy D'Souza, "What Is the Expanded LGBT Acronym? And What Does It Stand For?," *Huffington Post*, June 27, 2016, https://www.huffingtonpost.ca/2016/06/27/entire-lgbt-acronym_n_10616392.html.

6. See also Cranston, "Are There Any Human Rights?," 1.

7. Richard Tuck, *Natural Rights Theories: Their Origin and Development* (Cambridge: Cambridge University Press, 1979), 5–31.

8. Jack Donnelly, *International Human Rights*, 3rd ed. (Boulder, CO: Westview, 2007), 21; A. John Simmons, "Human Rights and World Citizenship: The Universality of Human Rights in Kant and Locke," in *Justification and Legitimacy: Essays on Rights and Obligations* (Cambridge: Cambridge University Press, 2001), 185; Kenneth Roth, "Human Rights 101: What Are Human Rights?," *Human Rights Watch*, May 29, 2015, https://www.hrw.org/human-rights-101.

9. United Nations, Office of the High Commissioner, "International Covenant on Civil and Political Rights," preamble, December 16, 1966, effective March 23, 1976, https://www.ohchr.org/EN/ProfessionalInterest/Pages/CCPR.aspx; United Nations, Universal Declaration of Human Rights, Art. 1, December 10, 1948, https://www.ohchr.org/EN/UDHR/Documents/UDHR_Translations/eng.pdf.

10. Charles R. Beitz, *The Idea of Human Rights* (Oxford: Oxford University Press, 2009), 48.

11. The following section is based on Roger Woolhouse, *Locke: A Biography* (Cambridge:

Cambridge University Press, 2007); Steve Pincus, *1688: The First Modern Revolution* (New Haven, CT: Yale University Press, 2009); Barry R. Weingast, "The Political Foundations of Democracy and the Rule of Law," *American Political Science Review* 91, no. 2 (1997): 252–53; Van A. Mobley, "Two Liberalisms: The Contrasting Visions of Hobbes and Locke," *Humanitas* 9, no. 1 (1996): 6–34; Macpherson, *Political Theory of Possessive Individualism*.

12. Macpherson, *Political Theory of Possessive Individualism*, 249; Woolhouse, *Locke*, 116–17, 182; Mobley, "Two Liberalisms," 27, 23. Cohen calls Locke's vision a "property owner's state." Using an abstract analysis, he shows why the propertyless might consent to second-class citizenship, in part because there is still "some slight probability of [their] gaining property and political rights" in such a state. Joshua Cohen, "Structure, Choice, and Legitimacy: Locke's Theory of the State," *Philosophy and Public Affairs* 15, no. 4 (1986): 319. Chapter 7 suggests that this philosophical possibility may not be borne out in practice, at least not in American political history.

13. Arthur O. Lovejoy, *The Great Chain of Being: A Study of the History of an Idea* (Cambridge, MA: Harvard University Press, 1936).

14. Carl L. Becker, *The Declaration of Independence: A Study in the History of Political Ideas* (New York: Harcourt Brace, 1922), 21.

15. Alison D. Renteln, *International Human Rights: Universalism versus Relativism* (Newbury Park, CA: Sage Publications, 1990), 71; Sumner B. Twiss, "A Constructive Framework for Discussing Confucianism and Human Rights," in *Confucianism and Human Rights*, ed. W. Theodore de Bary and Tu Weiming (New York: Columbia University Press, 1998), 31; John McCain, "Why We Must Support Human Rights," *New York Times*, May 8, 2017, https://www.nytimes.com/20 17/05/08/opinion/john-mccain-rex-tillerson-human-rights.html?ref=opinion.

16. Hunt, *Invention of Human Rights*, 17; Moyn, *Last Utopia*; Hannah Arendt, *The Origins of Totalitarianism* (New York: Harcourt, 1968), 298.

17. Gary B. Nash, *The Forgotten Fifth: African Americans in the Age of Revolution* (Cambridge: Cambridge University Press, 2006), 16–23.

18. Janet Polasky, *Revolutions without Borders: The Call to Liberty in the Atlantic World* (New Haven, CT: Yale University Press, 2015); David Malet, *Foreign Fighters: Transnational Identity in Civil Conflicts* (Oxford: Oxford University Press, 2013).

19. Ignatieff, *Rights as Politics*, 9.

20. Gary J. Bass, *Freedom's Battle: The Origins of Humanitarian Intervention* (New York: Vintage, 2009).

21. Alan J. Kuperman, "A Model Humanitarian Intervention? Reassessing NATO's Libya Campaign," *International Security* 38, no. 1 (2013): 105–36.

22. Worth differentiating here are the ringing words of Martin Luther King: "injustice anywhere is a threat to justice everywhere." King's statement, in his eloquent "Letter from Birmingham Jail," referred only to racial segregation in the United States. King was a staunch proponent of nonviolence, opposing America's war in Vietnam despite the fact that it was justified in part as a way to preserve democracy and rights in Asia.

23. William F. Schulz, *In Our Own Best Interest: How Defending Human Rights Benefits Us All* (Boston: Beacon Press, 2001), 7, 36, xvii–xviii, 14.

24. Samantha Power, "U.S. Diplomacy: Realism and Reality," *New York Review of Books*, August 16, 2016, http://www.nybooks.com/articles/2016/08/18/us-diplomacy-realism-and -reality/. As discussed in chapter 6, Power's "objective" case is debatable, even if there is little question that self-interestedly universalist rights rhetoric can serve as a mobilizing tool for would-be intervenors.

25. Terence quoted in Anthony Appiah, *Cosmopolitanism: Ethics in a World of Strangers* (New York: W. W. Norton, 2006), 111, 113.

26. For a similar viewpoint, grounded in the liberal rationales for Britain's colonization of

India, see Uday Singh Mehta, *Liberalism and Empire: A Study in Nineteenth-Century British Liberal Thought* (Chicago: University of Chicago Press, 1999), 77–80.

27. Yael Tamir, "Hands Off Clitoridectomy," *Boston Review* 21, no. 3 (1996), 21–22; Charli Carpenter, *"Lost" Causes: Agenda Vetting in Global Issue Networks and the Shaping of Human Security* (Ithaca, NY: Cornell University Press, 2014), 124.

28. "World and Europe Day against the Death Penalty," European Union External Action Service, October 10, 2016, https://eeas.europa.eu/headquarters/headquarters-homepage_en/13174/World%20and%20Europe%20Day%20against%20the%20Death%20Penalty.

29. Gustave Le Bon, *The Crowd: A Study of the Popular Mind* (New York: Viking, 1960), 16; McCain, "Why We Must Support Human Rights"; Judith N. Shklar, *Legalism: Laws, Morals, and Political Trials*, rev. ed. (Cambridge, MA: Harvard University Press, 1986), x; Vaclav Havel, "The Power of the Powerless," in *The Power of the Powerless*, ed. John Keane (New York: Routledge 2015), 40. See also György Konrád, *Antipolitics: An Essay* (New York: Harcourt, 1984).

30. Ignatieff, *Rights as Politics*, 56; Aryeh Neier, "Misunderstanding Our Mission," *Open Global Rights*, July 23, 2013, https://www.opendemocracy.net/openglobalrights/aryeh-neier/misunderstanding-our-mission.

31. For a sympathetic chronicle of this approach, see Daniel J. Whelan, *Indivisible Human Rights: A History* (Philadelphia: University of Pennsylvania Press, 2010).

32. Immanuel Kant, *Lectures on Ethics*, ed. Peter Heath and J. D. Schneewind (Cambridge: Cambridge University Press, 1997), 178–179 (27:415); Dworkin, "Rights as Trumps," 153; Ronald Dworkin, *Taking Rights Seriously* (Cambridge, MA: Harvard University Press, 1977), xi.

33. Hopgood, *Endtimes of Human Rights*, 189–90 n. 21.

34. Hans Kelsen, "Absolutism and Relativism in Philosophy and Politics," *American Political Science Review* 42, no. 5 (1948): 913.

35. Charles R. Epp, *The Rights Revolution: Lawyers, Activists, and Supreme Courts in Comparative Perspective* (Chicago: University of Chicago Press, 1998), 44; Steven M. Teles, *The Rise of the Conservative Legal Movement: The Battle for Control of the Law* (Princeton, NJ: Princeton University Press, 2010).

36. Karen J. Alter, *The New Terrain of International Law: Courts, Politics, Rights* (Princeton, NJ: Princeton University Press, 2014).

37. World Court of Human Rights Development Project, http://www.worldcourtofhuman rights.net/.

Chapter 3. Rights as Shields and Parries: Countering Threats

1. Neier, "Misunderstanding Our Mission."

2. Among the many works examining the concept are Keck and Sikkink, *Activists beyond Borders*; Cullen S. Hendrix and Wendy H. Wong, "When Is the Pen Truly Mighty? Regime Type and the Efficacy of Naming and Shaming in Curbing Human Rights Abuses," *British Journal of Political Science* 43, no. 3 (2013): 651–72; Jacob Ausderan, "How Naming and Shaming Affects Human Rights Perceptions in the Shamed Country," *Journal of Peace Research* 51, no. 1 (2014): 81–95.

3. Right to the City Alliance, "History and Mission," https://righttothecity.org/about/mis sion-history/; Henri Lefebvre, "The Right to the City," in *Writings on Cities*, trans. Eleonore Kofman and Elizabeth Lebas (Oxford: Blackwell, 1996), 147–59. I am grateful to Alex Bob for alerting me to this case.

4. Louis de Bonald quoted in Jean-Yves Pranchere, "The Social Bond According to the Catholic Counter-Revolution: Maistre and Bonald," in *Joseph de Maistre's Life, Thought, and Influence*, ed. Richard A. LeBrun (Montreal: McGill-Queens University Press, 2001), 193–94.

5. Edmund Burke, *Reflections on the Revolution in France* (Oxford: Oxford University Press, 2009), 60; see also Russell Kirk, "Burke and Natural Rights," *Review of Politics* 13, no. 4 (1951): 441–56.

6. Jeremy Waldron, ed., *Nonsense upon Stilts: Bentham, Burke, and Marx on the Rights of Man* (Abingdon: Routledge, 2015), 53, 73–74; Jeremy Bentham, *The Works of Jeremy Bentham*, vol. 3 (Edinburgh: William Tait, 1843), 221.

7. Stanley Cohen, "Government Responses to Human Rights Reports: Claims, Denials, and Counterclaims," *Human Rights Quarterly* 18, no. 3 (1996): 522. See also Stanley Cohen, *States of Denial: Knowing about Atrocities and Suffering* (Oxford: Blackwell, 2001).

8. Rachel Wahl, *Just Violence: Torture and Human Rights in the Eyes of the Police* (Stanford, CA: Stanford University Press, 2017), 104.

9. Wahl, *Just Violence*, 105, 102–3, 192. Sanders, *Plausible Legality*, 33, 73.

10. Sniderman, *Clash of Rights*, 78; Scheingold, *Politics of Rights*, xxxii; Tarrow, *Language of Contention*, 83.

11. Daniel T. Rodgers, *Age of Fracture* (Cambridge, MA: Harvard University Press), 127.

12. Colonial Office, *Nigeria: Report of the Commission Appointed to Enquire into the Fears of Minorities and the Means of Allaying Them* (*Willink Commission Report*) (London: Her Majesty's Stationery Office, 1958; reprint, Port Harcourt: Southern Minorities Movement, 1996).

13. Perugini and Gordon, *Human Right to Dominate*, 7, describe a similar phenomenon as "mirroring" by contending sides to conflict.

14. Wahl, *Just Violence*, 177.

Chapter 4. Rights as Camouflage: Masking Motives

1. Unless otherwise noted, all translations are my own.

2. James Jasper and Jan Willem Duyvendak, *Players and Arenas: The Interactive Dynamics of Protest* (Amsterdam: Amsterdam University Press, 2015); Neil Fligstein and Doug McAdam, *A Theory of Fields* (Oxford: Oxford University Press, 2012).

3. Michael Saward, "Shape-Shifting Representation," *American Political Science Review* 108, no. 4 (2014): 723–36.

4. Ian Haney López, *Dog Whistle Politics: How Coded Racial Appeals Have Reinvented Racism and Wrecked the Middle Class* (Oxford: Oxford University Press, 2014).

5. Alan J. Kuperman, "The Moral Hazard of Humanitarian Intervention: Lessons from the Balkans," *International Studies Quarterly* 52, no. 1 (2008): 49–80. See generally Alan J. Kuperman and Timothy W. Crawford, eds., *Gambling on Humanitarian Intervention: Moral Hazard, Rebellion, and Civil War* (New York: Routledge, 2014).

6. English Defence League, "Halal Meat: Say 'NO' to Halal!," 2016, http://www.english defenceleague.org.uk/islam/halal-meat/ (accessed September 22, 2017).

7. John Mearsheimer, *Why Leaders Lie: The Truth about Lying in International Politics* (Oxford: Oxford University Press, 2011), 50–52.

8. Joe Palazzolo, "ACLU Will No Longer Defend Hate Groups Protesting with Firearms," *Wall Street Journal*, August 17, 2017, A7, https://www.wsj.com/articles/aclu-changes-policy-on -defending-hate-groups-protesting-with-firearms-1503010167.

9. Amnesty International USA discussed its rationale for urging NATO to "keep the progress going" toward women's rights in Afghanistan in Vienna Colucci, "We Get It," Human Rights Now blog, May 19, 2012, https://blog.amnestyusa.org/asia/we-get-it/ (accessed August 4, 2018). For opposition to such uses of women's rights, see Malalai Joya, with Derrick O'Keefe, *A Woman among Warlords: The Extraordinary Story of an Afghan Who Dared to Raise Her Voice* (New York: Scribner, 2009); Lila Abu-Lughod, *Do Muslim Women Need Saving?* (Cambridge,

MA: Harvard University Press, 2013), 81–112. For more discussion of the Afghanistan case, see chapter 6.

10. See Flemming Rose, *The Tyranny of Silence: How One Cartoon Ignited a Global Debate on the Future of Free Speech* (Washington, DC: Cato Institute, 2014).

11. Jytte Klausen, *The Cartoons That Shook the World* (New Haven, CT: Yale University Press, 2009), 167.

12. Klausen, *The Cartoons That Shook the World*, 182.

13. See, for example, Alexander Trowbridge, "French Arrests Draw Charges of Free Speech Hypocrisy," *CBS News*, January 15, 2015, http://www.cbsnews.com/news/french-arrests-draw -charges-of-free-speech-hypocrisy/.

14. "Rightsifying" local claims for international consumption and support contrasts with what other scholars have called "vernacularizing": the transformation of international human rights principles by domestic movements to advance their causes in local settings. Peggy Levitt and Sally Merry, "Vernacularization on the Ground: Local Uses of Global Women's Rights in Peru, China, India, and the United States," *Global Networks* 9, no. 4 (2009): 441–61.

15. Marc Howard Ross, *Cultural Contestation in Ethnic Conflict* (Cambridge: Cambridge University Press, 2007), 9.

16. Will Kymlicka, *Liberalism, Community, and Culture* (Oxford: Oxford University Press, 1991); Liav Orgad, *The Cultural Defense of Nations: A Liberal Theory of Majority Rights* (Oxford: Oxford University Press, 2015).

17. This section is based in part on Ross, *Cultural Contestation*, 88–126; Jennifer Curtis, *Human Rights as War by Other Means: Peace Politics in Northern Ireland* (Philadelphia: University of Pennsylvania Press, 2014).

18. Parades Commission, "Parading in a Peaceful Northern Ireland: Forward View and Review of Procedures," 2006–2007, http://www.paradescommission.org/getmedia/377b73f5-74 bc-4e52-beed-e8a9804ecabe/NorthernIrelandParadesCommission.aspx, 8.

19. Portadown District LOL No. 1, "Civil Rights and Drumcree," http://www.portadown districtlolno1.co.uk/Civil_Rights_and_Drumcree.htm.

20. Portadown District LOL No. 1, "Civil Rights and Drumcree"; "Parading," *Parades Commission*, 6; "Civil Rights and Drumcree," *Portadown District*.

21. Ross, *Cultural Contestation*, 123.

22. This paragraph and other general information on Catalan politics is based on Marc Howard Ross, "Where Is Barcelona? Imagining the Nation without a State," in Ross, *Cultural Contestation*; Michael Eaude, *Catalonia: A Cultural History* (Oxford: Oxford University Press, 2008); Alexander Alland, Jr., *Catalunya, One Nation, Two States: An Ethnographic Study of Nonviolent Resistance to Assimilation* (New York: Palgrave MacMillan, 2006); John Hargreaves, *Freedom for Catalonia? Catalan Nationalism, Spanish Identity, and the Barcelona Olympic Games* (Cambridge: Cambridge University Press, 2000); David D. Laitin, "Linguistic Revival: Politics and Culture in Catalonia," *Comparative Studies in Society and History* 31, no. 2 (1989): 297–317.

23. The Tripartito consisted of the Socialist Party of Catalonia (PSC), affiliated with one of Spain's two largest parties, the Socialist Workers Party of Spain (PSOE); the Republican Left of Catalonia (ERC), a left-wing nationalist party; and the eco-socialist Initiative for Catalonia Greens–United and Alternative Left (ICV-EUiA). CiU included two nationalist parties, the Democratic Convergence of Catalonia (CDC) and the Democratic Union of Catalonia (CDU). The CiU broke up in 2015 over disagreements about whether to seek an independence referendum, as the CDC demanded.

24. After the declaration of independence, the Spanish government arrested leading Catalan politicians. Raphael Minder, "Catalonia's Leader, Facing Deadline, Won't Say if Region Declared

Independence," *New York Times,* October 16, 2017, https://www.nytimes.com/2017/10/16
/world/europe/catalonia-spain-independence.html.

25. Background information on bulls and bullfighting in Spain is based in part on Carrie B.
Douglass, *Bulls, Bullfighting, and Spanish Identities* (Tucson: University of Arizona Press, 1997);
Stanley Brandes, "Torophiles and Torophobes: The Politics of Bulls and Bullfights in Contempo-
rary Spain," *Anthropological Quarterly* 82, no. 3 (2009): 779–94.

26. Toni Strubell and Lluís Brunet, *What Catalans Want: Could Catalonia Be Europe's Next
State?* (Ashfield, MA: Catalonia Press, 2011), 145.

27. Dan Mihalopoulos, "Spain's Sacred Cow: Animal Rights Groups Raise a Cry against Bullfighting," *Chicago Tribune,* November 23, 1994.

28. ADDA quoted in Edward Schumacher, "Spain Questions Fascination with Matadors'
Deadly Dance," *New York Times,* September 29, 1985; Mihalopoulos, "Spain's Sacred Cow."
See generally Anima Naturalis, "Antitauromaquia," http://www.animanaturalis.org/f/1719/anti
tauromaquia (accessed June 1, 2017); Le Comité Radicalement Anti Corrida (CRAC) (France),
"Qui sommes-nous?," http://www.anticorrida.com/crac-europe/qui-sommes-nous/ (accessed
June 1, 2017); CAS (Anti-Bullfighting Committee) International (Netherlands), http://www
.stieren.net/EN/ (accessed June 1, 2017).

29. Prou, "The Law," http://www.prou.cat/english/index.php?c=proposta.php (accessed
August 6, 2012) (author's files).

30. Prou, "Principles Declaration," http://www.prou.cat/english/index.php?c=declaracio
.php (accessed October 12, 2011) (author's files); Prou, "The Prou Union," http://www.prou.cat
/english/index.php?c=plataforma_prou.php (accessed October 13, 2011) (author's files).

31. Much of the information on Prou strategies comes from my joint interview with two
Prou leaders, Leonardo Anselmi and Alejandra García, Barcelona, June 8, 2012. Anselmi, an
Argentine, holds a degree in marketing. See also Marius Kolff, CAS International director, inter-
view with the author, Madrid, June 13, 2012.

32. Anselmi, interview with the author.

33. Unless otherwise noted, all quotations in this paragraph are from Prou, "The Law," or
Prou, "Principles Declaration."

34. Giles Tremlett, "Catalonia Votes to Ban Bullfighting," *Guardian,* July 28, 2010, http://
www.guardian.co.uk/world/2010/jul/28/bullfighting-ban-spain-catalonia.

35. Anselmi and García, interviews with the author.

36. Joaquim Nadal, Socialist Party of Catalonia (PSC) deputy, interview with the author,
Barcelona, June 8, 2012.

37. Pablo de Lora, Professor of Legal Philosophy, Universidad Autónoma de Madrid, and
witness for the ILP, interview with the author, Boston, May 22, 2012. Testimony from the hearings is available on YouTube; see, for example, https://www.youtube.com/watch?v=pkVxiHr
d9SY.

38. Lourdes Lopez, "El Parlament de Catalunya aprueba gracias al voto de CiU prohibir las
corridas de toros a partir de 2012" [Catalonian Parliament approves prohibition on bullfighting
starting in 2012 thanks to the CiU vote], *Vanguardia,* July 28, 2010, http://www.lavanguardia
.com/politica/20100728/53973561269/el-parlament-de-catalunya-aprueba-gracias-al-voto-de
-ciu-prohibir-las-corridas-de-toros-a-partir-de.html.

39. Tremlett, "Catalonia Votes to Ban Bullfighting."

40. Myles Burke, "Flaming Bull Festivals Backed by Spanish Lawmakers," *Telegraph* (UK),
September 23, 2010, http://www.telegraph.co.uk/news/worldnews/europe/spain/8020479/Fl
aming-bull-festivals-backed-by-Spanish-lawmakers.html.

41. ADDA, "Catalan Parliament Shields the Correbous," September 23, 2010, http://www

.addaong.org/en/news/archive/ (accessed October 12, 2011) (author's files); Anselmi, interview with the author.

42. Strubell and Brunet, *What Catalans Want*, 146.

43. Kolff, interview with the author.

44. "El PP se propone dejar sin efecto en las cortes la prohibición de las corridas" [The PP proposes to nullify the ban in the courts], *Vanguardia*, July 28, 2010, http://www.lavan guardia.com/politica/noticias/20100728/53973601208/el-pp-se-propone-dejar-sin-efecto-en-las-cortes-la-prohibicion-de-las-corridas.html; see also "Espontánea Esperanza Aguirre: El Futuro de la Lidia" [Spontaneous Esperanza Aguirre: The future of the bullfight], *El País*, March 3, 2010, https://elpais.com/diario/2010/03/05/cultura/1267743601_850215.html; "Esperanza Aguirre: 'Algunos antitaurinos lo son por ser antiespañoles,'" [Esperanza Aguirre: "Some bullfighting foes are anti-Spanish"], *El Periódico*, April 20, 2014, http://www.elperiodico.com/es /noticias/politica/esperanza-aguirre-antitaurinos-antiespanoles-feria-taurina-sevilla-3254159 (accessed March 3, 2016).

45. Prou, "Prou Responds to Esperanza Aguirre," April 9, 2010, http://www.prou.cat/engli sh/index.php?c=n.php&id_noticia=25&idiom=cast (accessed April 26, 2012) (author's files).

46. All quotations in this paragraph are from Prou, "Prou Responds to Esperanza Aguirre." See also "Leonardo Anselmi, portavoz antitaurino: 'El respeto al animal figura en la identidad moral de Catalunya,'" [Leonardo Anselmi, anti-bullfighting spokesperson: "Respect for animals figures in Catalonia's moral identity"], *El Periódico*, July 25, 2010, http://www.elperiodico.com /es/noticias/sociedad/20100725/leonardo-anselmi-portavoz-antitaurino-respeto-animal-figu ra-identidad-moral-catalunya/403351.shtml; Anselmi, interview with the author.

47. Tremlett, "Catalonia Votes to Ban Bullfighting."

48. Williams Cardenas Rubio, interview with the author, Madrid, June 11, 2012.

49. Francis Wolff, *50 Razones para defender la corrida de toros* [50 reasons to defend bullfighting] (Córdoba: Almuzara, 2011), 82.

50. As the president of one of Spain's bullfighting fan clubs had earlier stated, "The bull lives like a king, enjoying the largest, best pastures, in a state of total liberty. . . . The brave bull has never seen a barn. And he has the chance to die fighting, like a hero. Given a choice, any bull would fight." Mihalopoulos, "Spain's Sacred Cow."

51. "Espontánea Esperanza Aguirre," *El País*. Later, Aguirre organized a Madrid art exhibit, "Bullfighting's Female Gaze," dedicated to women's role in *la corrida de toros* (and drawing scores of angry female protesters). GEVHA, "Protesta de mujeres contra la 'mirada femenina del toreo,'" [Women's protest against "bullfighting's female gaze"], May 20, 2011, http://www.gevha .com/opinion/1119-protesta-de-mujeres-contra-la-qmirada-femenina-del-toreoq.

52. Íñigo Crespo, "La Tauromaquia ya es oficialmente Patrimonio Cultural" [Bullfighting now is officially Cultural Heritage], *El Mundo*, July 11, 2013, http://www.elmundo.es/cultura/20 13/11/06/527ab20e68434te70a8b4576.html.

53. UNESCO, "Text of the Convention for the Safeguarding of the Intangible Cultural Heritage," https://ich.unesco.org/en/convention; Cardenas, interview with the author; "Spanish Bullfighting Should Have UNESCO Protection: Pro-Bulls Group," *The Local*, December 7, 2015, http://www.thelocal.es/20151207/fans-must-lead-fight-to-save-bullfighting-from-extinction -pro-bulls-group. In 2011, after a campaign by the French bullfighting association, UNESCO recognized bullfighting in southern France as part of the world's intangible cultural heritage. "UNESCO Honours French Bullfighting," *French News Online*, April 25, 2011 (author's files). In 2015, after a lawsuit, a French court removed bullfighting from the country's UNESCO cultural heritage list. Sylvia Edwards Davis, "France Drops Bullfighting from Cultural Heritage List," *Frenchly*, June 28, 2015, http://frenchly.us/france-drops-bullfighting-from-cultural -heritage-list/.

54. Marín and Masedo quoted in Tremlett, "Catalonia Votes to Ban Bullfighting"; Aguirre quoted in "El PP se propone dejar," *Vanguardia*.

55. Cardenas, interview with the author.

56. Kolff, interview with the author; Alessandro Zara, EquaAnimal director, interview with the author, Madrid, June 12, 2012; La Tortura No Es Cultura, "Bienvenida," http://www.latortu ranoescultura.org/es/ (accessed June 1, 2017).

57. Serafín Marín, "Queda la batalla más grande" [The biggest battle is still to come], *El Mundo*, October 20, 2016, http://www.elmundo.es/cultura/2016/10/20/5808c33a468aebad65 8b4599.html.

58. Joanna Swabe, "Catalonia's Bullfighting Ban Overturned by Spain's Constitutional Court," HumaneSocietyInternational–Europe,October20,2016,http://www.hsi.org/world/europe/news /releases/2016/10/catalonia-bullfighting-ban-overturned-102016.html?referrer=https:// t.co/vWVWtN5Qyg.

59. Salvadó quoted in Raphael Minder, "Spanish Court Overturns a Ban against Bullfighting in Catalonia," *New York Times*, October 20, 2016, https://www.nytimes.com/2016/10/21/world /europe/spain-bullfighting-ban-catalan.html?_r=0; Rull quoted in Stephen Burgen, "Spanish Court Overturns Catalonia's Bullfighting Ban," *Guardian*, October 20, 2016, https://www.the guardian.com/world/2016/oct/20/spanish-court-overturns-catalonia-bullfighting-ban.

60. Minder, "Spanish Court Overturns a Ban against Bullfighting."

Chapter 5. Rights as Spears: Overturning Laws

1. There is a vast literature on social movements, their tactics (including public protest and the use of courts), and their impacts. For overviews, see Charles Tilly and Sidney Tarrow, *Contentious Politics*, 2nd ed. (Oxford: Oxford University Press, 2015); Sidney G. Tarrow, *Power in Movement: Social Movements and Contentious Politics*, 3rd ed. (Cambridge: Cambridge University Press, 2011).

2. Alter, *New Terrain of International Law*.

3. Andrew Legg, *The Margin of Appreciation in International Human Rights Law: Deference and Proportionality* (Oxford: Oxford University Press, 2012).

4. In his study of the American civil rights movement, McAdam referred to this as the "critical dynamic." The movement provoked its opponents into "flagrant displays of public violence," which in turn helped "sustain member commitment, generate broad public sympathy, and mobilize financial support from external groups." McAdam, *Political Process*, 174.

5. Epp, *Rights Revolution*; McCann, *Rights at Work*; Scheingold, *Politics of Rights*.

6. By the same token, the case can say little about the use of mass protest to bring about social change. For a study of the long-term effects of failed rights litigation, see Jules Lobel, *Success without Victory: Lost Legal Battles and the Long Road to Justice in America* (New York: New York University Press, 2003).

7. Senato della Repubblica, "Constitution of the Italian Republic," Arts. 7 and 8, https:// www.senato.it/documenti/repository/istituzione/costituzione_inglese.pdf.

8. "Agreement Between the Italian Republic and the Holy See (1985)," signed February 18, 1984, Art. 9 (2), http://home.lu.lv/~rbalodis/Baznicu%20tiesibas/Akti/Arvalstis_ligumi/Italijas &Sv.Kresla_konkordats.pdf.

9. "Agreement Between the Italian Republic and the Holy See (1985)."

10. Article 118 of royal decree 965 of April 30, 1924 (internal regulations of middle schools) and Article 119 of royal decree 1297 of April 26, 1928. These decrees regularized practices laid down by various Italian governments in the mid-nineteenth century. See *Case of Lautsi and Others v. Italy*, application 30814/06, Grand Chamber, European Court of Human Rights (2011)

(hereinafter cited as *Lautsi II*), paras. 17–18, http://hudoc.echr.coe.int/sites/eng/pages/search .aspx?i=001-104040#{"itemid":["001-104040"]}.

11. Pew Forum on Religion and Public Life, "The Global Religious Landscape," Pew Research Center, December 2012, 47, http://www.pewforum.org/files/2014/01/global-religion -full.pdf.

12. Raffaele Carcano, interview with the author, Rome, December 3, 2012.

13. Unless otherwise noted, empirical information and quotations about the UAAR and the *Lautsi* case in this section are from my interview with Carcano.

14. Public letter on "Lautsi v. Italy" case, n.d., (author's files).

15. The Court also found that the presence of crucifixes in polling places might suggest state favoritism toward certain political parties that included crosses in their symbols. *Lautsi II*, para. 23, p. 11, citing and quoting Court of Cassation, Judgment 439 (March 1, 2000). In its ruling, the Court of Cassation expressly rejected government arguments that the crucifix symbolized "an entire civilization or the collective ethical conscience" or "a universal value independent of any specific religious creed."

16. Carcano, interview with the author.

17. Carcano, interview with the author.

18. All quotations in this paragraph are from European Humanist Federation, "Open Letter by Massimo Albertin and Soile Lautsi," n.d., http://humanistfederation.eu/wp-content/uploads /2011/10/162-Lautsi-Albertin-statement.pdf (author's files).

19. *Lautsi II*, para. 12.

20. *Lautsi II*, para. 24.

21. *Lautsi v. Italy*, Veneto Administrative Court, Judgment 1110 (2005), paras. 11.9, 11.5, 11.6, translated and quoted in *Lautsi II*, 5–6.

22. *Lautsi v. Italy*, *Consiglio di Stato*, Judgment 556 (2006), translated and quoted in *Lautsi II*, 7–9. Those values include "tolerance, mutual respect, valorization of the person, affirmation of one's rights, consideration for one's freedom, the autonomy of one's moral conscience vis-à-vis authority, human solidarity and the refusal of any form of discrimination."

23. European Convention on Human Rights, Protocol 1, Art. 2.

24. European Convention on Human Rights, Protocol 1, Art. 9.

25. *Case of Lautsi v. Italy*, application 30814/06, Second Section, European Court of Human Rights (2009), paras. 48, 55, 57, http://hudoc.echr.coe.int/sites/eng/pages/search.aspx?i=001 -95589#{"itemid":["001-95589"]}.

26. Carcano, interview with the author; Gabriel Andreescu and Liviu Andreescu, "The European Court of Human Rights' *Lautsi* Decision: Context, Contents, Consequences," *Journal for the Study of Religions and Ideologies* 9, no. 26 (Summer 2010): 47–74, 67.

27. European Humanist Federation, "Lautsi v. Italy (No. 30814/06)—Request for Third Party Intervention (Article 44.2 of the Rules of Court)," May 23, 2010, 4 (author's files).

28. ADF also highlighted the case's implications in the United States: "Lawsuits that seek to tear down religious symbols simply because one person says he or she has been 'offended' are very common in the U.S. In addition to the concerns directly related to this case, ADF wants to head off any opportunity for activists in the U.S. to cite foreign court decisions as patterns to follow. We will continue fighting that battle in all of the cases in which we are involved." ADF, "European Court of Human Rights: Crosses Can Stay in Italy's Classrooms," March 18, 2011, http://www.adfmedia.org/News/PRDetail/?CID=24739.

29. "Ignazio La Russa—Possono morire. Il crocifisso resterà in tutte le aule!!!" [Ignazio La Russa: They can die. The crucifix will remain in all the classrooms!!!], *Rai Uno*, November 9, 2009, https://www.youtube.com/watch?v=wwA4sR6kzGM.

30. European Humanist Federation, "Open Letter by Massimo Albertin and Soile Lautsi."

31. Luca Volontè, interview with the author, Rome, December 18, 2012.

32. Volontè, interview with the author.

33. CNN, "Italy Vows to Fight for Classroom Crucifixes," *CNN*, November 4, 2009, http://edition.cnn.com/2009/WORLD/europe/11/04/italy.crucifixes/.

34. Puppinck, "*Lautsi v. Italy*," 3. All quotations in the remainder of this paragraph are from Volontè, interview with the author. The effort described here was part of a broader international campaign to strengthen governmental attention to the rights of Christians in Europe, the Middle East, and elsewhere. See generally Pasquale Annicchino, "Winning the Battle by Losing the War: The Lautsi Case and the Holy Alliance between American Conservative Evangelicals, the Russian Orthodox Church, and the Vatican to Reshape European Identity," *Religion and Human Rights* 6, no. 3 (2011): 213–219.

35. Grégor Puppinck, "*Lautsi v. Italy*: An Alliance against Secularism," *L'Osservatore Romano*, July 28, 2010, 6–7, https://7676076fde29cb34e26d-759f611b127203e9f2a0021aa1b7da05.ssl.cf2.rackcdn.com/eclj/ECLJ-LautsivItaly-crucifix-case-20110315.pdf, quoting Patriarch Cyril Moscow and Metropolite Hilarion in "Interview," *Inside the Vatican*, April 24, 2005.

36. Volontè, interview with the author.

37. Unless otherwise noted, the remaining quotations in this paragraph and the next are from Puppinck, "*Lautsi v. Italy*," 6–7, 1–2, 2–3.

38. Carcano, interview with the author.

39. European Humanist Federation, "Open Letter by Massimo Albertin and Soile Lautsi."

40. See, for example, *Leyla Şahin v. Turkey*, application 44774/98, European Court of Human Rights, Grand Chamber (2005), http://hudoc.echr.coe.int/sites/eng/pages/search.aspx#{"dm docnumber":["789023"],"itemid":["001-70956"]}; see generally Legg, *Margin of Appreciation*.

41. Eyal Benvenisti, "Margin of Appreciation, Consensus, and Universal Standards," *NYU Journal of International Law and Politics* 31 (1998): 843–44.

42. *Case of Z. v. Finland*, Appl. 22009/93, Judgment of February 25, 1997, Dissenting Opinion of Judge De Meyer, para. III.

43. Grégor Puppinck, "The Case of Lautsi v. Italy: A Synthesis," *Brigham Young University Law Review* 873 (2012): 893–94, http://digitalcommons.law.byu.edu/lawreview/vol2012/iss3/7.

44. Roger Kiska (ADF), "The Threat to Religious Liberties and the International Institutions," *Revista Sfera Politicii* 161 (July 2011), http://www.sferapoliticii.ro/sfera/161/art01-Kiska.php.

45. "Russian Patriarch Protests Court Ruling to Ban Cross from Italian Schools," *Interfax*, November 26, 2009, http://www.interfax-religion.com/?act=news&div=6675.

46. *Lautsi II*, paras. 44–46.

47. *Lautsi II*, para. 46.

48. International Commission of Jurists, Interights, and Human Rights Watch, written submissions, *Lautsi v. Italy*, application 30814/06, 1, http://www.interights.org/document/128/index.html (author's files).

49. *Lautsi II*, paras. 61, 68.

50. *Lautsi II*, paras. 70, 69.

51. *Lautsi II*, paras. 71, 72.

52. See Jean-Marc Piret, "Limits of Supranational Jurisdiction: Judicial Restraint and the Nature of Treaty Law," in *The Lautsi Papers: Multidisciplinary Reflections on Religious Symbols in the Public School Classroom*, ed. Jeroen Temperman (Leiden: Martinus Nijhoff, 2012), 59–89.

53. Volontè, interview with the author.

54. Volontè, interview with the author.

55. Carcano, interview with the author.

Chapter 6. Rights as Dynamite: Destroying Cultures

1. Centre for Laws of the Federation of Nigeria, "Same Sex Marriage (Prohibition) Act, 2014," http://www.lawnigeria.com/LawsoftheFederation/Same-Sex-Marriage-Prohibition-Act ,-2014.html; Ogala Emmanuel, "No Going Back on Criminalizing Same-Sex Marriage—David Mark," *Premium Times* (Abuja), January 7, 2013, http://www.premiumtimesng.com/news /114085-no-going-back-on-criminalizing-same-sex-marriage-in-nigeria-david-mark.html; Datti quoted in "Nigeria Criminalizes Gay Marriage, Advocacy," *CBS News*, November 29, 2011, http:// www.cbsnews.com/news/nigeria-criminalizes-gay-marriage-advocacy/; "The Anti-Homosexuality Act (Uganda), 2014," http://www.refworld.org/pdfid/530c4bc64.pdf.

2. "Statement on British 'Aid Cut' Threats to African Countries That Violate LBGTI Rights," *Pambazuka News*, October 27, 2011, http://www.pambazuka.org/activism/statement-british -aid-cut-threats-african-countries-violate-lbgti-rights.

3. Perugini and Gordon pioneered such an analysis, focusing on how Israel and certain Israeli NGOs have used human rights to "help institutionalize, legitimize, normalize, and reproduce existing relations of domination" over Palestinians. Perugini and Gordon, *Human Right to Dominate*, 24.

4. Max Boot, "American Imperialism? No Need to Run Away from Label," *USA Today*, May 5, 2003, https://usatoday30.usatoday.com/news/opinion/editorials/2003-05-05-boot_x.htm.

5. Joan Wallach Scott, *Sex and Secularism* (Princeton, NJ: Princeton University Press, 2018).

6. Human Rights Watch, "'They Do Not Own This Place': Government Discrimination against 'Non-Indigenes' in Nigeria," *Human Rights Watch Reports* 18, no. 3A (August 2006); Myron Weiner, *Sons of the Soil: Migration and Ethnic Conflict in India* (Princeton, NJ: Princeton University Press, 1978). Other countries, such as Fiji, have similar policies. In Europe, policies protecting powerful cultural majorities have been justified by conservative philosophers under the rubric of "differentialism." Alain de Benoist, "Différents mais inégaux, réponse à A. Jacquard," *Éléments* 26 (Spring 1978): 3–7; Alberto Spektorowski, "The New Right: Ethno-Regionalism, Ethno-Pluralism, and the Emergence of a Neo-Fascist 'Third Way,'" *Journal of Political Ideologies* 8 (2003): 111–30.

7. John Gray, *Two Faces of Liberalism* (New York: New Press, 2000), 13.

8. Liav Orgad, *The Cultural Defense of Nations: A Liberal Theory of Majority Rights* (Oxford: Oxford University Press, 2015).

9. Donald L. Horowitz, *Ethnic Groups in Conflict* (Berkeley: University of California Press, 1985), 175–81.

10. Bob, *Marketing of Rebellion*, 26-41.

11. Kenneth Roth, "The Dangerous Rise of Populism: Global Attacks on Human Rights Values," *Human Rights Watch World Report*, 2017, https://www.hrw.org/sites/default/files/world _report_download/wr2017-web.pdf, 1.

12. Orgad, *Cultural Defense of Nations*.

13. Roth, "The Dangerous Rise of Populism," 8.

14. Liav, *Cultural Defense*; Wahl, *Just Violence*.

15. John Mearsheimer makes a similar point with regard to the use of "liberal lies" in international politics. Mearsheimer, *Why Leaders Lie*, 50–52.

16. Jervis, *Perception and Misperception*, 7.

17. See generally Sara R. Farris, *In the Name of Women's Rights: The Rise of Femonationalism* (Durham, NC: Duke University Press, 2017).

18. Assemblée Nationale, "Rapport d'information fait en application de l'article 145 du Règlement au nom de la mission d'information sur la pratique du port du voile intégral sur le terri-

toire national," January 26, 2010, http://www.assemblee-nationale.fr/13/pdf/rap-info/i2262.pdf, 28–29.

19. *Deutsche Welle,* "French Commission Recommends Banning the Burqa," trans. *Deutsche Welle,* January 26, 2010, http://www.dw.com/en/french-commission-recommends-banning -the-burqa/a-5169860; Jean-François Copé quoted in *Le Figaro,* Agence France-Presse, trans., "France Plans Law to 'Liberate' Women from Full-Face Veil," *Sydney Morning Herald,* December 19, 2009, http://www.smh.com.au/world/france-plans-law-to-liberate-women-from-fullface -veil-20091217-l02b.html.

20. Unless otherwise noted, quotations in this paragraph and the next two are from Library of Congress, "France: Highlights of Parliamentary Report on the Wearing of the Full Veil (Burqa)," last updated June 9, 2015, http://www.loc.gov/law/help/france-veil.php#f3.

21. See generally Abu-Lughod, *Do Muslim Women Need Saving?*

22. Sara Farris argues as well that governments have "seized on the opportunity opened up by the identification of women's rights as a 'migrant/Muslim-woman only issue' to decrease funds for more universal programs aimed at tackling gender injustice more generally." Farris, *In the Name of Women's Rights,* 9; see also Scott, *Sex and Secularism.*

23. Éric Raoult quoted in *Deutsche Welle,* "French Commission Recommends Banning the Burqa"; Olivier Roy, *Secularism Confronts Islam,* trans. George Holoch (New York: Columbia University Press, 2007), 4; Pew Research Center, "Widespread Support for Banning Full Islamic Veil in Western Europe," *Pew Global,* July 8, 2010, http://www.pewglobal.org/2010/07/08 /widespread-support-for-banning-full-islamic-veil-in-western-europe/.

24. Major European states have recently undertaken multiyear public processes to discover or invent their national identities. Orgad, *Cultural Defense of Nations,* 87–112.

25. Michèle Alliot-Marie quoted in Lizzy Davies, "France: Senate Votes for Muslim Face Veil Ban," *Guardian,* September 14, 2010, https://www.theguardian.com/world/2010/sep/14/france -senate-muslim-veil-ban.

26. Farris, *In the Name of Women's Rights*; Éric Fassin, "National Identities and Transnational Intimacies: Sexual Democracy and the Politics of Immigration in Europe," *Public Culture* 22, no. 3 (2010): 507–29; Jasbir K. Puar, *Terrorist Assemblages: Homonationalism in Queer Times* (Durham, NC: Duke University Press, 2007).

27. Rod Dreher, *The Benedict Option: A Strategy for Christians in a Post-Christian Nation* (New York: Sentinel, 2017).

28. There is debate about whether the current animus against homosexuality in African countries is indigenous or imported from the era of European colonialism and stoked by the contemporary influence of international activists from America's Christian Right. Rahul Rao, "The Locations of Homophobia," *London Review of International Law* 2, no. 2 (September 1, 2014): 169–99; Kapya Kaoma, "Globalizing the Culture Wars: U.S. Conservatives, African Churches, and Homophobia," Political Research Associates, 2009, http://www.publiceye.org /publications/globalizing-the-culture-wars/pdf/africa-full-report.pdf; Marc Epprecht, *Heterosexual Africa? The History of an Idea from the Age of Exploration to the Age of AIDS* (Athens, OH, and Scottsville, South Africa: Ohio University Press and University of KwaZulu-Natal Press, 2008).

29. Theresa Okafor, "Address to World Congress of Families VI Conference," Madrid, 2012, https://www.youtube.com/watch?v=UwUMjX7_ubk; Russell Goldman, "Ahmadinejad: No Gays, No Oppression of Women in Iran," *ABC News,* September 24, 2007, http://abcnews.go.com /US/story?id=3642673.

30. UN, Office of the High Commissioner for Human Rights, "Born Free and Equal: Sexual Orientation and Gender Identity in International Human Rights Law," 2012, http://www.ohchr

.org/Documents/Publications/BornFreeAndEqualLowRes.pdf, 9 n. 2; Rachel Bergenfield and Alice M. Miller, "Queering International Development? An Examination of New 'LGBT Rights' Rhetoric, Policy, and Programming among International Development Agencies," *LGBTQ Policy Journal*, Harvard Kennedy School (March 2014): 4–5, 12–13.

31. David Cameron, interview by Andrew Marr, *The Andrew Marr Show*, BBC, October 30, 2011, http://news.bbc.co.uk/2/hi/programmes/andrew_marr_show/9627898.stm; Kerry quoted in "Kerry Likens Uganda Anti-Gay Law to Anti-Semitism and Apartheid," *Reuters*, February 26, 2014, http://www.reuters.com/article/us-usa-uganda-kerry-idUSBREA1Q03U20140227.

32. NOI Polls, "About 9 in 10 Nigerians Support the Proposed Anti-Same-Sex Marriage Bill," June 11, 2013, http://www.noi-polls.com/root/index.php?pid=287&ptid=1&parentid=66; Mark quoted in Emmanuel, "No Going Back on Criminalizing Same-Sex Marriage."

33. "Ghana's President Slams David Cameron: You Can't Threaten Us with Gay Aid!" *Vibe-Ghana.com*, November 2, 2011, http://vibeghana.com/2011/11/02/ghanas-president-slams-david-cameron-you-cant-threaten-us-with-gay-aid.

34. *VibeGhana.com*, "Ghana's President Slams David Cameron"; Pamela Ankunda, "Gays Bill: Uganda Is Being Judged Too Harshly," *Daily Monitor*, January 11, 2010, http://www.monitor.co.ug/OpEd/Commentary/-/689364/839592/-/ak0cekz/-/index.html.

35. Ekpenyong and Mark quoted in Camillus Eboh, "Anti–Gay Marriage Bill Polarizes Debate in Nigeria," *Reuters*, November 1, 2011, http://uk.reuters.com/article/uk-nigeria-antigay-bill-idUKTRE7A03SB20111101; Okafor, "Address to World Congress of Families VI Conference."

36. NOI Polls, "About 9 in 10 Nigerians Support the Proposed Anti-Same-Sex Marriage Bill"; Pew Research Center, "The Global Divide on Homosexuality: Greater Acceptance in More Secular and Affluent Countries," June 4, 2013, http://www.pewglobal.org/2013/06/04/the-global-divide-on-homosexuality/. A 2017 NOI poll found a slight warming of Nigerian attitudes toward homosexuality. Adaobi Tricia Nwaubani, "LGBT Acceptance Slowly Grows in Nigeria, Despite Anti-Gay Laws," *Reuters*, May 16, 2017, http://www.reuters.com/article/us-nigeria-lgbt-survey-idUSKCN18C2T8.

37. "Statement on British 'Aid Cut' Threats to African Countries That Violate LBGTI Rights," *Pambazuka News*, October 27, 2011, http://www.pambazuka.org/activism/statement-british-aid-cut-threats-african-countries-violate-lbgti-rights. Except where otherwise noted, all quotations in this and the following three paragraphs are from this document.

38. Julian Pepe Onziema quoted in "Briefing: Punitive Aid Cuts Disrupt Healthcare in Uganda," *IRIN News*, April 2, 2014, http://www.irinnews.org/report/99878/briefing-punitive-aid-cuts-disrupt-healthcare-uganda#.U0DdRKMpDJs.

39. Madeleine Bunting, "Can the Spread of Women's Rights Ever Be Accompanied by War?" *Guardian*, October 2, 2011, https://www.theguardian.com/commentisfree/2011/oct/02/women-rights-afghanistan-war-west.

40. Laura Bush, "The Weekly Address Delivered by the First Lady," November 17, 2001, American Presidency Project, http://www.presidency.ucsb.edu/ws/?pid=24992; Hillary Clinton, "New Hope for Afghanistan's Women," *Time*, November 24, 2001, http://content.time.com/time/nation/article/0,8599,185643,00.html.

41. Clinton, "New Hope for Afghanistan's Women"; U.S. Department of State, "Secretary Clinton Remarks at the TEDWomen Conference," December 8, 2010, http://m.state.gov/md15 2671.htm. See also Hillary Clinton, "Remarks to the UN Commission on the Status of Women," quoted in "Hillary Clinton at UN: 'Women's Progress Is Human Progress,'" *Christian Science Monitor*, March 12, 2010, https://www.csmonitor.com/USA/Foreign-Policy/2010/0312/Hillary-Clinton-at-UN-Women-s-progress-is-human-progress.

42. Samantha Power, "U.S. Diplomacy"; Valerie M. Hudson and Patricia Leidl, *The Hillary*

Doctrine: Sex and American Foreign Policy (New York: Columbia University Press, 2015), 35, 34–35.

43. Hudson and Leidl, *The Hillary Doctrine*, 68–109. To their credit, Hudson and Leidl also give space to critiques of the doctrine.

44. Crocker, quoted in Hudson and Leidl, *Hillary Doctrine*, 265, 257, 264.

45. Vienna Colucci, "We Get It," Amnesty International, Human Rights Now blog, May 19, 2012, https://blog.amnestyusa.org/asia/we-get-it/ (accessed August 4, 2018). This campaign was controversial within Amnesty, sparking calls for the resignation of Amnesty International USA director Suzanne Nossel, a former deputy assistant secretary of state. Nossel, who had earlier worked as chief operating officer of Human Rights Watch, left Amnesty in 2013 after one year in her position.

46. Laura Bush, "NATO Should Not Abandon Afghanistan's Women," *Washington Post*, May 18, 2012, https://www.washingtonpost.com/opinions/nato-should-not-abandon-afghanistans-women/2012/05/18/gIQAmDh9YU_story.html?utm_term=.382a7d91adcc; Martha Roby and Niki Tsongas, "Afghan Women Worry as the U.S. Departure Looms," *Wall Street Journal*, July 22, 2013, https://www.wsj.com/articles/SB10001424127887323368704578596371748087486. Channeling the Hillary Doctrine, Roby and Tsongas write that "women's equality is more than a moral issue: The investment in women and girls is a matter of national security for Afghanistan and America."

47. Hudson and Leidl, *Hillary Doctrine*, 277, 266, 270.

48. See, for example, Alissa J. Rubin, "Afghan Policewomen Struggle against Culture," *New York Times*, March 2, 2015, https://www.nytimes.com/2015/03/02/world/asia/afghan-police women-struggle-against-culture.html; Alissa J. Rubin, "Afghan Policewomen Say Sexual Harassment Is Rife," *New York Times*, September 16, 2013, http://www.nytimes.com/2013/09/17/wor ld/asia/afghan-policewomen-report-high-levels-of-sexual-harassment.html.

49. Andrew Beath, Fotini Christia, and Ruben Enikolopov, "Empowering Women through Development Aid: Evidence from a Field Experiment in Afghanistan," *American Political Science Review* 107, no. 3 (2013): 540–57.

50. Azim and Akrami quoted in Amnesty International, "Afghanistan: Don't Trade Away Women's Human Rights," August 2011, http://www.refworld.org/docid/512251lf2.html, 4.

51. Anne E. Brodsky, *With All Our Strength: The Revolutionary Association of the Women of Afghanistan* (New York: Routledge, 2004); Rosemarie Skaine, *The Women of Afghanistan under the Taliban* (Jefferson, NC: McFarland Books, 2001). Testifying to RAWA's bona fides, Cheryl Benard, a strong proponent of the Afghanistan War and wife of Zalmay Kahlilzad, a National Security Council official and ambassador to Afghanistan and Iraq under the George W. Bush administration, devoted an entire book to the group—before its strong opposition to a U.S. war for women's rights became widely known. Cheryl Benard, *Veiled Courage: Inside the Afghan Women's Resistance* (New York: Broadway Books, 2002).

52. Spogmai Akseer, "Afghan Women: Identity and Invasion," *Feminist Review* 98, no. 1 (2011): 20; Malalai Joya, *A Woman among Warlords: The Extraordinary Story of an Afghan Who Dared to Raise Her Voice* (New York: Scribner, 2011), 161, 5; RAWA, "Let Us Drive Away the U.S. and NATO Occupiers with Our Unity!," October 7, 2014, http://www.rawa.org/rawa/2014/10 /06/rawa-statement-on-us-invasion-oct-2014-english.html. See also Susan Faludi, *The Terror Dream: Myth and Misogyny in an Insecure America* (New York: Picador, 2008).

53. Malalai Joya interview, *Democracy Now!*, October 3, 2013, at 9'25", https://www.you tube.com/watch?v=x6Dk6XclZUA&t=595s.

54. Joya interview, *Democracy Now!*; Joya, *Woman among Warlords*, 169; Rafia Zakaria, "'The Lovers: Afghanistan's Romeo and Juliet,' by Rod Nordland" (book review), *New York*

Times, January 13, 2016. See also Lina Abirafeh, *Gender and International Aid in Afghanistan: The Politics and Effects of Intervention* (Jefferson, NC: McFarland Books, 2009).

Chapter 7. Rights as Blockades: Suppressing Subordinates

1. "Grassroots Labour Revolt over All-Women Shortlist" (letter to the editor), *The Times*, May 1, 2018, https://www.thetimes.co.uk/article/amber-rudd-and-reform-of-the-home-office -f28xrscbh; "Labour: Row over Inclusion of Trans Women in All-Women Shortlists," *BBC News*, May 1, 2018, http://www.bbc.com/news/uk-politics-43962349; "Keep All-Women Shortlists Female!" GoFundMe, https://www.gofundme.com/fighting-for-female-representatives. The Labour Party instituted all-women short lists in 1993. However, protests and litigation by male party members led to their nullification in 1996, for violating discrimination laws. In 2002, Tony Blair's Labour government changed those laws, passing the Sex Discrimination Act. The Labour Party then reestablished its all-women short lists.

2. In this chapter, I follow conventional, if perhaps changing, practice and generally refer to people born anatomically female as "women" rather than as "cis women." The latter and the broader term "cisgender" is preferred by the trans movement but has not come into general usage at this time. I reserve its use to sections of the chapter that present the trans movement's perspectives.

3. McAdam, *Political Process*, 43–48.

4. For the dynamics of coalition-building within and among movements, see Suzanne Staggenborg, "Coalition Work in the Pro-Choice Movement: Organizational and Environmental Opportunities and Obstacles," *Social Problems* 33, no. 5 (1986): 374–90; Holly McCammon and Karen Campbell, "Allies on the Road to Victory: Coalition Formation between the Suffragists and the Woman's Christian Temperance Union," *Mobilization: An International Quarterly* 7, no. 3 (2002): 231–51; Phillip M. Ayoub, "Intersectional and Transnational Coalitions during Times of Crisis: The European LGBTI Movement," *Social Politics: International Studies in Gender, State, and Society*, March 26, 2018, https://doi.org/10.1093/sp/jxy007.

5. For examples of the "minimal basis of group differentiation[,] group feeling and discrimination," see Horowitz, *Ethnic Groups in Conflict*, 144.

6. Horowitz, *Ethnic Groups in Conflict*, 357–59; Randall Kennedy, *Sellout: The Politics of Racial Betrayal* (New York: Vintage, 2008).

7. Sheryl Gay Stolberg, "Views on Abortion Strain Calls for Unity at Women's March on Washington," *New York Times*, January 18, 2017, https://www.nytimes.com/2017/01/18/us /womens-march-abortion.html; Jia Tolentino, "The Somehow Controversial Women's March on Washington," *New Yorker*, January 18, 2017, https://www.newyorker.com/culture/jia -tolentino/the-somehow-controversial-womens-march-on-washington; Rosie Campos, "Dear White Women: This Is Not about Us," *Medium*, November 21, 2016, https://medium.com/ @PghRCampos/dear-white-women-this-is-not-about-us-bc80f8dca74b. Within movements, similar rifts are often found between more and less privileged members. See Dara Z. Strolovitch, *Affirmative Advocacy: Race, Class, and Gender in Interest Group Politics* (Chicago: University of Chicago Press, 2007).

8. Joshua Gamson, "Messages of Exclusion: Gender, Movements, and Symbolic Boundaries," *Gender and Society* 11, no. 2 (1997): 178–99; Marshall Kirk and Hunter Madsen, *After the Ball: How America Will Conquer Its Fear and Hatred of Gays in the '90s* (New York: Doubleday, 1989), 184, xxv.

9. Rogers M. Smith, "Beyond Tocqueville, Myrdal, and Hartz: The Multiple Traditions in America," *American Political Science Review* 87, no. 3 (1993): 549–66; Rogers M. Smith, " 'One

United People': Second-Class Female Citizenship and the American Quest for Community," *Yale Journal of Law and the Humanities* 1, no. 2 (1989): 229–93.

10. Human Rights Watch, "'They Do Not Own This Place,'"; Christophe Jaffrelot, *India's Silent Revolution: The Rise of the Lower Castes in North India* (New York: Columbia University Press, 2003).

11. Erving Goffman, "On Cooling Out the Mark: Some Aspects of Adaptation to Failure," *Psychiatry* 15, no. 4 (1952): 451–63, 459.

12. "Open Letter from Archbishop Emeritus Desmond Tutu to Ms. Aung San Suu Kyi," September 7, 2017, *Scribd*, https://www.scribd.com/document/358311066/Desmond-Tutu-Letter #from_embed; Jacob Judah, "Strip Aung San Suu Kyi of Her Nobel Prize," *New York Times*, September 7, 2017, https://www.nytimes.com/2017/09/07/opinion/strip-aung-san-suu-kyi-of-her -nobel-prize.html.

13. Jaffrelot, *India's Silent Revolution*, 19–25; Oliver Mendelsohn and Marika Vicziany, *The Untouchables: Subordination, Poverty, and the State in Modern India* (Cambridge: Cambridge University Press, 1998), 77–117; Ravinder Kumar, "Gandhi, Ambedkar, and the Poona Pact, 1932," *South Asia: Journal of South Asian Studies* 8, nos. 1–2 (1985): 87–101. Less successfully, as Nigerian independence neared in the 1950s, numerically small minority groups in the colony sought guarantees that their rights would not be trampled by the three much larger ethnic groups soon to rule the country. Colonial Office, *Willink Commission Report*; "Ogoni Bill of Rights," reprinted in Ken Saro-Wiwa, *A Month and a Day: A Detention Diary* (New York: Penguin Books, 1995), 67–70.

14. Unless otherwise cited, this section is based on an interpretation of the following works, especially the primary sources cited therein: Faye E. Dudden, *Fighting Chance: The Struggle over Woman Suffrage and Black Suffrage in Reconstruction America* (Oxford: Oxford University Press, 2014); Alexander Keyssar, *The Right to Vote: The Contested History of Democracy in the United States*, rev. ed. (New York: Basic Books, 2000); Laura J. Scalia, "Who Deserves Political Influence? How Liberal Ideals Helped Justify Mid Nineteenth-Century Exclusionary Policies," *American Journal of Political Science* 42, no. 2 (1998): 349–76; Elna C. Green, *Southern Strategies: Southern Women and the Woman Suffrage Question* (Chapel Hill: University of North Carolina Press, 1997); Aileen S. Kraditor, *Means and Ends in American Abolitionism: Garrison and His Critics on Strategy and Tactics 1834–1850* (New York: Pantheon, 1969); and Allison L. Sneider, *Suffragists in an Imperial Age: U.S. Expansion and the Woman Question, 1870–1929* (Oxford: Oxford University Press, 2008).

15. Keyssar, *Right to Vote*, 21 n. 83.

16. Keyssar, *Right to Vote*, 10, 8–21, 29; Spencer quoted in Scalia, "Who Deserves Political Influence?," 369, 363. Spencer's words came in an 1821 debate in the New York legislature over a bill to restrict voting for senators to men owning more than $250 in property. For similar sentiments from other states, see Scalia, "Who Deserves Political Influence?," 362–70; Keyssar, *Right to Vote*, 8–21, chap. 2; Kammen, *Spheres of Liberty*, 25.

17. Spencer quoted in Scalia, "Who Deserves Political Influence?," 363.

18. "Memorial of the Non-Freeholders of the City of Richmond," quoted in Keyssar, *Right to Vote*, 29–30.

19. Keyssar, *Right to Vote*, 11, 31.

20. For discussion of the Rhode Island dispute, see Dudden, *Fighting Chance*, 175; Keyssar, *Right to Vote*, 59–60. American Woman Suffrage Association resolution, May 12, 1870, reprinted in Elizabeth Cady Stanton, Susan B. Anthony, and Matilda Joslyn Gage, eds., *History of Woman Suffrage*, vol. 2, *1861–1876* (1881), 780; Scalia, "Who Deserves Political Influence?," 374.

21. C. Vann Woodward, *The Strange Career of Jim Crow* (Oxford: Oxford University Press, 2002), 20.

22. Dudden, *Fighting Chance*, 18–19.

23. Dudden, *Fighting Chance*, 20.

24. Elizur Wright Jr. quoted in Kraditor, *Means and Ends*, 57.

25. Dudden, *Fighting Chance*, 20, 63.

26. Dudden, *Fighting Chance*, 63, 82, 186.

27. *Report of the Proceedings of the Colored National Convention Held at Cleveland, Ohio, on Wednesday, September 6, 1848* (Rochester, NY: John Dick, North Star Office, 1848), quoted in Martha S. Jones, *All Bound up Together: The Woman Question in African American Public Culture, 1830–1900* (Chapel Hill: University of North Carolina Press, 2007), 60.

28. Dudden, *Fighting Chance*, 19.

29. Stanton quoted in Dudden, *Fighting Chance*, 43.

30. Stanton quoted in Dudden, *Fighting Chance*, 44. For more on this "priority" argument, see Aileen S. Kraditor, *The Ideas of the Woman Suffrage Movement, 1890–1920* (New York: Columbia University Press, 1965), 167. For their part, opponents of black suffrage repeatedly used the disfranchisement of women to claim that voting was not a natural right but a privilege and therefore should be denied to blacks as well.

31. Dudden, *Fighting Chance*, 49.

32. Dudden, *Fighting Chance*, 62.

33. For detailed historical discussion of this debate, see Dudden, *Fighting Chance*, chap. 3.

34. Dudden, *Fighting Chance*, 62.

35. "Elizabeth Cady Stanton for Congress," October 10, 1866, in Ann D. Gordon, ed., *The Selected Papers of Elizabeth Cady Stanton and Susan B. Anthony: In the School of Anti-Slavery 1840–1866*, vol. 1 (New Brunswick, NJ: Rutgers University Press, 1997), 594.

36. Dudden, *Fighting Chance*, 148.

37. Henry B. Blackwell, *What the South Can Do: How the Southern States Can Make Themselves Master of the Situation: To the Legislatures of the Southern States* (New York: Robert J. Johnston, 1867), 2, 3, 4 (emphasis omitted), https://www.loc.gov/resource/rbpe.12701100/?sp=1; Kraditor, *Ideas of the Woman Suffrage Movement*, 168–89. As Kraditor writes, this paralleled a similar blockade argument, used in the North, "that woman suffrage would insure the supremacy of the native born" over immigrant voters because statistically there were more native-born women than foreign-born men and women combined.

38. Quoted in Dudden, *Fighting Chance*, 98, 169–71, 196. See also Kraditor, *Means and Ends*, chap. 3; Lori D. Ginzberg, *Elizabeth Cady Stanton: An American Life* (New York: Hill and Wang, 2009), 129–31.

39. Dudden, *Fighting Chance*, 196; Phillips and Douglass quoted in Dudden, *Fighting Chance*, 175, 149. Stanton admitted at least once that "there seems to be a selfishness in our present position," but claimed that in attacking black male suffrage she spoke "not for ourselves alone" but for "all womankind, in poverty, ignorance and hopeless dependence, for the women of this oppressed race too." Quoted in Dudden, *Fighting Chance*, 169.

40. Stanton and Anthony quoted in Dudden, *Fighting Chance*, 8; Ginzberg, *Elizabeth Cady Stanton*, 131.

41. Equal Suffrage Association and Williams quoted in Green, *Southern Strategies*, 92 n. 90.

42. Michael Kammen, *A Machine That Would Go of Itself: The Constitution in American Culture* (New York: Alfred A. Knopf, 1986), 121.

43. *Richmond Evening Journal* quoted in Green, *Southern Strategies*, 96–97 (reprinted in *Woman Patriot*, June 8, 1918, 8).

44. NAWSA, proceedings, 1903, 59, quoted in Kraditor, *Ideas of the Woman Suffrage Movement*, 165–66 n. 3, 212; Garrison, letter to *Woman's Journal*, May 21, 1903, quoted in Kraditor, *Ideas of the Woman Suffrage Movement*, 203.

45. Kate Gordon, "Federal Law Called Useless by the Era Club," n.d., quoted in Green, *Southern Strategies*, 137–38; Kraditor, *Ideas of the Woman Suffrage Movement*, 216–17; White quoted in Kraditor, *Ideas of the Woman Suffrage Movement*, 216 n. 96; Du Bois, *The Crisis*, April 1915, quoted in Kraditor, *Ideas of the Woman Suffrage Movement*, 198 n. 69.

46. Green, *Southern Strategies*, 88.

47. "Keep All-Women Shortlists Female!," GoFundMe.

48. Radical feminists focus most of their activism on trans women and have spent less time criticizing female-to-male transgenders because they are fewer in number and less prominent in the transgender movement. Nonetheless, they hold that "female-bodied transgenders" also pose a threat to feminism's efforts to dismantle patriarchy. This "tiny minority" among the transgendered, radical feminists argue, "raise their [individual] status" by joining the "superior caste" rather than seeking to topple the hierarchy itself. Sheila Jeffreys, *Gender Hurts: A Feminist Analysis of the Politics of Transgenderism* (London: Routledge, 2014), 101–2. In this section of the book, I do not consider these cases but instead focus on trans women.

49. Until recently, of course, "woman" was viewed as a clear and stable category grounded in biology and reinforced by socialization from birth. In this view, "narrowing" would have been unnecessary or even inconceivable.

50. Neela Ghoshal and Kyle Knight, "Rights in Transition: Making Legal Recognition for Transgender People a Global Priority," *Human Rights Watch*, January 2016, https://www.hrw.org/world-report/2016/rights-in-transition.

51. U.S. Department of Education and U.S. Department of Justice, "Dear Colleague Letter on Transgender Students," May 13, 2016, https://www2.ed.gov/about/offices/list/ocr/letters/colleague-201605-title-ix-transgender.pdf. The guidance was revoked early in the Trump administration.

52. As India's minister for rural development, Jairam Ramesh, has stated, "Toilets are women's fundamental right, for her privacy and her dignity." Ramesh quoted in "India's Tough Toilet Challenge," *OneIndia News*, November 18, 2013, http://www.oneindia.com/feature/india-s-tough-toilet-challenge-1343275.html. See also Barbara Penner, "A World of Unmentionable Suffering: Women's Public Conveniences in Victorian London," *Journal of Design* 14, no. 2 (2001): 35–43; Sheila Jeffreys, "The Politics of the Toilet: A Feminist Response to the Campaign to Degender a Women's Space," *Women's Studies International Forum* 45 (2014): 42–51.

53. Jeffreys, *Gender Hurts*, 5, 15.

54. "#1: The Right to Define Gender Identity," International Bill of Gender Rights, adopted July 24, 1996, http://www.transgenderlegal.com/ibgr.htm.

55. Jeffreys, *Gender Hurts*, 3, 29–32.

56. Jeffreys, *Gender Hurts*, 185, 157, 145; Ruth Barrett, "The Attack on Female Sovereign Space in Pagan Community," in *Female Erasure: What You Need to Know about Gender Politics' War on Women, the Female Sex, and Human Rights*, ed. Ruth Barrett (Pacific Palisades, CA: Tidal Time Publishing, 2016), 375; Patricia McFadden, "Why Women's Spaces Are Critical to Feminist Autonomy," in Barrett, *Female Erasure*, 309. See also Janice G. Raymond, *The Transsexual Empire: The Making of the She-Male* (Boston: Beacon Press, 1979), xxi.

57. Jeffreys, *Gender Hurts*, 145, 7, 1; Raymond, *Transsexual Empire*, xviii; "#2: The Right to Free Expression of Gender Identity," International Bill of Gender Rights, adopted July 24, 1996, http://www.transgenderlegal.com/ibgr.htm.

58. Barrett, *Female Erasure*, 2, 3, 375; Jeffreys, *Gender Hurts*, 6, 42; Raymond, *Transsexual Empire*, xvii. See also "Suspects Sought after Brawl between Transgender Activists and Radical Feminists," *Guardian*, October 26, 2017.

59. Raymond, *Transsexual Empire*, xvii; Jeffreys, *Gender Hurts*, 6.

60. "Judith Butler Addresses TERFs and the Work of Sheila Jeffreys and Janice Raymond," The TERFs, May 1, 2014, http://theterfs.com/2014/05/01/judith-butler-addresses-terfs-and -the-work-of-sheila-jeffreys-and-janice-raymond/; *BBC News*, "Labour: Row over Inclusion of Trans Women."

61. Jeffreys, *Gender Hurts*, 148.

62. Raymond, *Transsexual Empire*, 188 n. 5; Mary Daly, *Gyn/Ecology: The Metaethics of Radical Feminism* (Boston: Beacon Press, 1978), 68; "Sheila Jeffreys Speaks on Beauty Practices and Misogyny," Sheila Jeffreys's speech to the Andrea Dworkin Commemorative Conference, April 7, 2006, *Feminist Reprise*, http://feminist-reprise.org/library/appearance-and-beauty -practices/sheila-jeffreys-speaks-on-beauty-practices-and-misogyny/.

63. Jack Halberstam, *Trans*: A Quick and Quirky Account of Gender Variability* (Berkeley: University of California Press, 2018), 109.

64. "History of the International Bill of Gender Rights," International Bill of Gender Rights, adopted July 24, 1996, http://www.transgenderlegal.com/ibgr.htm.

65. Halberstam, *Trans**, 108–19; *Vancouver Rape Relief Society v. Nixon*, 2005 British Columbia Court of Appeals 601 (2005).

66. National Center for Transgender Equality, "Issues: Anti-Violence," http://www.transe quality.org/issues/anti-violence, and "Issues: International," http://www.transequality.org/issues /international; "Judith Butler Addresses TERFs"; Rebecca Tuvel, "In Defense of Transracial-ism," *Hypatia: A Journal of Feminist Philosophy* 32, no. 2 (2017): 263–78; Jesse Singal, "This Is What a Modern-Day Witch Hunt Looks Like," *New York*, May 2, 2017, http://nymag.com/daily /intelligencer/2017/05/transracialism-article-controversy.html.

Chapter 8. Rights as Wedges: Breaking Coalitions

1. "Who You Get in Bed with—Human Rights, Gay Rights," June 23, 2011, http://www.you tube.com/watch?v=vhmBbGFJleU&feature=youtu.be (accessed June 1, 2016).

2. Robert Mackey, "Israeli Video Blog Exposed as a Hoax," *New York Times*, June 27, 2011, https://thelede.blogs.nytimes.com/2011/06/27/israeli-video-blog-exposed-as-a-hoax/?ref =world.

3. D. Sunshine Hillygus and Todd G. Shields, *The Persuadable Voter: Wedge Issues in Presidential Campaigns* (Princeton, NJ: Princeton University Press, 2008); Roger W. Cobb and Marc Howard Ross, eds., *Cultural Strategies of Agenda Denial: Avoidance, Attack, and Redefinition* (Lawrence: University Press of Kansas, 1997); E. E. Schattschneider, *The Semisovereign People: A Realist's View of Democracy in America* (Boston: Wadsworth, 1975), 64; Timothy W. Crawford, "Preventing Enemy Coalitions: How Wedge Strategies Shape Power Politics," *International Security* 35, no. 4 (2011): 155–89. See also Eric A. Posner, Kathryn E. Spier, and Adrian Vermeule, "Divide and Conquer," University of Chicago Law and Economics, Olin Working Paper 467; Harvard Public Law Working Paper 09-24; Harvard Law and Economics Discussion Paper 639, May 26, 2009, available at SSRN: https://ssrn.com/abstract=1414319 or http://dx.doi.org/10.21 39/ssrn.1414319.

4. Hillygus and Shields define a wedge issue as "any policy concern that is used to divide the opposition's potential winning coalition." Hillygus and Shields, *Persuadable Voter*, 367. In this chapter, I sometimes refer to "crowbar" instead of "wedge" politics to highlight that activists use the tactic to bruise and batter a coalition, even if they cannot achieve their maximal goal of breaking it apart.

5. Glendon, *Rights Talk*, 15.

6. For more on gatekeeper groups in transnational advocacy, see Bob, *Marketing of Rebellion*, 18–19.

7. Clifford Bob, ed., *The International Struggle for New Human Rights* (Philadelphia: University of Pennsylvania Press, 2009).

8. This section relies in part on the following historical scholarship: Laura A. Belmonte, *Selling the American Way: U.S. Propaganda and the Cold War* (Philadelphia: University of Pennsylvania Press, 2008); Mary L. Dudziak, *Cold War Civil Rights: Race and the Image of American Democracy* (Princeton, NJ: Princeton University Press, 2000); Carol Anderson, *Eyes off the Prize: The United Nations and the African American Struggle for Human Rights, 1944–1955* (Cambridge: Cambridge University Press, 2003).

9. Quoted in Dudziak, *Cold War Civil Rights*, 38 n. 48

10. *To Secure These Rights: The Report of the President's Committee on Civil Rights* (New York: Simon & Schuster, 1947), 148; amicus brief of the United States in *Brown v. Board of Education of Topeka*, quoted in Aryeh Neier, "Brown v. Board of Ed: Key Cold War Weapon," *Reuters*, May 14, 2014, http://blogs.reuters.com/great-debate/2014/05/14/brown-v-board-of-ed-key-cold-war-weapon/; Thomas W. Zeiler, *Dean Rusk: Defending the American Mission Abroad* (Lanham, MD: Rowman & Littlefield, 1999), 90–91; U.S. State Department official Pedro Sanjuan quoted in Dudziak, *Cold War Civil Rights*, 169; Bowles quoted in Dudziak, *Cold War Civil Rights*, 78 n. 66

11. See, for example, "Explosive FBI Report on Martin Luther King Jr. among Documents in JFK Files," *CBS News*, November 4, 2017, https://www.cbsnews.com/news/explosive-fbi-report-on-martin-luther-king-jr-among-documents-in-jfk-files/.

12. Anderson, *Eyes off the Prize*, 5–6, 149–152, 167.

13. National Association for the Advancement of Colored People, *An Appeal to the World! A Statement on the Denial of Human Rights to Minorities in the Case of Citizens of Negro Descent in the United States of America and an Appeal to the United Nations for Redress* (New York: NAACP, 1947); Anderson, *Eyes off the Prize*, 108.

14. Daniels quoted in Anderson, *Eyes off the Prize*, 110.

15. *A Study of USIA Operating Assumptions*, vol. 3, TC19–20 (1954), quoted in Belmonte, *Selling the American Way*, 167 (emphasis in original). See also Dudziak, *Cold War Civil Rights*, 142.

16. See Dudziak, *Cold War Civil Rights*, 65–77; Acting Assistant Secretary of State Ben Brown quoted in Dudziak, *Cold War Civil Rights*, 69; USIA officials quoted in Dudziak, *Cold War Civil Rights*, 70–71.

17. Pinkwatching Israel, "General Assembly Declaration—Queer Visions at the World Social Forum: Free Palestine," December 10, 2012, http://www.pinkwatchingisrael.com/2012/12/10/wsf-declaration/ (accessed June 1, 2017).

18. I am grateful to Jackie Smith for alerting me to this case.

19. SWU, "About Us," https://www.standwithus.com/aboutus/; SWU, "Why Does Israel Look Like Paradise to Gay Palestinians?," August 28, 2002, https://www.swuconnect.com/insys/npoflow.v.2/_assets/pdfs/flyers/whydoesIsrael.pdf; Mackey, "Israeli Video Blog Exposed."

20. USPCN, "About," Facebook, https://www.facebook.com/pg/USPCN/about/; USPCN, "About USPCN," http://uspcn.org/about/.

21. For general information on the U.S. Social Forum and WSF, see Jackie Smith, Ellen Reese, Scott Byrd, and Elizabeth Smythe, eds., *Handbook on World Social Forum Activism* (New York: Routledge, 2015).

22. U.S. Social Forum, "LGBTQI Liberation in the Middle East" (workshop information), http://organize.ussf2010.org/ws/lgbtqi-liberation-middle-east (author's files).

23. Roz Rothstein and Roberta Seid, "U.S. Social Forum 2010: The Stench of Hypocrisy," SWU, n.d., http://www.standwithus.com/app/iNews/view_n.asp?ID=1532 (accessed June 1, 2017).

24. All quotations are from Helem [Lebanese Protection for LGBT] et al., "U.S. Social Forum Gives 'Stand With Us' Platform to Bash Arabs, Pinkwash Israel," *Palestine Today*, June 10,

2010, http://palestinetoday.tumblr.com/post/719775070/us-social-forum-gives-stand-with-us -platform-to-bash (accessed October 10, 2011) (author's files).

25. For a sample of this mostly internal debate, see Nada Elia, "Reflections from Detroit: Standoff with StandWithUs," *Incite!*, August 2, 2010, https://inciteblog.wordpress.com/2010/08 /02/reflections-from-detroit-standoff-with-standwithus/; American Leftist, "Zionists Welcome at the U.S. Social Forum (Part 2)," June 19, 2010, http://amleft.blogspot.com/2010/06/zionists -still-welcome-at-us-social.html.

26. All quotations in this and the next paragraph are from Rothstein and Seid, "The Stench of Hypocrisy."

27. For general information on this network and its tactics, see Clifford Bob, *The Global Right Wing and the Clash of World Politics* (Cambridge: Cambridge University Press, 2012), chaps. 3–4.

28. Scott W. Long, "Anatomy of a Backlash: Sexuality and the 'Cultural' War on Human Rights," *Human Rights Watch World Report 2005* (New York: HRW, 2005), 71, 75.

29. Andrew R. Lewis, *The Rights Turn in Conservative Christian Politics: How Abortion Transformed the Culture Wars* (Cambridge: Cambridge University Press, 2017).

30. NOM, "Board Update 2008–2009," n.d., 6, https://archive.org/stream/NationalOrgani zationForMarriageDocuments/Nom2#page/n0; "Miss California's Opinion on Same-Sex Mar- riage," May 3, 2009, https://www.youtube.com/watch?v=0s-jO1iO0IQ. Her equivocal response prompted Hilton to take to YouTube, where he maligned her as a "dumb bitch" who had given the worst answer in pageant history. See also NOM, "National Strategy for Winning the Mar- riage Battle," August 11, 2009, https://archive.org/details/NationalOrganizationForMarriage Documents, 16.

31. NOM, "Marriage: $20 Million Strategy for Victory," April 22, 2015, https://archive.org /stream/NationalOrganizationForMarriageDocuments/Nom4#page/n0; Robert P. Jones, "At- titudes on Same-Sex Marriage by Religious Affiliation and Denominational Family," PRRI, April 22, 2015, https://www.prri.org/spotlight/attitudes-on-same-sex-marriage-by-religious-affiliation -and-denominational-family/, 8–9.

32. NOM, "Board Update 2008–2009," 5–6, 10.

33. NOM, "National Strategy for Winning the Marriage Battle," 24; NOM, "Board Update 2008–2009," 11.

34. NOM, "National Strategy for Winning the Marriage Battle," 4.

Chapter 9. Conclusion

1. Abraham Lincoln, "Address at Sanitary Fair in Baltimore: A Lecture on Liberty," April 18, 1864, American Presidency Project, http://www.presidency.ucsb.edu/ws/?pid=88871. This elo- quent address came days after the massacre at Fort Pillow, Tennessee, when Confederate troops summarily executed hundreds of captured African American soldiers fighting for the Union. Al- though Lincoln had earlier issued an Order of Retaliation for such killings in violation of the laws of war, after much cabinet debate, no retaliation ensued. The massacre became a rallying cry for the North, whereas its very occurrence was roundly denied by the South, both during and after the Civil War. John Cimprich and Robert C. Mainfort Jr., "Fort Pillow Revisited: New Evidence about an Old Controversy," *Civil War History* 28, no. 4 (1982): 293–306.

2. See Jennie L. Schulze, *Strategic Frames: Europe, Russia, and Minority Inclusion in Estonia and Latvia* (Pittsburgh: University of Pittsburgh Press, 2018); Erin K. Jenne, *Ethnic Bargaining: The Paradox of Minority Empowerment* (Ithaca, NY: Cornell University Press, 2007).

3. Nancy F. Cott, *The Grounding of Modern Feminism* (New Haven, CT: Yale University Press, 1987), 68.

4. "UN Human Rights Chief Points to 'Textbook Example of Ethnic Cleansing' in Myanmar," *UN News*, September 11, 2017, http://www.un.org/apps/news/story.asp?NewsID=57490 #.WjqJu7Q-eRs.

5. Strolovitch, *Affirmative Advocacy*.

6. Stephen Hopgood, *Keepers of the Flame: Understanding Amnesty International* (Ithaca, NY: Cornell University Press, 2006), 61–62.

7. United Nations Population Fund, "Human Rights Principles," 2005, http://www.unfpa .org/resources/human-rights-principles.

8. Kathryn Sikkink responds to recent critics of human rights such as Samuel Moyn and Stephen Hopgood by faulting them for holding human rights up against an "implicit ideal." Kathryn Sikkink, *Evidence for Hope: Making Human Rights Work in the 21st Century* (Princeton, NJ: Princeton University Press, 2017), 22–51.

9. I thank Will Kymlicka for urging me to think about these and related issues.

INDEX

A NOTE ON THE TYPE

This book has been composed in Adobe Text and Gotham. Adobe Text, designed by Robert Slimbach for Adobe, bridges the gap between fifteenth- and sixteenth-century calligraphic and eighteenth-century Modern styles. Gotham, inspired by New York street signs, was designed by Tobias Frere-Jones for Hoefler & Co.